ORIGINAL MIND

DEE JOY COULTER, EdD

ORIGINAL MIND

UNCOVERING YOUR NATURAL BRILLIANCE

sounds true
BOULDER, COLORADO

Sounds True
Boulder, CO 80306

Published 2014

Jacket design by Jenny Miles
Book design by Beth Skelley

The excerpt by Walter Littlemoon, from *They Called Me Uncivilized: The
Memoir of an Everyday Lakota Man from Wounded Knee,* is reprinted with
permission from the author.

All quotes from *Cognitive Development: It's Cultural and Social Foundations*
by A. R. Luria pp. 25, 27, 56, 75, 81–82, 108–109, Cambridge, Mass.:
Harvard University Press, Copyright © 1976 by the President and Fellows
of Harvard College, are reprinted by permission from the publisher.

Printed in the United States of America
          Library of Congress Cataloging-in-Publication Data
Coulter, Dee Joy.
  Original mind : uncovering your natural brilliance / Dee Joy Coulter, EdD.
     pages cm
  Includes bibliographic references and index.
  ISBN 978-1-62203-194-8
  1. Philosophy of mind. I. Title.
  BD418.3.C68 2014
  128'.2--dc23
                                        2013043266

Ebook ISBN: 978-1-62203-217-4

10 9 8 7 6 5 4 3 2 1

Dedicated to kindling three fires:

the love of your own mind,
a deep appreciation of others' minds,
the creativity to bring fresh possibilities into the world.

For the great doesn't happen through impulse alone,
and is a succession of little things that are brought together.

VINCENT VAN GOGH
in a letter to his brother, ca. 1889

CONTENTS

CONTENTS

ACKNOWLEDGMENTS

I AM INDEBTED to all of my former students who were such profound teachers about mind, as they developed their own minds and engaged in experiments with me along the way. I would also like to thank those acquaintances and even strangers who were willing to answer my many questions about the wonders of their minds and to share their stories with me.

However, it was one thing to gather all these teachings and quite another to weave them into written form for others to read and enjoy. Writing is an intense, solitary undertaking. Had I not gathered five wonderful readers together to support me, I doubt I could have persevered with the journey as it stretched into an unexpected three full years.

This amazing group of readers actually offered more than mere support. Their unique contributions deeply informed my writings. In the end, their minds joined mine in creating the voice for the book.

One of the readers, Christina Pacheco, gave valuable feedback for the early chapters before stepping down and remained a part of the audience in my mind throughout. Always the final test of clarity was whether it would make sense to Chrissy yet.

And the four incredible friends and colleagues who continued on for the entire three-year journey included:

Dr. Anne Forrest Ketchin, anthropologist, who provided invaluable help with the chapter on orality-based cultures and was as fond of systems thinking as I was. I always knew when I had written a piece she would especially enjoy and would await her feedback with delight.

Mary Lou Faddick, education leader, whose vision and enthusiasm for the project never wavered. Her uncanny intuition always sensed when my energy was flagging and needed a boost. Then we'd schedule a lunch, and somehow she would revive my stamina once again.

Susan House, teacher trainer and writing coach, who used her English-major background to set the standards for my writing with her early edits. I added her lens to my inner editor early on and wrote with much more precision because of it. Her influence brought the manuscript much closer to publication mode than it ever would have reached otherwise.

Trudy Walter, a longtime Buddhist practitioner, who had the uncanny ability to ferret out any ideas that still needed more integrity, even when I had given them the green light. She kept me honest in the most compassionate way imaginable. I deeply appreciated her wise counsel and ability to guide me as I explored the secret realms of the book.

I had one dream publisher in mind and sent the manuscript only to them—Tami Simon and her team at Sounds True. I was thrilled when they expressed their enthusiasm and offered me a contract! They even assigned their senior editor, Haven Iverson, to help me take it the last few steps toward publishable form. She is a master! Her refined suggestions elevated the manuscript to heights I could never have reached on my own. The whole journey from manuscript to published book is on track to flow just as well with continued synchronicity and grace. What an honor to be one of their authors!

Preface

WELCOME TO THE WONDERS OF YOUR MIND

Love the questions themselves as if they were locked
rooms or books written in a very foreign language.
The point is, to live everything. Live the questions now.
Perhaps . . . someday . . . you will gradually,
without even noticing it, live your way into the answer.

RAINER MARIA RILKE
Letters to a Young Poet

YOU ARE INVITED to travel a clear path through a mysterious land.
The title of this book, *Original Mind,* speaks to this paradox. The name
Original Mind is as impossible to explain as the emptiness within the
circle on the cover. The journey begins and ends in this emptiness, traveling from the fresh emptiness of the newborn baby's mind to exploring
the return to this empty mind at the journey's end. Yet, as the author,
I have provided you with a subtitle, offering a clear path through this
mystery: *Uncovering Your Natural Brilliance.* Traveling the path between
these two poles, you will encounter rich stories of the brilliant minds of
others and discover a great deal about how the mind works.

Before your journey even begins, you must make a choice. You can choose to simply *read* this book, in which case you will come away fascinated by the amazing brilliance of the minds of others and have fresh knowledge about the brain itself, or you can choose a slower, more demanding path. You can choose to *experience* this book, in which case you will also awaken your own mind's amazing brilliance.

The process of uncovering your own natural brilliance involves practices of many sorts, each one revealing yet another facet of that brilliance. You will discover these practices tucked away all along the journey. To take this practice-filled approach, you would be wise to bring along a blank journal. In each section within the book, you will usually find at least one practice. Jot it down in your journal and begin practicing it. You might even come up with ideas for practices of your own to add.

The uncovering process will range from the clarity of acquiring new outer skills and lenses that make sense from the outset, to inner ones that work their wonders on you in slower and subtler ways. And like every wisdom teaching, there is also a third, more hidden, learning experience as well. Wisdom teachings are said to contain outer, inner, and *secret* realms. The secret realms are really impossible to explain but can bubble up as understandings and transformations unexpectedly. Once they arise for you, it becomes clear why they are often called *self-secret*. If they had been named before you experienced them, they would make no sense, and after you've experienced them, there is no need for an explanation. In that spirit, perhaps by the journey's end even the mysterious nature of original mind will be revealed to you.

While scientific and historical research have informed much of my writing, I have chosen to put a detailed bibliography online at SoundsTrue.com/OriginalMind rather than interrupt the flow of your reading with endnotes and footnotes. The online site will give you, the reader, abundant resources for continuing to explore any questions or interests you may want to pursue in greater depth. I am deeply indebted to Angela Palermo, a reference librarian at the University of Colorado, for her careful work in compiling this extensive bibliography for the readers' benefit.

RECLAIMING OUR
EARLIEST MIND

If your mind is empty, it is always ready for anything,
it is open to everything.
In the beginner's mind there are many possibilities,
but in the expert's mind there are few.

SHUNRYU SUZUKI
Zen Mind, Beginner's Mind

OUR JOURNEY BEGINS with a great challenge. We must set aside all we know in order to experience the world with the freshness a baby does. When we look at the world, we tend to see what we expect to see. It is as if we are taking inventory, recognizing the elements in our surroundings, and silently naming them to ourselves. Our minds thrive on order, and this naming process gives us a measure of comfort. Highly creative thinkers have reclaimed the ability to see what they can't name, to notice with a freshness that takes in confusing elements, and to savor the puzzlement that arises. Out of that uncertainty, new ideas are easily born. They have discovered how to see as a baby does.

We can learn to do this too. It is an unlearning process, where we drop the naming of objects in order to perceive them without our inner chatter. Then we must drop the associations that trigger those perceptions in order to reawaken the pure sensations that precede any kind of knowing at all.

These pure sensations can only arise in moments when we have a truly fresh encounter with the world.

We begin this chapter with just such an encounter by a practicing monk. Then we will see what we can learn from babies and from individuals who are seeing for the first time after eye surgery. We will close with ideas, stories, and practices that can strengthen our own ability to see in this incredibly valuable, fresh way.

ZHANGI ZHINGI

By 1993, I'd been teaching at Naropa University in Boulder, Colorado, for ten years. Naropa is a Buddhist-inspired university that was founded by Chögyam Trungpa Rinpoche, a Tibetan monk credited with a major role in bringing Buddhism to the West. Interest in the link between Buddhist thought and neurology was beginning to grow. The Mind and Life Dialogues between scientists, monks, and His Holiness the Dalai Lama were in their sixth year, and a young Tibetan monk had come to Boulder for a brief visit. He had a question about the mind, and since I had the strongest neurological background on the faculty at the time, I was summoned.

After very brief greetings through his translator, I was invited to sit next to him to hear his question. He spoke in Tibetan, turning his head to look across the empty room at some imaginary object. "I look," he paused and then went on, "I see a flower. First time. What's happening?" I started to explain how the eyes carry information back to the visual cortex, but as the translation began, it was clear this was *not* what he wanted.

He interrupted, shaking his head, and tried again. "I look. [pause] I see a flower. First time," he said, using the same head motion, but this time he went on, turning his head as before and again said, "I look. [pause] I see a flower. First time. What's happening?" I was stunned! (We will have to examine several pieces to unpack the pattern that fell into place in my mind at that moment, but for now I'll continue sharing what happened.)

He was telling me that when he looks at a flower, at first he doesn't see it, and then the flower takes form. He seemed to be aware of his mind organizing a signal out of the light waves coming from the flower. Scientists call that *feature binding,* and we all do it, but it happens so quickly that, unlike him, we are usually completely unaware of the process. I thought he might want to know how this organizing process worked, so I explained how signals in the brain organize against the backdrop of lots of noise, a kind of neurological static. The cells chatter randomly, and when a cluster of them organizes in response to a stimulus, it sends a signal through the noise. That signal carries information that is coherent, meaning that it holds together as a wave pattern, setting it apart from all the chatter. That chatter or noise creates a chaotic background against which even the faintest of coherent signals will stand out extremely well.

It was obvious right away that he was pleased with this explanation, and he looked intently at me as the translator worked his way through my words. Unfortunately, however, the translator was at a loss to explain the word *chaos.* There didn't seem to be a Tibetan correlate for it. The monk knew that word held the key and finally spoke. "Ah, zhangi zhingi, zhangi zhingi," he said with delight.

"Yes," I replied, certain that those z's had to be describing chaos in some way. That was the end of the interview. I was thanked and dismissed.

Four years later, at a Naropa faculty retreat, I was sitting next to Sarah Harding, an outstanding Tibetan language scholar, and recalled the story for her. "So what's zhangi zhingi, then?" I asked her.

"Well, it means 'tangled hair'," she replied.

What a satisfying image of chaos that was. And what a wonderful question he had asked. It shed light on a core difference between his mind, refined by years of meditative practices, and the strange limitations he must have been discovering in the Western mind. Typically, the Western-educated mind refuses to let images dissolve. It works hard to construct its understanding of the world and becomes quite attached to its accumulated knowledge and expertise. Images remain fixed, and a second glance at a flower registers automatically as the same flower.

This story raises two important questions. If at first the monk saw no flower, what was he seeing before the image of the flower emerged?

Secondly, how could he erase the image of the flower once he saw it so that the second time was a "first time" all over again? Hold these questions as you continue reading. They are part of the pattern that fell into place in my mind when I heard the monk's question.

While this story is describing a very advanced mind skill, here is a beginning exercise you can practice. Once or twice a day, interrupt your habitual activities and shift your focus. See if you can pay attention simply to the light, color, and motion around you for just a moment before the voice in your head starts naming what you are seeing. You may think you need to be taking a walk in nature to let this happen, but it should be just as easy in the grocery store, in an office, or at home. These isolated sensations are actually everywhere! The following sections will guide you in reclaiming this skill again.

TO SEE AS A BABY DOES

> Look at things as a baby does, without foreknowledge . . . let it
> come in and experience it fully and totally, without understanding it.
>
> MURSHID FAZAL INAYAT-KHAN
> leading Sufi teacher, former head of Sufi Movement International

Babies aren't looking at objects as we know them but rather at the movement traces they leave. They are especially fascinated with biological motion paths. How do we know they are doing this? Some very clever researchers came up with this ingenious experiment: They dressed a person totally in black, blackened the face and hands, and then attached tiny LED lights to key joints—elbows, wrists, shoulders, hips, and so on. Then they filmed the person walking in a darkened room, against a black backdrop. The resulting film only registered a moving trace of all the joint movements. Babies *loved* looking at that film and fixed their gaze on it for a long time. But then the researchers altered the film slightly, changing only the motion path of the elbow light, so it would indicate a "freak" elbow that was jutting forward and returning back to center rather than the natural movement of backward and returning. The babies were visibly upset by this and quickly averted their gaze. The altered film violated the natural flow of human motion paths, and the babies could sense that, even though there was no image of a person on the film. This response of staring at or turning away from a film or object is the main way researchers can tell what a very young baby likes.

A young baby's reaction to beauty may not involve actual images either. Researchers asked college students to sort through one hundred pictures of college-age males and one hundred of college-age females, picking out the ten most attractive and ten least attractive faces in each stack. They then flashed slides of these faces onto a screen. They showed each of these slides to a large number of six-week-old babies, one baby at a time. Once again, each baby would fix his or her gaze on the faces college students identified as most attractive and would be distressed and avert his or her gaze when shown the ones deemed least attractive. Portrait artists maintain that the distinction between beauty and ugliness is largely a matter of proportion. Alter one feature slightly, and a face can suddenly lose its beauty. Somehow this small alteration violates the mathematical formula or template for facial beauty. So what were the babies seeing? Babies can learn to recognize the face of their mother, but it will take months before they can generalize to the point that other faces come into focus easily enough to be recognized. These babies were too young for that, so it means they weren't actually seeing faces in this experiment. They seemed to be responding to the harmony or dissonance embedded in the proportions of each face.

It is very hard for us to observe these motion paths with our conscious minds. And here is why: As an infant, you were dazzled by the motion paths that surrounded you and devoted all of your waking life to engaging your senses in varied combinations. Gradually, you learned to recognize the objects behind all those motion paths. You learned to identify their sounds, their touch, their look, and sometimes even their smell and taste. Your brain was generating a neural program to translate motion paths and waves into objects. By the time you entered school, you were converting these waves into objects so quickly that you no longer realized the world was actually coming to you as waves. This leaves us with a puzzling problem. How can we possibly know what our eyes would be seeing if our brains hadn't developed this translation program?

Perhaps the experiences of a unique population of newly sighted adolescents and adults who were just beginning to develop a visual translation program can teach us. Many of them have described what their eyes saw as they experienced sight for the first time and began their struggle to make visual sense of the world. And what they saw was fascinating.

When the bandages came off, there was no face greeting them—only a blur when they looked in the direction of a familiar voice. For weeks, color was the most captivating sensory stimulus, since touch and hearing couldn't prepare them for that phenomenon. The visual stimulation around them seemed overwhelming at times, a dazzling mixture of light, color, and movement. Learning to convert from touch to sight posed an unusual challenge. Feeling a statue of an elephant, for example, could not prepare them for the look of the whole statue. Their minds were organized to study an object part by part in a kind of time sequence. Sight should enable them to see these parts all at once, assembled in space, but it wasn't that easy. With great effort, they might learn to recognize the elephant statue by sight, but if the statue were turned, it would again be unrecognizable at this new angle. Their brains had not yet developed a visual program to rotate objects spontaneously.

Furthermore, if an object didn't move, they couldn't register depth perception. Distance then had to be analyzed by the size of an object. Stairs appeared as a single flat surface with parallel stripes. One subject described navigating through his home by constructing lines or paths in his mind that connected all the rooms and key furniture and then following these mental paths as he walked. If he veered off from one of his paths, he would easily get lost. Overall, the wave features of color, light, and motion paths dominated their visual world. Only with much practice would some newly sighted individuals learn to bind these features together and see objects easily. As you work with the practices suggested in the first two chapters, your ability to sense waves and motion paths may return. For your first practice, try turning your attention toward observing very young infants more carefully. Notice how often lights, tones, movements, and breezes seem more interesting to them than the objects around them.

You will find practices such as this throughout the book, some clearly stated at the close of a section and others embedded within the text. Some sections, like the ones in chapter 6, are absolutely filled with possible practices for you to consider.

LEARNING TO MATCH

There was a child went forth every day,
And the first object he look'd upon, that object he became,
And that object became part of him for the
day or a certain part of the day,
Or for many years or stretching cycles of years.

WALT WHITMAN
Leaves of Grass

As you practice observing the world with fresh eyes, you may discover that you are becoming one with what you are observing at times. This is terrific! We can call that *matching* for now. Later, we will look at some exciting research on mirror neurons and take this skill even further.

Matching is an ability you were born with and relied on heavily in your first few years of life. Gradually, other cognitive abilities took over, and your ability to match grew weaker. Some remnants of matching remain, however. As spectators when we watch athletic events or dance programs, we naturally imitate their leaps, spins, tosses, and other actions inwardly. We can actually feel ourselves getting quite a workout as we do this physical matching. It is part of the satisfaction that draws us back to the next performance. This matching phenomenon can also occur on the emotional level. When we extend our sympathy or share in a joyful celebration with friends and family, our feelings can rise to the level of true matching. Then we can honestly say we feel their pain and joy along with them.

With practice it will even be possible to match with the *mind* of another at times, although this is more challenging. Ironically, even *this* understanding cannot be achieved with intellect and requires an inner, felt sensing by our body, much like when we matched with feelings and movements. The intellect can analyze, categorize, and spot weaknesses in a mind, but you need to awaken the ability to match before you can embrace the mind of another. Perhaps some stories about how others work with matching will help clarify this idea so you can begin to develop your own practice.

The idea of matching is not new. Buddhists have often called it *exchanging self for other.* Paracelsus, the sixteenth-century medical therapist and mystical philosopher, spoke eloquently about it five centuries ago.

> Understanding arises not from intellection, but from
> sympathetic rapport. It is our duty in our quest for wisdom to
> know things according to their own natures or essences, and not
> their appearances.

Paracelsus is suggesting that to really understand another, the observer must connect so deeply with a person or object that the true nature of that person or object is revealed. Eastern traditions often speak of "masters" and "apprentices" rather than "teachers" and "students." The apprentice receives transmissions rather than lessons and must match with or be on the same wavelength as the teacher in order to receive the teaching. Jane Faigao, a beloved tai chi chuan teacher at Naropa University, used to tell her students, "Just steal it off my body," as they struggled to learn the form. The essence of tai chi could not be known by merely imitating the outer postures.

I once interviewed a nearly olympic-caliber young equestrian who demonstrated the power of this sympathetic rapport very well. She so loved the dressage performance routines that she would doodle them in her school notebooks, she would dream about them, she would envision doing them forward and backward, she would do them in slow motion in her mind and on the horse. She even resorted to getting down on all fours and running through the routine to find out how the horse felt doing it.

There are still a few professions that rely heavily on transmitting skills by matching. When I asked a gifted master gardener how he went about arranging flowers in landscape gardens, he confessed to holding the bulbs or plants in his hand until he could sense where they longed to be planted.

In sports, this capacity to match with an opponent can bring about a higher level of engagement. In *Zen and Japanese Culture,* D. T. Suzuki quoted a Japanese swordsman who described this exchange as follows:

> When the identity is realized, I as swordsman see no opponent confronting me and threatening to strike me. I seem to transform myself into the opponent, and every movement he makes as well as every thought he conceives are felt as if they were all my own and I intuitively . . . know when and how to strike him.

This idea of trying to get inside the person or object you are observing may still seem rather strange and limited in its usefulness, but its importance is growing. Leading scientists, for example, have found it to be extremely valuable in advanced scientific research.

Consider the examples of the two Nobel laureates Joshua Lederberg and Barbara McClintock. Joshua Lederberg, whose discoveries established the genetics of microorganisms, described his approach to observation this way:

> One needs . . . the ability to imagine oneself *inside* a biological situation. I literally had to be able to think, for example, *What would it be like if I were one of the chemical pieces in a bacterial chromosome?*

Barbara McClintock's discovery of genetic transposition in corn, which became known in popular terms as *jumping genes,* revolutionized the field of molecular biology. She spoke of her approach in very similar terms:

> I found that the more I worked with them the bigger [the chromosomes] got, and when I was really working with them I wasn't outside, I was down there. I was part of the system. . . . I even was able to see the internal parts of the

chromosomes. . . . It surprised me because I actually felt as if I were right down there and these were my friends. . . . As you look at these things, they become part of you. And you forget yourself. The main thing about it is you forget yourself.

While you may have no need for such refined matching skills as these, I encourage you to practice matching with the simple elements of your daily life. Let nature, cherished objects, and the endearing qualities of the people in your life capture your attention. Savor them, however briefly, and your skill in matching will begin to grow.

The art of matching with the minds of others is an especially valuable skill. In the stories that follow, if you read about a mind skill you would like to have, do not hesitate to take Jane Faigao's advice and "steal it" from the story. Try it out. With practice, your natural brilliance can expand enormously!

OUTVISIBLE AND INVISIBLE

My first teacher about the "invisible world of children" was my own son. Scottie was four when I wanted to introduce him to gardening. Unfortunately, I was a terrible gardener. I began to muse about Findhorn, an extremely successful gardening project in Scotland that insisted they were following the guidance of elemental beings and plant spirits in their work. I longed for help like that, so one day, as we were preparing the soil, I asked Scottie if he saw any creatures. "No-o-o," he said, bewildered at the question.

I persisted out of desperation, "Don't you, don't you see *any* critters?"

"Critters! Oh, I see lots of critters," he said, delighted that I was finally making some sense.

"Well, do you see any now?"

"Yeah," he said, beginning to squint a bit as he looked around the yard. He said some were doing tricks on the roof, others were hunkered down by the tree roots, and still others were hovering around the flowers. I confessed that I really couldn't see them, and he just looked at me as if he had no idea I had this defect. For days after that, he tried to point them out to me. His search finally culminated one day when he peered under a huge spruce tree in our front yard and cried out, "C'mere, Mom. I think I finally see one you can see!"

I looked under there and tried blurring my eyes, squinting—everything I could think of before finally having to say, "Scottie, I just can't see it."

He stood up, sighed, and declared, "Well, Mom, that's just how it is. See, grown-ups, they see outvisible things, and kids, they see outvisible and *invisible* things."

Evidence for this childhood skill pops up all around us if we just keep an open mind. All too often we tend to dismiss their observations if they aren't based on any outer sign that we can see. One day in the grocery store, I overheard another young child of about five announce to his mom, "That's not a very nice man!" The mother tried to hush him and pulled him aside to ask why he said that. "Well, if my mind makes the pictures his mind makes, that's not very nice!" How many young children are doing that every day?

When I was teaching a special education class, my room was just across from the teacher's lounge. I opened my classroom door just as a former nun who was new to the faculty came out of the lounge with hands folded in front of her and made a sharp turn to go down the hall to her classroom. As I watched her disappear around the corner, the eight-year-old student beside me, who knew nothing of her background, asked, "Doesn't she ever want to get married?"

Here's a chance to play detective along with me. I was observing a special reading class one day that included a very autistic young boy of about eight. He had some beginning language skills but spent most of his time in his own little world. That morning he seemed to be all over the place. First he went over to the aquarium, rocked it back and forth, and then stood back delighted. He was about to do it again when the teacher directed him away from it. He ran over to the shiny metal door of the supply closet and began waving it back and forth vigorously. Then he was asked to sit on the floor with the group to join a discussion about calendars. Behind him a child tucked a therapy ball snugly into the top of a toy barrel, and the boy became hysterical, insisting that the ball be removed. It was, and he calmed back down until snack time a few minutes later when he raced to a seat right next to the radiator.

Can you see the *invisible* pattern? If you stop looking at the objects and think about the waves they were generating, you can see that he was actually quite focused. It wasn't the fish but the waves he created on top of the water that delighted him. And the metal door rippled when it shook, creating wind and wavy lights from the shiny surface. The ball? It was smothering the barrel—he could hear the whoosh of the barrel's last breath as the ball was pushed down. The barrel couldn't breathe until he rescued it. And at snack time, he delighted in the heat waves that rose from the radiator on cold days.

The world is actually filled with these threshold phenomena, events that can be experienced both invisibly and outvisibly. Look for opportunities to share them with young children. Rainbows, for instance, look like real objects, but they are actually just light waves arranged prismatically. Streams and waterfalls are also flowing waves made especially visible. Echoes are no more than sound waves, but they can play back our voices too. Most children under the age of six live in a realm of direct experiencing, engaging the senses, and becoming absorbed in events as they occur without activating the constant mental chatter of the adult mind. For them, these waves and motion paths are natural aspects of the images and percepts that surround them. To fully develop this ability, however, they need our help. We need to notice what they are sensing in the world about them and resist being their tour guide all the time. With that understanding, the great naturalist Rachel Carson gave this advice:

> If a child is to keep his inborn sense of wonder, he needs
> the companionship of at least one adult who can share it,
> rediscovering with him the joy, excitement, and mystery
> of the world we live in.

The following practice gives you the opportunity to serve one young child in this way. I invite you to take what I have been calling a *silent walk* with the child you choose. This activity has surprised and delighted hundreds of my college and adult students over the years, rekindling their ability to observe the world with fresh eyes. Take the time to read these instructions thoughtfully, so you will be ready to take your own silent walk whenever an opportunity arises.

THE INSTRUCTIONS

Plan a thirty to forty-five minute walk with a child between the ages of two-and-a-half and five-and-a-half. It can be around the block, in the child's backyard, or in a nearby park. If you don't really know the child well, you may want to stay close to the child's home. Let the child set the tempo throughout. Let the child initiate any conversations. While the goal is to quiet the conversation down so the child will almost forget you are there and begin to relate naturally to the surroundings, be sure to be friendly and social with the child as you begin your walk. Being completely silent would seem too awkward and might be unsettling for the child. Just avoid leading the conversation or elaborating on what is said—no teaching! Ideally, the conversation will die down shortly, and the walk will become largely silent. Be sure to keep your awareness gently focused on the child and the child's interaction with the environment during the entire walk, whether you have a talkative or silent child.

If you find you have chosen a child who talks almost constantly during the walk, your challenge will be to give quality attention to the child and the child's activity without giving focused attention to the child's words. The child may be right at the peak of language acquisition and full of the joy of naming his or her universe for you and explaining its wonders. In this case, just relax your attention to the words and resist the urge to join in on the conversation as much as you can. As you actively savor the child between comments, even the extremely talkative child can begin to realize that there is such a thing as nonverbal attention.

As you enter the child's world on this walk, notice the nature of the objects and activity the child attends to, how long the child attends to these matters, and the observations and discoveries the child seems to make. Notice, also, what it does to *your* tempo and mental activity when you enter the child's world in this way.

Many of my former students reported on their walks in great detail. Here are a few excerpts, reprinted with their permission. Notice how these young children were observing their world.

> She picks up a rock and throws it in the street. She becomes obsessed with rock throwing. (two-year-old child)

> The stimuli I expected to entertain him did not. It was the can and a cigarette butt and tapping that occupied him more. (five-year-old child)

> People on the street did not hold her attention as much as a blade of grass, a tall tree, or motion. (five-year-old child)

> We stopped to look at the wet newspaper on the lawn. At the next house we smelled the flowers in front of the porch. (three-and-a-half-year-old child)

Just before the children selected these objects to notice, their eyes caught a bit of movement or a vague glimmer that seemed more like an array of sensations than an organized perception. As their attention settled on an object, an important shift occurred. Those isolated features bound together to create conscious perceptions, claiming their focused attention.

We do the same thing as adults, but it happens so quickly that we are no longer aware of this *feature binding* process. The practices we have worked with so far have begun to help us slow that process back down so it can once again become a conscious process. In the next chapter, we will take a close look at feature binding and discover how each of our senses binds features together to create perceptions and, more importantly, how we can *unbind* them once again.

FROM SENSATIONS TO PERCEPTIONS AND BACK AGAIN

We sense infinitely more things than we perceive. . . .
We are bathing in a pool of sensations from which our
perception only extracts what is useful right now.

SERGE CARFANTAN
Philosophy and Spirituality

WE HAVE BEEN making an important distinction between sensations, which arise before we even fix our attention on them, and perceptions, which form once we bring our awareness and our naming skills to bear on the stimulus. The act of shifting from sensations to perceptions is a natural one and happens very quickly as we become more familiar with our surroundings. Think about the last time you returned from a long trip and caught yourself wandering through your home, taking inventory. You wanted to see that it was all there. Your mind was making rapid-fire perceptions as it took stock of all those familiar objects.

However, if we look deeply at sensations before they morph into perceptions, it allows us to explore an action not often identified—the act of shifting *backward* from perceptions to sensations once again. We are essentially learning to cross a rarely considered threshold in our consciousness!

This threshold-crossing skill underlies nearly all truly intuitive processes. As you practice it, you may find your own intuition improving rather dramatically. This emergent skill belongs to the secret layer of our journey, mentioned in the book's preface. It cannot be taught directly, but once it arises and you experience it, it can become a valued part of your natural brilliance. This chapter presents a rich array of possible practices for you to explore in your quest to uncover your amazing intuitive capacities.

EXPLORING THE TERRITORY BETWEEN TWO MYSTERIES

How the brain "binds" information to create a coherent
perceptual experience is an enduring question.

DAVID WHITNEY
Center for Mind and Brain, University of California, Davis

Many scientific fields encounter mysteries at their polar extremes. In these farther reaches of each field, the rules can change abruptly. The ideas of Newton, first published in 1687, served physics researchers well for almost three centuries, with very few changes until the field began to explore extremely small subatomic particles or extremely vast interactions between moving celestial bodies. Quantum mechanics arose to address the microuniverse while Einstein's theory of relativity helped address the macrouniverse.

The study of population growth also contains two mysterious extremes. When a population faces the possibility of dying out, there is often a surge of births. At the other extreme, when overcrowding and overpopulation threaten to cause a different kind of extinction, birthrates may again shift radically. At that point, fertility mysteriously declines, and the birthrate, which had been climbing steadily, can suddenly drop off.

The study of feature binding runs into similar mysteries at its two extremes. On a cellular level, neuroscientists still struggle to explain how the brain binds features like color, motion, shape, and sound together to form a perception. Looking at the larger picture, cognitive theorists are locked in debate about the role feature binding might play in explaining the nature of consciousness. They question whether consciousness can even exist until unbound features are combined in some way. However, just as scientists continue to study the sizeable territory between the extremes in physics and population growth, it is also possible to explore the many fascinating aspects of feature binding that fall between its two mysteries.

In fact, we have already begun exploring these features. The motion paths and wave patterns that engage newly sighted individuals are actually unbound features. Once a perception arises, whether it is a flower or a mother's face, we say that those features have bound together. Our challenge is to find a way to experience these features *before* they bind together, realizing that our minds tend to bind features almost instantly.

Let's experiment. Listen to the sounds around you right now and make note of two or three that seem to be simple sounds. For instance, right now I can hear a clatter . . . of dishes, a whirr . . . of the refrigerator, and a ping . . . of my computer registering an incoming e-mail. No matter what I just listened to, I instantly paired it up with its source if I could. That is feature binding at work. The very act of *attending* to one's environment usually causes this binding to happen.

However, a rabbit will startle at all sounds and run off instinctively without bothering to identify the source. Consider what you do when an unexpected sound startles you. In that moment before you even think "What was that?" you too are experiencing pure sound.

Not every simple sound is so fleeting or so startling, however. Middle Eastern music has an element called a drone that comes close to being a pure sound. It is a constant background hum around which a melody dances. It grounds the song or *rag* without carrying any information of its own. The melodies themselves carry forms that the ear reaches out to notice and then to recognize if heard a second time, but the drone doesn't engage the ear in that way.

Several Western twentieth-century composers were also intrigued with the search for unbound or unpredictable tones. Keith Jarrett, a renowned pianist, would meditate before a performance, striving to drop all musical patterns from his mind, so he could begin without any expectations, starting with whatever tones arose when he lowered his hands onto the keyboard.

Another uncomposer, John Cage, strove for what he called *indeterminacy,* randomizing single tones, tone clusters, and intervals of silence, often incorporating mechanical and environmental sounds. He was always inviting listeners to drop focused listening and allow pure sounds to reach their ears instead. However, not even the audience at a contemporary piano music recital in New York was prepared for Cage's most extreme experiment. That evening he introduced a piece he called *4' 33"* (four minutes, thirty-three seconds) that contained three carefully timed movements. A pianist entered the stage, sat down at the piano, set up his stopwatch and sheets of music, opened the lid to the keyboard for the first movement, and began turning pages but playing nothing, closed it, opened it again for the next movement, turned more pages, closed it, and opened it a final time for the third movement. Unfortunately, this opportunity to listen without a focus was lost on much of the audience. John Cage reminisced about that premiere as follows: "They missed the point. . . . What they thought was silence, because they didn't know how to listen, was full of incidental sounds. You could hear the wind stirring outside during the first movement. During the second, raindrops began pattering on the roof, and during the third people themselves made all kinds of interesting sounds as they talked or walked out."

You can practice listening without a focus whenever you want. The secret is to let sound come to you instead of going out to meet it. Take a walk in nature, and allow the random sounds to reach your ears. You can even take in city traffic noises in the same relaxed manner. Veteran teachers have learned to use this approach on playground duty, letting the ordinary sounds fade into a drone. If a problem arises, it will stand out from the drone, and they can quickly address it.

Before we move on to explore other senses, it is fascinating to consider how babies register sounds. Two key sounds are especially powerful at soothing and engaging them. These sounds were identified by researchers as they measured the strength of the immune response in newborns, taking a measurement called the *vagal tone index*. The higher the index, the stronger the baby's chances of survival became. They found that high-risk babies in intensive care units showed a dramatic rise in vagal tone at the sound of their mothers' voices, an effect that no other sounds could match.

Along with the mother's voice, one other sound always stands out in utero—the sound of the mother's heartbeat. Tapes of music incorporating the sound of a relaxed adult's heartbeat are often used in hospital nurseries to calm fussy babies. And if the pregnant mother had watched a particular soap opera to relax, researchers discovered that her baby would calm within thirty seconds of hearing that theme music. These findings seem to suggest that the ear's first crucial task is to foster bonding by registering sounds linked to the mother. A newborn's first experiences with feature binding, anchoring key sensory stimuli to the mother, has begun.

WAYS OF SEEING

The will that controls thinking must cease to flow from subject
to object and begin to flow from object to subject. . . .
This purification of subjective experience is achieved through the
practice of wonder, reverence, at-oneness, and complete surrender.

JOHN GARDNER
Right Action, Right Thinking

The eye has two basic mechanisms for processing sight. The first is a focal mechanism that uses the center of the eye and is excellent at targeting in and attending to fine detail. In nature, predators rely heavily on this focal vision to identify, track, estimate lunging distance, and capture their prey. The second mechanism is used by the prey and involves peripheral vision, which is much more useful to them since it spots any movement in their surroundings so much faster than focal vision can. While predators have front-facing eyes that can join together to focus on a single object, prey animals like rabbits and horses have eyes on the sides of their heads. Rabbits' eyes are set so far back that their line of sight doesn't overlap, and they can't really focus on objects directly in front of them at all. Horses can and do focus on objects at some distance, but not on any objects closer than three feet in front of them. Horses that are trained to jump over obstacles are exhibiting profound trust that their riders will signal exactly when to lift off the ground because they can no longer see those obstacles at that point.

As humans, we can use both mechanisms well. Our peripheral vision system uses the sides of our eyes, is much faster, and picks up on the slightest movements. So birdwatchers cock their heads to the side, soldiers patrolling enemy lines walk back and forth with the enemy lines off to the side, and good teachers monitor classroom behavior with "eyes in the back of their head." Team-sport athletes also rely heavily on this system in moments of peak performance, instantly picking up on the changing movements of their opponents and teammates. All of these motions happen quickly and unexpectedly and are not paired with other features at first, so they qualify as pure visual sensations or unbound features. While our peripheral mechanism alerts us rapidly to faint motion cues, it doesn't register color and cannot make out the details very well at all. For that, we turn toward the movement, switching to our focal vision, which uses the central part of each eye. Now we can process color, fine details, and information about distance or spatial perception.

It will not be easy to find a way to observe pure visual sensations with our highly analytical visual system. The strongest possibilities are the experiences of light and color. Light was the first profound sensation to greet newly sighted individuals, and it appears to captivate babies as well. We are probably trying to recapture that pure, dazzling sensation when we watch fireworks, scan the sky for shooting stars, or gather to see a holiday parade of lights. These light shows have a way of inviting us to experience pure sensations, but it took some dedicated artists to find a way for viewers to experience color as a sustained sensation.

During the twentieth century while some composers were searching for the pure experience of sound, a few visual artists attempted to share their love of color as a pure or unbound experience. Yves Klein, a French painter, was especially moved by a particular shade of blue and even worked with a chemist to create a bonding agent that allowed the pigment's color to shine through in all its brilliant intensity. Klein went on to create nearly two hundred canvases using only this color, which he named International Klein Blue. Some of the canvases were simply blanketed with this blueness, inviting the viewer to give up on looking *at* the painting and to discover the pure sensation of color coming *from* the painting instead.

American writer, antiwar activist, and visual artist Ad Reinhardt was searching for a way to remove all the form and information from visual art, in the same way John Cage tried with music. Deeply upset by the oppositional thinking of the Vietnam War, he attempted to rise above that kind of polarized thinking through his writing and his artwork. Reinhardt described his intention as an effort to create "an unmanipulated, unmanipulatable, useless, unmarketable, irreducible, unphotographable, unreproducible, inexplicable icon." He devoted the last thirteen years of his artistic life to painting large canvases of barely discernable black-on-black squares with extremely careful brush strokes. At a recent exhibition of his life and works, one of his large canvases, which had been carefully preserved for over fifty years, was the featured exhibit. Even now it has the power to mesmerize viewers. They would stand motionless for long moments in front of the canvas, letting go of analytic perception, and simply allow themselves to take in the blackness that arose from the painting.

We might say that most of this section has been an exploration of the world of visual *events* that also have a strong relationship to pure *waves*. Perhaps the consideration of light itself can be considered a wave experience, but that is just a beginning. With practice, you can train your eyes to enjoy seeing the wave world more fully. The secret is in letting the world come to you rather than going out in search of it. Feel the surging sensation when you see a horse break into a run; savor the flow of traffic moving by, the meandering motion of shopping carts moving through a store, the downward motion of snow and rain. Let your eyes soften their gaze and discover the motion paths embedded in the world around you.

HOW THE NOSE KNOWS
The Remarkable Olfactory System

Our nose is linked to its own specialized organ called the *olfactory system,* located within our larger brain. This organ, made up of a bulbous region with various branches, operates surprisingly freely, insulated from influences that shape the rest of our brain. If brain territories have so-called status, then the olfactory bulb, along with its branches, is located in a very elite region. Its neighboring brain organs include the hippocampus, which is the brain's main memory center; the frontal cortex, which regulates all of our higher-level thinking; and the amygdala, which serves as an emotional gatekeeper, storing trauma memories and scanning for new dangers.

Folklore has always given the nose special powers to discern truth, as if realizing it was less likely to be swayed by outside influences. The word *sage* that we use to describe a wise person originated from the Latin root *sagax,* which means one who has a keen sense of smell. Several slang expressions honor the truth-detecting powers of the nose. We say that a reporter has a "nose for the news," and we have sayings like "That smells fishy," "That stinks," and "I smell a rat."

Police interrogators pay special attention to whether suspects touch their noses. Lying raises a person's stress level, which then engorges the blood vessels in the nose. Only by rubbing or pulling at the nose will the swelling go down. The key to one's facial identity is also the nose, and changing it will make a person unrecognizable. Covering it with a red bulb was originally a shaming device that has since become the vehicle for transforming a performer into a clown personality.

When we inhale through the nose, the air travels back to a nasal cavity near the olfactory bulb that serves as a small refrigeration unit for the frontal cortex. One branch of the carotid artery travels through this cavity on its path from the heart to the frontal cortex, carrying fresh, hot blood upward. If that blood can be cooled by as little as two-tenths of a degree, it will allow a person to operate with a cool head. Otherwise, the person can literally become hotheaded and less able to think before acting. Recall the many newspaper clippings you've seen of the faces of rioters. They are breathing through their mouths and grimacing with anger. These two behaviors guarantee that they will remain hotheaded.

The nasal cavity's refrigeration process depends on two behaviors that are opposite to the ones the rioters are using. First, it definitely needs the cool air coming in from the nose, so nose breathing is very important. But it is also counting on a visit from the cooler vein blood that is leaving the brain and returning to the heart for more oxygen. When a person grimaces, the blood drops straight into the carotid vein, bypassing the nasal cavity. If a person smiles on the other hand, the facial muscles will route that blood back to the nasal cavity through a network of facial veins. The Vietnamese monk and Nobel Peace Prize nominee Thich Nhat Hanh is known for advising everyone to "Seek Peace. Smile, breathe, and go slowly." Not only is he offering wise philosophical advice, he is actually offering wise neurological advice as well. You might want to test the power of his recommendation by experimenting with the impacts nose versus mouth breathing and smiling versus grimacing have on your state of mind.

This air pathway from the nose back to the nasal cavity is the only unprotected route into your brain. The fact that it enters such a sensitive region of your brain has medical professionals both concerned and excited. They are concerned because polluted air can carry contaminants like lead from gasoline, fumes from sprayed pesticides, and black mold from wet drywall and cardboard into your brain where they can cause serious neurological damage. The region surrounding the olfactory bulb is the first place Alzheimer's plaque builds up and includes the area where Parkinson's disease develops as well. Because these disease processes crowd the olfactory bulb, a loss of smell is often their first symptom. In the past, medical researchers tried to deliver medicines to these regions of the brain through the blood stream, but they were stopped by the blood-brain barrier that blocks foreign substances from reaching the brain. Researchers are now developing chemical inhalants that can be delivered through the nose to treat conditions like these directly.

While nasal cavity properties have drawn many neuroscientists into the study of the olfactory system, another intriguing discovery has created even more excitement. Brain cells can repair themselves to a certain extent, but it is rare for them to completely replace themselves and their connections to other cells. This process of cell replacement, called *neurogenesis,* has only been found to occur in two brain regions, the hippocampus (the major memory center) and the olfactory system.

Recent findings show that approximately 10 percent of the hippocampal cells will replace themselves on a regular basis. However, 100 percent of the olfactory system refreshes itself by creating identical replacement cells every six months. Researchers still don't understand why this occurs, but they do know that if this process is blocked, the olfactory bulb will wither dramatically. This capacity to rebuild has led to promising research with rats using the cell sheaths that coat their olfactory pathways to wrap spinal cords that have been severed. Early results indicate that the cells are able to mend the injury and restore the rat's ability to walk, creating hope that a way to heal spinal cord injuries in humans can someday be developed. While twenty years ago there seemed to be no future in olfactory research, today it has become a neurological goldmine.

The next section will consider smells themselves, how we register them, and whether we can discover any unpaired olfactory sensations.

FROM PERFUMES TO PHEROMONES

The tendency of the nose to identify whatever it smells, pairing it up with a name or an association, is so strong that the search for a conscious scent that hasn't been paired up seems hopeless. Instead, the nose serves as a powerful memory trigger because its olfactory bulb is located right next to the primary memory center of the brain, allowing scents to connect with memories easily. Aromatherapy can reawaken the fading memories of Alzheimer's patients and can activate a flood of memories for an author like Marcel Proust, whose memoir *Remembrance of Things Past* was inspired by experiencing a single scent from his childhood.

However, not all smells fall into the same category. The environmental smells that connect easily to memories are being detected by the nose's primary olfactory system. Smells like perfume, flowers, skunks, gasoline fumes, and cooking odors are all carried back to the olfactory bulb and link easily with the frontal cortex to get identified and with the hippocampus to form memories.

Some anthropologists claim that two particular scents are more primitive than this and play a genuine survival role: the smell of smoke and the smell of spoiled food. They even suggest that the original purpose of the nose may have been to detect these two scents. In today's technological environment, however, the need for these skills is fading. Smoke alarms detect smoke for us, and grocery stores remove spoiled food from the shelves and counters before we arrive. The end result, for much of the population, has been a diminished ability to discern smells.

Decades ago, most Western medical schools included a course on diagnosis by smell, since many disease conditions have very distinct body odors that can serve as diagnostic clues. Diabetes, bowel obstructions, liver conditions, kidney failure, and lung cancer all release molecular markers in the breath. While students in Eastern medical training programs continue to be taught to use smell as an important diagnostic tool, these courses gradually disappeared from the Western curriculum. Fewer medical students seem to have the keen sense of smell needed to learn this skill. Meanwhile, diagnosis came to rely on visual observations, on patient self-reports, and on data from progressively more advanced technological instruments. With the resurgence of interest in olfactory properties, electronic noses and canine noses are joining the battery of diagnostic tools. The earliest electronic noses, or scent-reading devices, were adaptations from the equipment developed by the perfume industry. State-of-the-art devices are now much simpler, more portable, and less costly. One promising approach involves using laser beams to assess the molecules in a single breath. Therapy dogs have been used for some time to detect changes in their companions' breath patterns before epileptic seizures and to signal when their diabetic human companions are suffering from high or low blood sugar levels. Now, trainers are discovering that they can teach some dogs to identify the presence of cancer on the breath of patients with a remarkable 99 percent accuracy.

There is a good reason why humans will never reach that level of skill, though. The human nose is only able to hold the trace of any scent for a few minutes without making a special effort. Because the nose cannot shut out smells, its way of protecting us from overload is to require that we actively sniff every few minutes to refresh our awareness of the scent.

Think back to a time when you passed through your front door only to have your nose alert you that the garbage needed to be taken out. If you decided to read your mail first, the scent message faded, and you likely forgot all about the garbage.

Dogs experience the world of smells very differently. They have a unique breathing pattern that lets them monitor their surroundings and track important scents continuously. Their nostrils quiver to stir up the air on each in-breath, and their side slits flutter to create a breeze on each out-breath, refreshing the scent for the next in-breath.

The noses of dogs and most other animals have two separate systems for smell. One resembles our primary mechanism and registers the many strong scents in their environment. The other mechanism is devoted to handling a collection of extremely faint scents. This collection of scents is called *pheromones.* Pheromones include all the body's odors from the breath to urine, feces, vaginal odors, vomit, blood, and decaying flesh to the scent of emotional states like fear and aggression and the many odors given off by the health problems mentioned earlier. If the pheromones are strong, the main system handles them, but if they are extremely faint, a more primitive olfactory system called the *vomeronasal organ,* or VNO, takes over. This little organ consists of a very small pit located deep inside the nose in mammals and on the roof of the mouth in reptiles. It is tied into the olfactory bulb by its own pathways and is devoted entirely to detecting and tracking pheromones. These pheromones may be as close to an unbound feature as the nose can get, so can humans detect them too?

Because this vomeronasal organ is so incredibly small and well hidden, researchers didn't realize it even existed in humans until fairly recently. Following this discovery, they began isolating key pheromones, hoping it would lead to powerful perfume ingredients, but this research has been disappointing. At least with adults, it appears that pheromones are not being registered very clearly. Babies show much stronger sensitivity to pheromones, detecting and responding to the smell of their own amniotic fluid and their own mother's milk easily. Their amniotic fluid calms them immediately, while the smell of the milk they seek causes them to cry in frustration if they can't find it. This keen sensitivity to the smells of the mother seems to play a major role in early bonding and may even qualify as a pure sensation.

This is as far as current research can take us in identifying the human response to pheromones, but please continue to explore your own hunches. Can humans smell fear? Does "animal magnetism" play a part in choosing a mate? Do some emotional encounters actually cause bad breath?

EXPLORING TASTE, TOUCH, AND MOTION

One must ask children and birds
how cherries and strawberries taste.

JOHANN WOLFGANG VON GOETHE

Much of our sense of taste is based on our memories of past experiences and our associations with those tastes. Did we like it, when did we first taste it, and is this a good example of that taste or not? So it might seem impossible to find an unbound taste sensation at all. From enjoying the comfort of familiar foods, to taste-testing recipes and new dishes, to using the sense of taste to detect spoiled food or the bitter taste of possible poisons, we are always pairing up taste with smells or with memories of past experiences. If we look to a baby's experiences with taste, however, we can discover what it is like to have a true, unpaired taste sensation. There are three taste reactions that babies display immediately as newborns, and some research even suggests they have the same responses in utero. Even newborn babies who have not yet been nursed will pucker their mouths, wrinkle their noses, and blink their eyes rapidly when given a swab of mild acetic acid that tastes sour. If they are first presented with a swab of sugar water, the babies will lick their lips, begin to suck, and show contentment. And finally, if swabbed with a mild dose of quinine, which has a very bitter taste, they will thrust their tongue out, make a gagging, spitting motion, and close their eyes tightly.

Some researchers speculate that this primitive rejection of bitter is to protect the baby from poisons since most poisons are bitter. Babies and young children typically continue to dislike all bitter tastes, but as adults we often outgrow this and begin to enjoy coffee, bitter chocolate, or salad greens. However, bitter foods that are not toxic to adults can still harm fetuses in very small doses, so even without knowing this, most women will instinctively develop a dislike for bitter tastes during pregnancies.

While we know what a baby's face does with tastes, this still does not tell us how they experience taste. However, I may have discovered the answer. During the 1970s I took part in a group therapy program that included reparenting, a therapy process designed to give healthy parenting messages to participants when they are in a childlike state and likely to receive them more deeply. Each week the group would play for an hour in the presence of two therapists and then debrief about their experiences during the second hour. The participants all entered into a sort of waking half-hypnotic state where they actually felt like children and acted like them, playing with toys and asking the therapists child-like questions. Before the play hour began, the therapists would ask if anyone thought they would want a bottle. If so, the therapists would prepare a bottle of warm milk for them. Sure enough, at some point during the hour that person would become infant-like and cry out for a bottle. I was sure I would *never* do that. Besides, I hated the taste of warm milk and was certain I couldn't stay in the age-regressed state of an infant if I had to taste it. Six months later, I actually gave it a try, and it completely changed my understanding of what a baby experiences.

I made sure I was hungry before I came to the session. Then I curled up in a corner and drifted backward in time till I felt very young. Suddenly, I felt a radiating pain beginning in my abdomen and moving out to my whole body. Next, I was startled by a piercing howl in my ear. A brief flicker into an adult state told me that was actually *my* voice! Back to infancy I went. The sense of being held came next and then, the bottle. Again I flickered into an adult state long enough to realize my mouth wasn't tasting at all before returning to the pleasure of radiating warmth that seemed to pool in my hands and feet especially. When nursing babies curl their toes and flick their fingers, this is actually part of their "taste" experience. It is still a global experience, not yet a mouth sensation. The closest we come to that feeling of radiating warmth from taste may well be when we enjoy a cup of hot cider, cocoa, or coffee after having been out in the cold for a long time.

The last of our five senses, touch, is easier to experience as a pure sensation. We often pair up our sense of touch with some object to gain information as when we stroke velvet cloth, touch hot water from the faucet, lift a sack to see if we can carry it, or even feel the forehead of a fevered child. However, if we expand our quest to a search for full-body experiences, we can discover a rich array of unbound features. Playground equipment and amusement park rides capitalize on the pleasure these pure sensations give us. Sensations like buoyancy, spinning, falling, swinging, and bouncing can stand alone. They don't need to be paired up to be experienced, and even babies, who have only learned to pair a few features, usually love these sensations.

Sometimes these motions can arise unexpectedly as unpaired impulses. When a flock of birds takes flight, a school of fish darts about, or a group of hornets swarms, they are responding to what is called an *action impulse*. This may also explain two kinds of human behavior: being caught up in mob action or audience frenzy as a part of a group, and heroic actions as an individual. Often rescuers being honored for jumping into the water or running into a burning building or lifting a car off of a victim have no explanation for their actions. They don't recall thinking about it at all.

Another important, but unpleasant function of the sense of touch is to register pain. Most pain sensations have been paired and analyzed in some way, so they fall in the category of bound features. But what about the sense of well-being? Can it become a background quality that we cease to notice? The act of appreciating our health, as we do after a period of illness and pain, is definitely a paired sensation, registering clearly and happily in the brain. But perhaps when we take our health for granted and let this absence of pain settle into the background of our day, it may be acting like a drone state. Once again, we are experiencing the pure sensations of a baby's reality. When they feel no pain, they rest calmly, sleep, or attend to whatever stimulation their senses register. They, too, take their bodily comfort for granted until it gets disrupted.

MORE SENSATIONS TO SAVOR

The infant began experiencing the world as pure sensations and gradually created a large inventory of paired or bound features, while you have been striving to experience pure sensations once again. You have no doubt discovered how naming a sensation always turned it into a bound feature. We will begin referring to bound features as perceptions in the next chapter and explore the power of language to solidify these perceptions. As language became a dominant force in your childhood, the world of sensations grew increasingly difficult for you to access.

Fortunately, however, you can still experience special moments with each sense where speech falls away and you are once again open to pure sensations. Here are a few examples that can be helpful in your quest to experience pure sensations.

With taste, fine chefs strive to create gourmet magic for the diner, tastes so exquisite that they transport the diner into a speechless ecstasy. A number of memorable movie scenes capture this moment well, from *Tom Jones* to *Babette's Feast.*

Nature is able to transport the sensation of smell to this vast state as well. When an entire field of lavender sends its aroma everywhere or when the world smells completely fresh after a rain, it can give rise to a moment that resonates so deeply we again have no words.

Our eyes can encounter awe-inspiring beauty, perhaps being stunned by a powerful work of art in a museum or by the sight of a spectacular sunset.

Music has the power to transport the listeners and the performers to a speechless world as well and does it so often we almost come to expect it. Those who have not been touched by music in this way are missing a deeply fulfilling experience.

Lastly, the sense of touch can carry lovers into an ecstatic realm, and touch can also pick up on extremely subtle energy fields as well. It is possible to actually feel the profound energy surrounding a memorial site or spiritual center as it arouses a speechless state of reverence and awe.

We have been striving to reclaim the ability to experience pure sensations or unbound features. Now it is time to deepen our ability to bind features, or form perceptions, more consciously. A quality of focused attention and analysis arises as the mind forms perceptions, and there are ways to sustain that focus. The challenge is to engage a brain region called the *frontal cortex*. Before this journey ends, you will become deeply familiar with this region and know how to use it well. Your first set of practices involves playing with five great sensory triggers that can enhance your attention and focus.

If your ears are struggling to listen, raising your eyebrows will lift your ears slightly and tug on your eardrum, bringing your attention into focus. It triggers an alerting response in us just as it does in animals.

If your eyes are wandering and blurring up, squinting will bring them back into focus by activating focal vision. Observe what your eyes do next time you have to drive in poor visibility conditions or when you struggle to finish reading a page even though your eyes are exhausted. Very likely you will resort to squinting in both situations.

If your mind feels groggy and the world seems dull, try breathing deeply through the nose by sniffing. This activity does more than refresh your sense of smell. It also refreshes your mind so it can continue to think. College students, business executives, and elders wanting to enhance their aging brains are all experimenting with brain-aerobics breathing exercises.

If your mind needs to be alerted, your tongue can make a clicking sound against the roof of your mouth. As it turns out, animal researchers have discovered that all mammals click to their young to get their attention.

And finally, if your mind is having a hard time finding words, tapping the fingers on your right hand or snapping your right thumb and middle finger together will help. The brain region that operates those fingers is adjacent to a major speech center in the left frontal cortex, and this stimulates that center to search for words.

As we will discover in the next phase of the journey, many young children and indigenous people can look out at the formed world and then shift their focus so they only see the energetic properties behind those forms. *They are essentially moving back and forth across this threshold between sensation and perception.* This seems to be what the monk, mentioned earlier, was doing when he regarded the flower anew each time he turned toward it. As you work with these feature-binding explorations, see if you can find ways to cross this threshold also.

STEPPING STONES
TO FORMING
OUR CHARACTER

For every one step you take in the pursuit of
higher knowledge, take three steps in the
perfection of your own character.

RUDOLF STEINER
Knowledge of Higher Worlds

I have a dream that my four little children will one day
live in a world where they will not be judged by the
color of their skin but by the content of their character.

MARTIN LUTHER KING JR.

WHERE DOES CHARACTER come from, how is it formed, how
much do we inherit, and how much is learned? Can we coach our children in ways that guide them into developing strong characters, and can
we strengthen our own character at this late date in our lives? We know
character when we witness it. It propels the acts of kindness, goodness,
and heroism that bring tears to our eyes. We are clearly touched by these

displays of noble character, and when they arise in young children, they are even more precious. As parents, these acts by our children become stories to cherish and retell. As teachers, we rejoice if the social climate in our classrooms can call forth such compassionate behavior. We may strive to manifest these traits ourselves, aspiring to deepen our character so our natural tendencies have more nobility about them.

This chapter opens with new discoveries about the formation of our character, events that occur before we are even born. The second section, "The Quest for a Neurology of Peace," introduces a pattern that will lay the foundation for a profound journey into the developing character, will capacities, and social-engagement style of the young child. As you explore the four developmental challenges that must be met and handled effectively between birth and age five, you will be invited to explore how these four stepping stones have contributed to shaping your own character and personal style of relating to others. Fortunately, the strategies that help children develop well can be adapted to help us grow as adults too, allowing us to strengthen our own character and enhance our way of relating to others.

FIRST STEPS IN BUILDING OUR CHARACTER

The earliest contributions to your character occurred in utero and have only recently been discovered. These are the *epigenetic* influences, and they came to you in the form of chemical messages.

Epigenesis literally means *beyond genes* and explores the way your genes are programmed to perform their functions. While scientists have known for some time that altered forms of genes can result in emotional and physical disorders, they have only recently begun uncovering the much broader range of impacts arising from the genes' programming problems. Much of this programming occurs in utero. As the fetus develops, the genes receive their assignments in the form of chemical bonds that determine how they will be packaged within the cells, what their roles are to be, and how and when they are to activate these roles.

If the cells fail to remember these roles, cancer and other diseases can be the result. However, if the genes were packaged poorly or contained faulty instructions, then the cells could remember these poorly designed instructions perfectly and do their jobs exactly as programmed but still cause serious negative outcomes. So what could possibly be interfering with the normal chemical bonding and packaging process of the genes in an unborn fetus? Researchers discovered that the instructions to create abnormal modifications were actually coming from the parents! Here is a sampling from the many studies that helped them come to this realization.

In 2010, researchers at the University of Zurich reported an experiment in which they stressed a group of male mice for the first fourteen days of their lives by continuously and unpredictably separating them from their mothers. After that, they were fed and cared for normally, but as adults these mice still displayed a trauma pattern of isolating themselves and being overly jumpy. These mice were then bred with perfectly calm females and had nothing to do with the upbringing of the offspring. Nevertheless, these pups grew up to have the same behaviors, and their brains had the same genetic programming abnormalities as their fathers. This programming pattern was found to exist in the sperm of those fathers and had been passed on to the next generation at conception.

Mothers send their alarm messages differently. The human fetus is able to produce enzymes to shield itself from the ordinary ebb and flow of stress hormones it receives from the mother. However, when the mother faces extreme stressors or suffers from PTSD (post-traumatic stress disorder), this buffering capacity can be overwhelmed, causing the fetus to suffer from *fetal distress.* If the fetus endures this distressed state for very long, less oxygen reaches the fetus, and this can set off a cascade of reactions, from stunted growth and premature birth to a weakened immune system that will put the newborn at risk for infections, asthma, and digestive problems. Added to that, the newborn will now be programmed to be at high risk for PTSD just like the mother.

Researchers saw this pattern clearly in a study of mothers impacted by Hurricane Andrew in Florida in 1992. They studied fetal distress patterns of babies born to mothers who had been in their first, second, or third trimesters when the hurricane hit and compared them to babies born at those same times to mothers who had been living in areas not affected by the hurricane. Babies of mothers impacted in the first trimester showed no significant rise in fetal distress, but those impacted in the second trimester faced a 20 percent greater risk of fetal distress, and those in the third trimester had a 26 percent greater risk. Babies of African-American mothers in their third trimester faced an even higher risk of 45 percent, in large part because those mothers were most heavily impacted. They were less likely to evacuate, more likely to have been injured, more likely to have less insurance, and more likely to have been rendered homeless.

This trauma story is being told over and over as mothers and fathers face natural disasters, devastating poverty, violence, and war and then unwittingly pass their shock onto their children. This pattern can be reduced if mothers are better protected from trauma during pregnancy and if fathers, who produce new sperm every day, are helped to recover from their own traumas so their sperm can begin sending better messages. Epigenetics researchers are also searching for ways to reprogram some of these messages in children and adults. While the results are slow in coming, excitement is growing about the possibility of breakthroughs.

For now, we must learn to work with these original messages, softening any shadows they may be casting on our character. Fortunately, they play a fairly small part in forming the content of our character. Our character is in large part the result of the will qualities we have cultivated. Will is much more than simply the ability to resist temptations. It includes our ability to initiate, to endure, to compromise, to abstain, to act with courage. The list is long, and you may have some favorite qualities of your own that you have cultivated or aspire to develop. The rest of this chapter explores how our will qualities develop during our first five years, heavily shaping our character in the process. Unlike the epigenetic influences, the impact of these experiences can be modified later. If you are dissatisfied with the impact this phase of your life journey has made on your character, you will discover many practices that can help you improve its content over time.

THE QUEST FOR A NEUROLOGY OF PEACE

For years, I had a great rhythm operating in my public speaking. Propelled by my insatiable curiosity, I would frequently discover new research, make connections to the world of education, and then look for opportunities to share these insights with an audience. This process happened with a kind of ease. Sometimes I would be invited to keynote large conferences, and those invitations would come a year or two ahead of time. So I would make an educated guess about what themes I would have figured out by then and offer to shape the talk around those ideas. That way, I was spared from trying to breathe life into ideas that no longer excited me. This approach worked well until a few years ago when I finally pushed it too far. The invitation came with an eighteen-month lead time. The audience would be nearly two thousand Montessori educators, and at the time, I was puzzling about what the neurological underpinnings of peace might look like. Since their philosophy of education rested heavily on peace education, they were delighted when I offered to speak about awakening the neurology of peace.

I had several hunches about where to search. First, I returned to my study of the olfactory bulb, hoping that new findings on the olfactory tract leading to the frontal lobes had found it to be a truth detector of some sort. If so, it might serve as the basis for wise decision-making and more peaceful behaviors. So far, no such discovery. Then I pored over research on moral development to see if any of these studies were anchored to neurological processes. Those researchers were pretty certain that the frontal lobes played a significant role and often cited the work of Alexander Luria for evidence. But I had been studying Luria's work for years and knew it didn't have enough pieces to satisfy my quest.

By now, with only nine months left, I knew I was in trouble. I'm a vegetative scholar, not a speed-reader, so I was going to have to narrow my search to the works of no more than three key researchers and hope I could make the connections I needed that way. First, I chose Dr. Bruce Perry from Baylor University in Texas who was researching the impact of violence and trauma on the behavior and thinking skills of young children. Next, I chose Dr. Allan Schore, a child psychiatrist who had synthesized a vast amount of neurodevelopmental research and specialized in exploring the stages of affective development in children. My final choice was Dr. Stephen Porges, who had just recently published the results of his twenty years of research into the workings of the vagus nerve system.

After months of reading and study, I began distilling my extensive notes until a surprisingly simple pattern emerged. It looked as if there were four basic steps to developing both self-regulation and the ability to behave compassionately in the world. It turns out that babies are born without "brakes," as new mothers discover to their dismay when they try to calm their newborns. Not only that, they won't go on to handle the surges of energy from the sensory world or to manage their urges to move without some coaching. This pattern will make much more sense as we unpack it in the next few sections. For now, the emergent pattern can be crudely described as a set of on and off switches that need to be cultivated.

First, babies need to learn how to handle the sensory world of incoming stimuli. They need to be able to turn off the sensory world when it is too stimulating so they can calm down. We can call that a *sensory off switch*. Then they need to learn how to handle more and more stimulation from the world around them without overloading. We can call that a *sensory on switch*. That takes care of the first year of life. But then they begin crawling and exploring the world around them, and motor processing becomes the focus. At first they go through a period of following their impulses to move, which we can call *motor on switch* time. The second half of this period includes learning to speak so they can make deeper social connections to their world. Finally, the mechanisms are in place to allow them to develop their *motor off switches*, much to the relief of preschool teachers and parents. Those were the four basic steps.

With only two months to go and a possible pattern barely emerging, I had a very brief conversation with one of my colleagues at Naropa University that convinced me I was on the right track. Jane Carpenter was the chair of the BA psychology department at the time, a long-time Buddhist practitioner, and student of Buddhist philosophy, and I knew she would be fascinated with my findings. "You know how I think it is with child development," I said. "I think it goes from sensory off to sensory on to motor on to motor off." I expected that she would need much more elaboration than that, but she didn't.

Instead she quickly replied, "Oh, you mean pacify, enrich, magnetize, and destroy." I asked what she meant by destroy, and she said, "You know, overcome the desire nature." Then I knew we had a match. *Pacify* is like calming or sensory off. *Enrich* is like enjoying stimuli or sensory on. *Magnetize* is like engaging with the world or motor on, and *destroy* is like developing the impulse control to have a motor off switch.

My final question then was, "Yes, what are those?"

And her answer still delights me: "Those are the four karmas of enlightened activity."

These four conditions that we first meet in infancy are seen in Buddhist philosophy as karmas or practices to work on throughout life. This pattern will become very clear as you move through the next few sections, starting with a chance to take inventory of yourself!

And that keynote talk? It was down to the wire, but the findings came together well, and I was able to deliver a very satisfying presentation. Later in the book, we will be exploring how to bring ideas into form and how coherence can arise when we need it. This was a great example of that phenomenon.

REFLECTING ON OUR PERSONAL BALANCE

We will be exploring how babies, toddlers, and young children develop each of the four switches needed for the development of their will qualities and self-regulation skills. They need the ability to calm themselves, or turn the sensory switch off, to handle the sensory on switch so they can engage in the sensory world around them without becoming overstimulated, to work with their motor on switch so they can enjoy exploring their environment, and lastly, to activate their motor off switch so they can endure tasks, resist temptation, and control their impulses.

Before we study the child's journey through these four switches, it will be helpful to explore our current relationship to these same four switches. At various times throughout our lives, one or another of these switches can get out of balance or will need to be deepened.

In the following exercise, you will be reading descriptions of what the grown-up version of each switch looks like when it is truly in balance. But remember, the Buddhists refer to these qualities as practices, or karmas, of enlightened activity. This means they are ideal states, to be worked on throughout life, not qualities you should have mastered by now.

If you find that a particular switch needs special attention, you may already know what you need to do. If not, you could try one of that switch's strengthening exercises. Be kind to yourself, though. If you have several switches you'd like to address, just work on one at a time and choose practices that seem simple and workable so you can meet with success.

Sensory Off Switch: Calming/Pacifying

This is the ability to be at peace, to spread a feeling of peace to those around you, and to treat problems as workable when they come up. Since your sensory off switch is in balance, worry, fear, and frustration are not common emotional states for you. When others come to you with their worries, you are able to help them calm down so they can deal with their situations more easily.

How well does this describe you lately?

Not very well		Somewhat		Very well
1	2	3	4	5

If this quality is weak for you right now, here are some things you can do to strengthen it:
- Do relaxation practices: stretching, yoga, a minute or two of deep breathing, or meditating.
- Watch the flow of nature: clouds, streams, birds, or even aquarium fish.
- Take one-minute breaks: soften your eyes, relax your face, tongue, throat, and shoulders.
- Give yourself face rubs, gently rub your closed eyes, massage your hands.
- Add half an hour of sleep per night.

Sensory-On Switch: Delight/Enriching

This is the ability to see the basic goodness in others, to delight in the beauty of nature, and to feel nourished by the happiness of others. You take time to enjoy fine artwork and craftsmanship, to watch talented athletes and performers, and to appreciate the simpler skills of family and friends. You have a good sense of humor and notice the joy and comedy of everyday life.

How well does this describe you lately?

Not very well		Somewhat		Very well
1	2	3	4	5

If this quality is weak for you right now, here are some things you can do to strengthen it:
- Practice an "attitude of gratitude," noticing small bits of beauty and kindness each day.
- Be well rested (an unmet need for calmness will keep you from enjoying enrichment).
- Pet furry animals, get a massage, wear more lotion.
- Take up a hobby, anything from drawing to woodworking to a new style of cooking.
- Sing out loud at least five minutes a day (even privately—in the shower or in the car).

Motor On Switch: Engaging/Magnetizing

This is the ability to draw people to you and to play a key role in social gatherings. It is also the desire to seek adventure and explore new places and activities. Your curiosity is strong, and you are fascinated by what the world has to offer. It is easy for you to initiate actions, to enjoy the challenge of new projects, to learn new skills, and to work and play wholeheartedly.

How well does this describe you lately?

Not very well		Somewhat		Very well
1	2	3	4	5

If this quality is weak for you right now, here are some things you can do to strengthen it:

- Interrupt your habits and do an ordinary task in a new way, try something new, go somewhere new.
- Give and get more hugs.
- Give a small gift to someone—something you know they'll like.
- Make a list of things you want to accomplish, choose one, and begin it.
- Volunteer your time on a project that helps others.
- Organize and carry out a small event for family or friends (a party, a movie, a picnic, a hike).

Motor-Off Switch: Self Regulating/Destroying Desire

This is the ability to endure on tasks you don't enjoy and to control your impulses and resist temptations. You are patient, willing to work now and be rewarded later. You spend little time wishing for things you don't have. You have good willpower and follow through on projects you commit to doing. You are an even-tempered and trustworthy friend.

How well does this describe you lately?

Not very well		Somewhat		Very well
1	2	3	4	5

If this quality is weak for you right now, here are some things you can do to strengthen it:

- Save up for a major purchase instead of using a credit card to buy now and pay later.
- Resist the urge to quit an endurance task by continuing "just a few minutes longer."
- Relax your hands and shoulders and take three deep nose breaths to dissolve anger surges.
- Practice compromising—"I want this but I'll settle for that."
- Stop stressing over lost time in traffic jams or long lines—use this time to relax your muscles and breathe more deeply.

We are now ready to begin a detailed exploration of the infant and young child's developmental journey through these four switches. We will begin with the first two switches, the ability to turn the sensory world off and then to turn it on.

LEARNING TO CALM, LEARNING TO DELIGHT

Babies must learn how to regulate their behavior and to care for others. In the first few days, their most critical challenge is to learn to regulate their body heat. If they can't do that, they are not likely to survive. Caregivers help by adding blankets, cuddling them, and helping them cool off if they feel too hot, but this won't be enough. The baby's own body needs to do the fine-tuning, and miraculously it learns to do this very quickly. Then, with the help of their caregiver coaches, they are ready to begin the critical task of learning how to calm themselves.

Over the first six weeks, if they have been cared for consistently, they begin to relax whenever the mother appears. They have learned to associate her presence with comfort. Soon they will be fed, have their diaper changed, be held and stroked. They still aren't calming themselves, but this consistent care is teaching them what it feels like to be calm.

Self-calming gradually emerges if the babies continue to experience comfort and tranquility whenever their basic needs are met. They begin to spend blocks of waking time cooing or sucking their thumb contentedly. They are more often able to drift off to sleep once fed and cared for, without so much rocking, humming, or drives in the car to usher them to sleep. This milestone is a great comfort for the parents as well.

Now the fun can begin. Babies can begin developing more and more tolerance for stimulation. They are fun to play with; they enjoy new sights, new movements, perhaps being bounced to the rhythm of a song, or rocked to the sound of a lullaby. While sight is still more powerful than sound, and touch is the most powerful sense of all in these early months, they are gradually learning to delight in the world. However, they must count on their caregivers to protect them from getting overwhelmed. If they've had too much stimulation, their only choices are to cry or fall asleep to shut the world out.

Perhaps you have noticed a basic pattern developing here. In general, the excitatory, or on, switch will begin to work before the inhibitory, or off, switch does. Learning to calm (the sensory off switch) is not scheduled to engage until many weeks after birth even though the sensory on switch has been active since before birth. This means that shielding and coaching by the caregiver is vital. Without it, high doses of stimulation can be too startling and unpleasant, and the baby will either become agitated or withdrawn. Even with wonderful caregiving, this can occur if the baby's nervous system isn't well balanced at first. Babies are identified as being either neurologically "overly excited" or "well organized" at birth. If they begin life overly excited, it means they will need much more coaching to discover what calming feels like and how to self-calm.

We have been considering the experiences of healthy, well-cared-for babies, born into a peacetime situation and exposed to reasonable doses of neutral and pleasant stimulation. And if their sensory nervous systems are poorly organized at first, we are assuming they will have extremely patient caregivers who learn how to coach them in the art of calming. These babies are very likely to become calm and tranquil children, delighted to be alive. By ten or twelve months of age, their sensory system will be well organized, and they will be ready to focus on the motor switches.

Sadly, however, staggering numbers of children around the world have much more shocking beginnings. They are born into wartime conditions; live in violent environments; endure natural disasters; face neglect, poverty, and malnutrition; and are surrounded by adults who model the agitation and physical imbalances of chronic high stress. Without nurturing caregivers to shield them, babies are too young to fight or flee, leaving only two ways to protect themselves: they can stay open and exposed to their chaotic environments, or they can try to shut down and withdraw from it all. Staying open locks them into an over-reactive distress state. These babies soon learn to regard all stimulation as negative, become hypervigilant, begin to startle easily, and to cry from distress. They may try to self-calm by excessive rocking and head banging. Many reach the point where just being alive is upsetting to them. Shutting down is an even more costly choice. This response locks them into a withdrawn, nonresponsive "freeze response" state. In this state, they learn to become numb or sleep in order to stop taking in the world around them. They can become so physically depressed that even their bodies begin to shut down. Their immune systems collapse, their digestive systems function poorly, their resistance to disease is weak, and their very survival becomes uncertain. Only when facing starvation does this radical shutdown make sense—it uses so few calories that their bodies are able to hold on longer until food comes.

When these negative experiences occur regularly, they begin to shape the baby's ability to handle stress in the future as well. As Dr. Bruce Perry explains, "The state will become the trait" if it isn't resolved. The response will become a basic part of their neurology. The damage that can be done in those first few years is profound, but it doesn't have to be permanent. It is important to remember that we are only talking about the baby and toddler's *first* opportunity to engage the switches successfully. As we shall soon discover, there will be another opportunity to help children develop these qualities through effective coaching in preschool and kindergarten.

LEARNING TO ENGAGE WITH THE WORLD

The next step, which we are calling the *motor on switch* and which Buddhists call *magnetizing,* includes two monumental accomplishments. It spans the period from about nine months to three years of age during which the infant learns to walk and the toddler learns to talk. While talking will typically become the focus only after walking has begun, the newborn does offer a small sampler of the conversational skills to come.

Within the first six weeks of life, the first intentional conversational effort is seen—a radiant smile so contagious that it fills the recipients with happiness. This happiness arises by triggering a release of oxytocin, a chemical known to enhance a feeling of well-being, in both the smiling baby and the one receiving the smile. This reward explains how a formerly active mother will suddenly be willing to spend the countless hours involved in nursing, stroking, and caring for her helpless baby and honestly enjoy it.

Oxytocin not only offers the mother a sense of well-being, it aids in her digestion, warms her upper body so she can warm the baby easily, lowers her stress level so she can deeply relax, and activates her breast milk so she can nurse. At the same time, these bonding activities infuse the newborn with oxytocin as well, helping the baby to calm and feel content. Since calming is paired with increases in oxytocin, the baby will soon be drawn to discovering ways to self-calm as well. A whole array of self-calming activities await discovery, from cooing, sucking a thumb or pacifier, cuddling stuffed animals, petting furry animals, and watching slowly moving objects to gently rocking by themselves.

This has been a dazzling conversational beginning, but it will be another year or two before the neural mechanisms are in place to launch the burst of language that completes this motor on period. In the meantime, the baby's focus is on creeping, crawling, and finally walking.

If *tranquility* was the gift of learning to calm, and *delight* the gift of learning to enjoy stimulation, then *radiance* is the gift of learning to smile. Two more wonderful qualities arise to draw older infants and toddlers into exploring their surroundings. They become filled with a sense of *wonder* and of *curiosity* so strong that they go through incredible efforts to learn to move toward the objects of their attention.

Most of these early explorations occur before they can regulate their urges. This means the caregiver needs to be the brakes and the choice monitor, until the mechanisms for the motor off switch are activated around age four. At first, the infant's adventures may amount to nothing more than crawling to the other side of the room alone before hurrying back to the comfort of the caregiver's arms. The caregiver is not likely to expect much self-control from these young ones. But once they learn to speak, it will be much more tempting to expect them to control themselves and to shame them if they fail. We will be exploring the complex art of coaching young talkers in a later section, but we can look briefly at the impact of shaming now as well. If we lash out with a shaming reaction when children at this age do upsetting things, it can be very painful for the child and possibly sear itself into their very core. It is one thing to shame the behavior ("It's not OK to hurt the kitty") and quite another to shame the child ("Shame on *you* for hurting the kitty; you are not nice"). The shaming must not generalize to where it is accusing the *child* of being bad or unlovable. And if this is compounded by a refusal to comfort (go to your room, get out of my sight), it can be even more harmful, leading to intense reactions to any humiliations later in life. We will explore many constructive strategies when we look at the art of language coaching in a later section.

For now let's continue to consider young walkers. A series of triumphs of motor organization brought them to their feet. Many of these milestones were instigated by the onset of various reflexes that arose at different times, were practiced, and then were mastered. These reflexes act like theatrical prompts for movement practices that are worth trying. Then they mature or fade away, leaving these burgeoning mini-athletes with new capacities. The reflex to walk is a good example. You can hold a three-month-old baby upright, and the baby's little legs will go through a walking motion, as if nature were whispering, "You know, we have found this to be a really useful motor pattern." Then if you hold the same baby up at six months old, you might worry because that reflexive or fairly automatic walking pattern has faded away. However, this simply clears the way for the toddler to revisit that motor pattern on a voluntary basis. If it were still active, it would interfere with the toddler's efforts to be in charge.

Fortunately, children are naturally drawn to practice each reflex pattern as it arises, so they don't usually need to be coached. They will find a way to practice on their own. Many of the games children used to play involved movements that addressed these reflexes as well. Walking along rails, logs, and curbs strengthened balance and developed a sense of symmetry on the body. Games such as ring toss and clothes pins in the bottle refined the child's eye-hand coordination in preparation for writing later. Follow the leader gave children practice imitating novel movements. Simon says asked them to let language override their motor impulse to move. Seen through the eyes of an occupational therapist, almost all of their play was an organic approach to sensory integration. Since the culture of childhood is fading away, these games are no longer being passed on from older children to younger ones. However, a growing number of creative early childhood and primary-grade teachers are rediscovering these games and introducing them to children again.

While most young children need very little coaching about reflex patterns, they definitely need coaching to learn to handle the motor on switch. So how should a caregiver guide this fairly nonverbal but highly active toddler and two-year-old? Four words sum up what they need from their caregivers at this point: *modeling, repetition, permission,* and *protection.* If you received each of these in full measure, you probably found that you were fairly successful with your motor on switch.

Young children love to imitate what they see us doing, so take the time to move slowly and gracefully, approaching tasks very simply so they can copy you. As you *model* for them, use two hands to carry things. Show them many rhythmic tasks like pouring, scooping, sweeping, and washing tables and windows. They will love practicing these things, and the *repetition* will improve their skills, organize their behavior, and become a familiar activity that can calm them later. When things spill or break, if you can stay calm and let them help clean it up, you will be laying the foundation for them to become problem solvers rather than ashamed children later.

Because these young walkers want to explore everything, the caregivers need to guide their choices and become their brakes when needed. Given a healthy balance of *permissions* and *protections,* they will be able to go forth as upright toddlers, taking deliberate steps and pursuing their environment with their sense of curiosity and wonder intact.

However, this curiosity and wonder can be thwarted at a very early age if *permission* is not granted. Perhaps they have a fearful or overwhelmed caregiver who keeps them confined to cribs and playpens. Perhaps they are surrounded by violence or war, and their environment is simply too dangerous to explore. At the very worst, they may be among the orphans consigned to a crib without attention for long hours each day. Without consistent caregivers, these children are likely to collapse into apathy, resistance, and fearfulness.

Some infants encounter almost the opposite experience as they set out on their little adventures. They might have careless or neglectful caregivers who offer ample permission but no *protection.* Not only are these young adventurers more likely to be injured, they aren't being coached to protect themselves either. They are likely to become strong willed, reckless, much more prone to accidents, and less able to make compromises or use social engagement skills later. This will make mastery of the motor off switch much more challenging for them.

The work of three key researchers has been informing our discussion of the four switches. Bruce Perry's work will be more prominent later when we look at the final step, the motor off switch. Allan Schore's work has been valuable throughout, suggesting the stages we are calling *the four switches* and providing a deep understanding of how various coaching strategies by caregivers impact the development of infants and young children. The work of the third researcher, Stephen Porges, plays such a key role in understanding both walking and talking that the next section is devoted entirely to exploring his amazing findings.

THE DISCOVERIES OF STEPHEN PORGES

Some contexts may promote states related to
antisocial behavior and health vulnerability,
while other contexts may promote states related to
positive social behavior, health, and development.

STEPHEN PORGES

Scientists have long acknowledged two systems of nerves as regulators of our ability to mobilize for action and our ability to rest or become quiet. The mobilizing system is called the *sympathetic nervous system*. It is fueled by adrenaline and is capable of accelerating the heart, or cardiac function, to four times its resting state when needed so creatures can fight or flee. To accomplish this surge, it shuts down all unnecessary operations, including digestion, to divert all possible energy toward the limbs.

This works well for mammals because they are skilled at turning the surge on and off as needed. But humans tend to keep the adrenaline running in between events, which leads to chronic stress. This is very hard on the human digestive system and can lead to ulcers or colitis. It also interferes with impulse control because when adrenaline is running through our bodies, we focus on quick action rather than thinking first. This locks us into a chronic state of hypervigilance, thus exhausting our immune system.

The calming or quieting system is called the *parasympathetic nervous system*. The nerve network within the parasympathetic system that regulates this calming and quieting was identified as the mighty vagus nerve. Known to be the longest single nerve in the body, it is composed of many meandering branches. However, its behavior was for a long time confusing. On the one hand, it was linked with calming and the quiet alertness involved in learning and socializing, but somehow it was also involved in an extreme kind of quietness too—the complete immobilization involved in a freeze response. This response was designed as a "last ditch" response in the face of real and present danger, and it was never intended to be used as a regular response pattern. How could the same system behave in two such radically different ways?

It was this mystery that Stephen Porges, a neuroscientist known for his research on the neurobiology of social behavior, solved through his twenty-year study of the complex dynamics of the vagus nerve system. Porges discovered that there are two major vagal pathways, not just one as neuroscientists had been assuming. We will call them the *lower vagal pathway* and the *upper vagal pathway* because of the connections they make.

The lower vagal pathway originates in the brain stem and travels downward from there, linking to the esophagus where it can reverse the swallowing activity and trigger vomiting. As it reaches the gut region, it connects with the stomach, intestines, pancreas, gall bladder, and liver. Under ordinary conditions, it regulates digestion very effectively. In times of stress, however, it can bring digestion and defecation to a standstill, quelling any noises the stomach and intestines might otherwise make. Its connection to the heart and lungs allows it to break up the natural rhythm between them in order to slow the breath way down and reduce the heart rate to near death when needed for survival. This serves reptiles well. If they need to submerge in water, they need the ability to stay down for long periods without breathing, and if they want to use their camouflage coloring to remain invisible to a predator, they need to be still for long periods of time. For mammals, however, this response pattern can be life threatening. If we placed one hundred mice in a room and introduced a hungry cat, they would all freeze and feign death. Then if we removed the cat, we would discover that only about eighty of them would revive. Roughly twenty of those mice would have shocked their systems so severely by shutting down that they died of cardiac arrest. Premature babies have an equally intense response to shock and startle easily, so nurses in newborn intensive care units are extremely careful about how they touch them.

This immobilization technique, so well suited to more primitive animals like reptiles, is definitely a last resort for mammals and humans. They are much better off resorting to the sympathetic nervous system, even with all of its drawbacks. However, there is an even better strategy for ensuring safety for mammals and humans, and it doesn't have any of those drawbacks—no adrenaline, no wear and tear on the gut, no short-circuiting of the ability to think under stress. This optimal strategy involves the upper vagal pathway.

The upper vagal pathway is unique to mammals. It, too, originates within the brain stem but then it moves upward, connecting to the frontal lobes of the brain and to the facial and eye muscles where it regulates eye movements and facial expressions. It travels to the tongue and throat to control sucking and swallowing, and to the middle ear and larynx to coordinate listening and speech. From there it goes on to foster a rhythmic connection between the heart and lungs. It links up to a secondary branch that meanders past the tissues surrounding many organs throughout the body, picking up subtle information called *visceral movements* from these organs. It then carries this information back to the frontal lobes, allowing the brain to consciously track the body's sensations. It is this extraordinary connection that allows us to match with others, to have intuitive awareness, and to develop some remarkable cognitive skills we shall explore in later chapters.

This system has another extremely valuable feature. It can allow the individual to surge without using adrenaline. This lets the athlete or dancer engage in peak performances without becoming anxious, it allows the child to run without becoming overly aroused, and it allows us to learn new things, meet new people, and travel to new places without getting overwhelmed with excitement. This surge-and-restraint mechanism is first activated between sixteen and eighteen months of age, just in time to assist the young child in coming to speech. Naming the universe is as exciting to them as learning to sign was to Helen Keller in that incredible scene in *The Miracle Worker,* when she discovered that water had a sign. Without this surge feature, children would be overwhelmed by all these new words and be unable to develop a rich vocabulary. In adults, we see remnants of this problem in those who can't express their anger in words and resort to rage behaviors instead or are flooded with overwhelming feelings and experience an emotional meltdown.

However, two questions remain unanswered so far. First, how can Porges's theory address the neurology of peace? Is there something about the way it operates that fosters empathy, compassion, and bonding? And secondly, how can the upper vagal system offer an alternative for keeping us safe so we don't always have to resort to either the fight-or-flight response of the sympathetic nervous system or worse yet, to the freeze response of the lower vagal pathway?

The answer lies in those neck, facial, and throat connections of the upper vagal pathway. The upper vagal connections linking the various facial movements are so fundamental to bonding and social engagement that Porges calls them the "social engagement system." The interplay among them is elegant. As the baby's eyelids lift up to gaze at the mother, they pull on a set of middle ear muscles to tense the eardrum. Just as tightening a drumhead would raise the pitch on an actual drum, tensing the eardrum allows the ear to register the high frequency tones of the human voice rather than the low tones of the background environment. Now the baby can more easily attend to the mother's voice. The facial muscles, the larynx, and the pharynx help the baby show feelings and control vocal tone to create the smooth flow of cooing and babbling. Head-turning and eye-tracking are the beginning steps in orienting for conversation. Together, these subtle qualities combine to encourage loving social exchanges with the mother and other caregivers.

We continue to use these social engagement cues throughout life. In safe surroundings, when we meet someone new, our first option is to make eye contact, smile, and attempt to create safety by social engagement. Only when that fails do we need to resort to those more primitive options. For children who are locked in a stress response, our first goal is to create enough safety and warmth for them to relax, build trust, and begin to think and socialize again.

The same dynamics can be seen between countries, whenever the goal would be to elevate the response from a fight-or-flight response to the level of skillful social exchanges. Sitting at a round table where heads can turn, sharing a meal where chewing stimulates listening, making eye contact in culturally sensitive ways, and smiling all help to promote understanding. These are vital ingredients for fostering peace. The challenge, then, is to find ways to guide children into the miracle of speech so they can learn to get along with one another in similar harmony. The next section explores this incredible step in their development.

THE BRAIN PREPARES FOR SPEECH

The crowning glory of social engagement comes when children learn to speak. In less than two years, the typical child will acquire more language than adults tackling a second language could ever do in the same length of time. This burst of language learning can only happen because a surprising number of brain systems come on line within a few short months of each other and coordinate brilliantly. Here is the story of that unfolding miracle.

The brain is going to need a new storage system for handling all these words. Until now, the memory systems have been storing information from each sense separately—smells, tastes, touch, a few special sounds, and a growing number of images from the faces of parents and caregivers to favorite toys and familiar objects. Some connections and associations have been made but nothing like those needed for language. To store words, a special memory system will need to combine sight with sound and images with the names of those images. To handle that, both the eyes and the ears will need to make some advances.

Beginning at ten months of age, infants begin preferring visual stimuli over their former favorite, touch. Now their sight is strong enough and their focus accurate enough to process new information quickly. This means the eyes are now ready to begin addressing speech.

The ears will need another six to eight months, however. The ear has two very different functions: balance and hearing. For most children, learning to walk precedes learning to talk, so the ear dedicates itself to stabilizing the child's balance to make that happen. Only when walking has been accomplished can the ear shift its focus from the balance mechanisms in the inner ear to the region of the inner ear devoted to processing sound. By eighteen months, the ear is finally ready to prepare for listening and speaking. It begins by developing skill in shutting down distractions. It must learn to ignore vibrations and environmental sounds in order to attend to tones and then learn to ignore the voice tone and attend to words as long as the speaker sounds calm and friendly. Most children learn to ignore vibration easily, but sometimes they need music to help them make this transition. Here is a good example.

Some years back, I was teaching infant-toddler observation skills in a Montessori teacher training program. The students and I watched as several eighteen-month-old children entered the demonstration classroom for the first time. Most began to explore the space in expected ways, but one child was different. He didn't respond to his name, and later put his ear against a metal support pole, pounded on it, and then did the same thing against a metal file cabinet. Clearly, he was drawn to vibrations. Was he hard of hearing? That afternoon, as we debriefed the morning class, I asked if anyone had a recorder. Happily, one student did and agreed to sit at the back of the play area the next morning and alternate between playing a simple tune and being silent. When the children arrived, all but this boy noticed the music before beginning to play in the space. Later, as he watched his feet in a low mirror next to the recorder player, he happened to notice her fingers moving and then stopping. In those short moments he "discovered" tone! He ran to the play area, sat down with a little shell, and spun about in a little seated dance, stopping and starting in time with the music. After that, he responded to his name perfectly.

By eighteen months of age the eyes and ears are usually ready for language. A few more systems need to become operational before the language burst can happen, though. We have already learned that by sixteen to eighteen months, the resting heart rate slows down, and the *vagal brake* becomes available for the first time. It will soon play a crucial role in language learning. It is very exciting to begin naming one's universe, and this restraint mechanism will allow the learner to stay calm in the face of all this new learning.

Even the breath needs to shift from an automatic process to a manual one. In the beginning, the breath was strongly influenced by reflexes. For the first six months, the swallowing reflex blocked all mouth breathing so the baby wouldn't choke when nursing. A submerge-and-dive response stopped even nose breathing when the baby was underwater, making it easy to teach infants to swim. This response typically matures and disappears by about age two. Now the child will begin to use mouth breathing to learn to speak. By age four or five, breathing while speaking usually flows well (and swimming is again easy to teach).

However, this natural flow of breath as we speak isn't guaranteed. It only works if the upper vagal system is activated. But if a child's lower vagal system is engaged, triggering a freeze response, that child will want to shut down the breath and stay invisible. That same child will dread speaking, be hard to hear, and seem to run out of air by midsentence. Now consider a child whose fight-or-flight response system is activated. This child will have emotionally charged speech with held breaths and a tendency to blurt out words. The flood of emotion will make it very hard to wait for a turn to talk or to keep from talking too loud.

The final readiness step involves the brain's three language centers, all of which are located in the brain's left hemisphere. Two of them have been handling language for many months but just haven't been able to coordinate well. Broca's area, located just above the left ear, regulates speech production and allows babies to babble back when we talk to them. Meanwhile, Wernicke's area, located behind the left ear, has been learning to comprehend simple words and phrases rather well. Eighteen-month-old infants can have quite an extensive listening vocabulary even though they still aren't able to express themselves well in words. This frustrating disconnect between understanding and speaking is a major contributor to the tantrums of the "terrible twos." Some parents and preschools are introducing signing to tide them over until speech can catch up with understanding.

A band of fibers called the *archuate fasciculus* links the speaking and comprehension areas, but it doesn't get insulated until nearly age two usually. Once that finally happens, the clarity of signals traveling between these two areas improves dramatically, and the language burst is ready to launch.

One final speech area, the inner speech center, will join them and bring some incredibly advanced features with it. It is located in front of the left ear in the frontal lobe and until now has been operating as a high-level movement area. However, those same cells are now converting over to become a high-level language area. As its name implies, this inner speech center is not very social and is inner directed instead. It allows the language learner to pause, turn inward, and digest new words. For the first time, the child is actually *thinking* about the world rather than *responding* to it. This region will play a vital role in regulating the motor off switch as well.

Now that all these brain systems are operational, language learning can begin in earnest. As you reflect on your own early childhood and the stories your parents told about how you learned to speak, note whether or not you were able to meet these milestones with grace. Does your speech flow easily now and can you find the words you need in delicate situations, or do you wrestle, perhaps, with being tongue-tied or responding so quickly that you say things you wish you hadn't? If you long for more fluency and skill in speaking, you may discover that guiding a young child into the art of speaking will wash back on you and repattern your own speaking skills. The next section will give you all the guidance you need for helping a young child embark on this wonderful journey and for refining your own elocution in the process.

NAMING THE UNIVERSE

When a child encounters speech, every nuance matters. The tone and attitude of the caregiver who introduces all those special words, the wonder in discovering that everything seems to have a name, and the fact that this marvelous coach enjoys listening to them when they begin to speak turns what may seem quite ordinary to a grown-up into the miracle of learning to name the universe for the child.

If you have the opportunity to name the universe for a beginning speaker, how should you approach this noble task? We shall begin this exploration by understanding how young children build their vocabularies.

When children learn new words, they move back and forth from the outer world in which each word is introduced to the inner world of their own mind where the word is savored and filed away. After hearing a new word, a young learner must shut down the outside world, withdraw, and go inward to digest and store that word. Interestingly, this solitary phase has the same features as a shame response. In order to learn new words, children must use this mechanism without letting it collapse into a feeling of isolation, abandonment, and shame. Children who delight in their surroundings, who feel safe, and have good language coaches can easily avoid this problem and go on to build rich vocabularies.

But children living in stressful surroundings do not feel safe. They must remain vigilant and may be surrounded by arguments and meager language coaching as well. These children may not be able to stave off this shame response. For them, vocabulary building would be so unpleasant that they would settle for just enough words to get by. Many research studies point to the great value early childhood language programs have for these children. Now let's take those programs one step further and consider what the most elegant coaching skills for "naming the universe" might be. If you are able to offer such loving, mindful speech to a young child, it can uplift your relationship to your own speech at the same time.

SKILL 1 Cultivate Authentic Speech

Young learners are just beginning to learn how breath and speech come together, so they will be copying not only what you say but how you say it. You can give new words a special magic by speaking authentically. Authentic speech is actually an aerobic exercise. You are becoming a poet for the child, breathing life into each name you give. As adults, we may have almost forgotten about the power of naming, but a remnant still exists for all of us. When proud parents show us their newborn, we never ask, "And what have you labeled your baby?" We ask for the *name* and then listen carefully to how they speak the new baby's name. "This is Marissa Elizabeth, Javier Luis, George Adam, Nita Camille." And from those sounds, we catch a glimpse of their regard for their baby and perhaps a hint of their baby's destiny.

SKILL 2   Attend to Voice Tone

We can bring a similar regard to naming the objects and action words our young learners ask about. They savor the sounds of their favorite words as if they carry a special charge—*asparagus, equipment, investigate, excavate,* and, unfortunately, all the profanity they hear even once!

What do music teachers and kindergarten and first grade teachers all have in common? After decades of listening to teachers, I've noticed a consistent pattern. Their voices are almost always more lyrical than their colleagues. We would expect music teachers to have lyrical voices, but somehow elementary principals consistently place classroom teachers with the most lyrical voices in kindergarten and first grade as well. They may be intuitively sensing that these are the voices that will help the young learner fall in love with school.

Other factors matter as well. Facial expressions play a part. Even blind infants can sense the warmth in the voice of a smiling caregiver. Thoughts can influence our tone of voice. If we have an angry thought in the back of our mind, the young child will pick that up and may even tell us "that's not a very nice tone." The only solution is to clear those thoughts before repeating what we were saying. They can't hear the words when the tone is harsh. Avoiding tone altogether is no solution, however. It is the tone in our voice that teaches about feelings. A flat, monotone coaching voice fails to teach the children how to notice the feelings of others or express their own feelings. These varying tones play a key role in teaching them how to understand others and cultivate empathy.

SKILL 3   Be Aware of Mood and Intention

As we speak, we actually teach young children how to breathe. If we are inspired about life, they learn to *in-spire* or *breathe in* joyfully. If we are depressed and breathe irregularly, they entrain to that and become depressed too. Moods can be very contagious, and for babies with depressed mothers, this can be a problem.

Words and the gestures behind them are also powerful and can actually cause pain. I witnessed a stunning example of this while visiting a mother and her two children. Her eight-year-old son was studying karate and wanted his mother to swing her arm in a sharp arc. Her four-year-old daughter's leg was in the path of her arm but too far back to get touched. Nevertheless, she cried out, "You cut me," putting her hand right where the arc would have sliced. The mother was not intending to cause harm. She was just sending her energy, what the martial artists would call *chi* or *ki,* and its force was felt. Imagine how much more painful a scolding finger feels when pointed intentionally at a child.

If words and the gestures behind them can wound, they can also heal. In one of my courses, several teachers from one preschool were concerned about a little boy. He would walk in with his shoulders raised as if protecting his ears and withdraw into a small playhouse for the whole morning, never speaking to anyone. I asked what his mother's voice sounded like. Sure enough, it was raspy and nagging, so I asked them to greet him gently each morning, as if sending angel wings out to embrace him. Each morning they kindly spoke his name, "Hi, Harold." The first day he stopped, looked at them with surprise, said hi back, and went on to the playhouse. Each day he softened more. By next week's class, they reported that he was now sitting in their laps telling them stories and beginning to make friends.

SKILL 4   **Become a Kid Talker**

"My new teacher talks like a grown-up. She's not as good at talking to kids as Miss Williams was. What if she says a word I don't know?" This child voiced the fears of many kindergarteners and first graders who see grown-ups as being in one of two camps, either purely grown-up talkers or able to shift from grown-up to kid talk. By kid talk, it doesn't mean using baby talk at all. It just means that the adult is very good at putting information, stories, and explanations in words the child can understand. Listen to gifted kindergarten and first grade teachers talking to their classes if you ever get the chance. Very likely their great success is due in part to their outstanding ability to do kid talking.

SKILL 5   Know When to Talk, When to Be Silent

If you've ever tried learning a second language, you quickly learn how to say, "Speak more slowly, please." And you can only take so much talk before your ears become exhausted and can no longer process what native speakers are saying to you. Young first-language speakers have the same needs. Using too many words overwhelms them. Speaking too rapidly confuses them. But it is also possible to offer them too few words. Appalachian mothers tended to speak very little as a culture, and their children would enter school with minimal language skills. However, once these mothers were encouraged to talk more to their infants and toddlers, the children improved dramatically in language development and were much more successful when they reached school age.

Naming the universe has been a compelling triumph, but something can be lost as well. Each time we offer a name, we help to solidify that object, drawing the child more deeply into the world of form, fixed perceptions, and language and farther away from the world of pure sensation. We have been striving to reclaim an appreciation of that world of sensation now that we understand its importance. As we work with young language learners, we can take care to make sure they don't sacrifice those earlier skills as they gain these new ones. Artists, musicians, dancers, and nature lovers have found ways to keep the world of sensations alive, and if we bring nature, the arts, and playful experiences to children while they learn to name their universe, they may succeed in holding on to their awareness of the world of sensations better than most of us have.

MOTOR OFF
The Switch with No Guarantees

The drive to master walking and talking is intense, but the infant and toddler have a lot of biological support as well. Reflexes coach the early movements while new brain systems are laid down to support speech. Their natural longing to name the universe adds the final touch. The fact that babies are born with these preinstalled mechanisms suggests that nature places a very high value on the motor on switch.

Why, then, is the establishment of a strong motor off switch so uncertain? Nature seems to take a hands-off approach to this final switch, allowing it to develop based on experiences. This suggests that having a motor off switch isn't always a good idea. Perhaps there are some environments where the survival and safety of a child might be better served without the interference of such a switch. Indeed, many children are growing up with extremely weak motor off switches, and the implications for learning, for social behavior, and for cultural dynamics are profound.

Yet with the right coaching practices and warm-up skills, we can help a child create a strong motor off switch. The primary warm-up skills of self-esteem, curiosity, patience, and the ability to focus attention and to delay rewards come together with inner speech to create the ultimate motor off skill—impulse control. These warm-up skills are laid down in several stages that depend heavily on brain chemistry and the skillful coaching of caregivers. If these early efforts fail, there will still be one more opportunity to offer this critical coaching during preschool or kindergarten.

The first phase for establishing the motor off switch involves the period from ten to fourteen months. This is an absolutely thrilling time for most toddlers. They are the center of the universe, and the world is all theirs. It is a time of adventures and *reunions,* of going out to explore new things, getting a bit queasy out there all by themselves, and then rushing back to the loving arms of their bonded caregiver.

The caregiver's task is to have boundless energy, to protect them from burns, stairs, growling dogs, and traffic, and otherwise to rejoice in their discoveries with them. During this highly nurturing time, the exchanges are fueled by an increase in high-arousal brain chemicals in the infant-like opioids and dopamine, designed to register pleasure and dull the pain from all the bumps and bruises of learning to walk. If this coaching relationship continues to flourish, the toddler's brain will create an extensive filing system to process all of this information about pleasure. Neurologists would say they are building many receptor sites for registering pleasure. Of course, even optimal circumstances will fall short of this idealized picture. So what is good-enough coaching for this first phase or practice period?

Most toddlers will find enough joy and be protected enough from harm for their brains to develop a reasonably strong structural system for registering pleasure. For them, this coaching period has managed to keep their capacity for delight and wonder alive. Even if no caregiver seems terribly interested in them, the resourcefulness of toddlers is incredible. If anyone in their lives conveys delight—singing, tending to flowers, hugging them, laughing easily—they will find these special people and get their needs met. However, if children encounter a great deal of physical pain, spankings, or abuse during this period, their brains will create a much less elaborate structure for registering pleasure, and their social development will suffer.

Later, while others find enjoyment in small pleasures and can delight in discovering nuances of change in their environment, these children fail to pick up on such subtlety. They may seek greater stimulation so they can feel pleasure and may even be drawn into addictions in their search for intensity. On the other hand, they may prefer to avoid intense stimulation and choose to live a relatively flat emotional existence instead. In either case, they are missing out on all the wonderful subtleties of emotional life.

While this first practice period involved adventures and loving *reunions* with the caregiver, the next period, from fourteen to eighteen months, will involve distress and relationship repairs with the caregiver. These older toddlers must face a very unpleasant bit of news: Their days of narcissistic delight are over. Life actually has limits, and they are not the center of the universe after all. This second practice period is accompanied by a shift in brain chemistry away from the high-arousal pleasure-producing chemicals to lower-energy brain chemicals, like corticosteroids, that are much less arousing. They allow the toddler to slow down and learn about limits and to process the pain of negative emotions more easily.

This phase can strain the relationship bonds between caregiver and child as the wonderful words of *yes, go,* and *good* give way to increasing encounters with *no, stop,* and *bad.* Their left brains are not typically ready to store language for another six to eight months, so these highly charged emotional words are stored in the right brain where they make a deep impression. Therefore, they must be used very carefully and in small doses.

The brains of these fourteen- to eighteen-month-olds still lack a natural braking mechanism, so when they are told to stop something, they will become distressed, both at being deprived of the activity and at the caregiver's obvious disapproval. *This distress triggers a shame response.* They can endure this feeling of shame only briefly, before needing to be comforted. Their bond with the caregiver needs to be *repaired.* Caregiving begins to involve a very delicate alternation between the *no* that causes a shame response and the comforting that follows. This comforting removes the caregiver's anger from the equation. The child's feelings are soothed, the relationship is repaired, but the limit still stands.

Done well, the toddler moves through the distress and the comforting to an entirely new cognitive state that arises from the feeling of relief. This state is sometimes called *resting wakefulness, quiet alertness,* or *alert inactivity.* Every time this cycle of *distress, repair,* and *relief* is played out, the toddler's brain becomes more familiar with this new cognitive zone. In a few more months, the toddler will want to use this valuable zone for taking in, digesting, and storing new words.

Poorly coached toddlers, who experience too much stress and too little comforting, end up creating an overly extensive pain-registration system and fail to discover this important cognitive zone. Their brain chemistry may settle into a chronic stress response, overpowering their ability to find joy in life. Many of the warm-up skills needed for a strong motor off switch are also impacted. Their self-esteem is damaged, their ability to focus their attention is limited, and their need for vigilance makes it very hard to be patient.

Living with prolonged shame at this helpless young age can also lead to intense rage later if it becomes reactivated as humiliation. It is estimated that the typical rage-disordered child will have over forty serious rage episodes between adolescence and midadulthood. This severely affects their lives, the lives of those around them, and all of society.

There is an interesting practice you can use any time you want to deeply embed a teaching you encounter. Give the passage three slow readings in a row. The first reading serves the intellect as you glean the meaning from the passage. The second reading can then touch the heart as you savor the feeling tone of the words. Finally, the third reading can reach the will and infuse you with a sense of the truth embedded in the teaching.

Allan Shore has spoken eloquently about what happens when we fail to help children adjust to their encounters with limits, and I encourage you to give his words three slow readings to take them in fully.

> I see the products of unregulated unconscious primary
> narcissism and humiliation-induced narcissistic rage in
> both children and adults as the major threat to the further
> development of our species.

Clearly, we must find ways to support children in developing effective motor off switches. The following two sections offer ways to meet that challenge, both for well-coached children who are about to develop their own vagal brakes and for those children who need special care as they begin this coaching journey for the second time. These same qualities can help us as adults if we want to strengthen our own impulse control.

FINAL PREPARATIONS
Order, Wait Time, and Inner Speech

What is so special about *order?* Consider this true story. One year, nearly six weeks into the fall semester, two of my students at Naropa University came to see me, looking frantic. The excitement of leaving home, being in a new town, and making new friends was exhilarating, but somehow these first-year students hadn't done any assignments or even purchased their textbooks yet. They had no idea how they had let it go on so long and asked what they could possibly do now. My advice was simple: "Buy a box of cereal and some milk. Create a place to eat, a place for your keys, and another place for your shoes." This was on a Thursday. The next class was on Tuesday, and they were beaming. They had bought textbooks, done their first loads of laundry, and caught up on half of their assignments. Why? The familiarity of a few basic routines tempered all the novelty and allowed them to reactivate their natural impulse control.

Order is a powerful organizing device. Harnessed anger can be used to clean houses, organize offices, and whittle down long lists of dreaded tasks. Simple daily routines can comfort those who grieve, and the repetitive motions of walking, digging, and scrubbing can free up the stalled energy of depression. Giving young children the gift of order will continue to serve them for a lifetime. So, how do we do that?

The period from eighteen months to two-and-a-half years is an ideal window for coaching young children because they are incredibly drawn to repetition. Done with regularity, these repetitions will turn activities into routines, and the child will be comforted by their predictability. Begin by building physical routines from regular nap times to set times for meals, baths, and jammies before bedtime. If the rhythms of daily life keep changing, try telling "the story of tomorrow" at bedtime to make the next day more predictable.

During this period, young children love to master motor tasks and can spend long blocks of time filling buckets of sand, arranging a set of measuring cups by size, and fitting pegs into the right holes. The more time children spend absorbed in these practice sessions, the stronger their endurance and concentration will become and the easier later challenges will be.

Some daily routines can become especially enriching. Setting the table with a special place for each person, lighting a candle, having a moment of silence or grace before eating can turn ordinary routines into ceremonies. Not only are these young children learning about order, these ceremonial practices also include tiny natural wait times that lay the groundwork for developing the next preparatory skill—*learning to wait.*

One summer day as I was sitting with a mother and her two-and-a-half-year-old daughter on their porch steps, the aroma of cookies baking in the oven came wafting through the screen door. "Oh, it's so *hard* to wait for those cookies!" Missy exclaimed. She was practicing what we are calling *wait time* and what psychologists like to call *delayed gratification.*

If you do a computer search on that term, you will immediately uncover references to marshmallows and a simple study from the late 1960s.

It began at the nursery school attached to Stanford University when psychology professor Walter Mischel devised an experiment to study why some children could wait and others could not. In the study, four-year-old children entered an examination room one at a time and sat at a table that had a tempting marshmallow on it. They were told they could eat it at any time, but if they could wait a few minutes (until the examiner returned to the room) before eating it, they could have a second one as well. A few devoured the marshmallow within thirty seconds after the examiner left, while others were able to wait as long as fifteen minutes without eating the marshmallow. These long delayers would crawl under the table, cover their eyes, sing a song—anything to take their minds off of that marshmallow.

A decade later Mischel began to hear about the performance differences among the children in the experiment. Reviewing the data revealed significant differences between the very short and very long delayers. The short delayers went on to have more trouble paying attention, more behavioral problems, and more difficulty maintaining friendships. The longer delayers were much more successful academically. The SAT scores of those who had waited fifteen minutes averaged 210 points higher than those whose delay time had been only thirty seconds. Fortunately, their findings discovered a third group—ones who began as short delayers, later learned to be long delayers, and went on to be very successful.

So, aside from baking cookies, how can we stretch this tolerance for waiting? Caregiver coaches can begin with very small wait times like the gap that arises when rolling a ball back and forth. Next, look for activities that take a minute or two, like wrapping and unwrapping pretend presents. Then move on to longer wait times. Waiting for a friend to arrive, for a backhoe to begin digging, or for a butterfly to land on a flower—these are all golden moments. A gifted Montessori toddler trainer, Virginia Varga, loved making those moments fun. When she saw a toddler wanting to work with materials another child was using, she would kneel down beside the child and whisper delightedly, "We're *waiting!*" and then go on to say things like, "It is hard to wait. . . . You have to be strong to wait. . . . You are getting stronger." She would finish by seeing that the child actually did get a turn with those materials.

All of these activities have one thing in common—they are linked to a reward. Children will learn to wait because it *pays* to wait. Punishment can force children to wait, but it will not teach them to wait voluntarily, and that is our goal for them. Every dieter has discovered the truth in this—building in small treats can go a long way toward sustaining the willpower to keep the diet plan going.

These lessons about order and wait time have a calming effect, supporting young children as they experience a dramatic surge in language development during this same period. Three language centers participate in this work. The speech production center guides the pronunciation and is now able to work closely with the speech comprehension center that registers the meaning. However, it is the third language center, the inner speech center, that will pair up with the ability to wait or delay gratification. Together they will determine the strength of the motor off switch, but this merger cannot happen until the child is about four years old.

Inner speech develops gradually alongside ordinary social speech. In the beginning most speech is directed toward others, but occasionally toddlers can be heard using inner speech and talking to themselves. Plans are spoken aloud ("I'm going to get my teddy bear"), and rules are recited ("No, no. Don't touch"), but not obeyed yet. This is when child abuse is most common because it is so hard for caregivers to realize that these young children can repeat rules, but their brains are not yet able to apply those rules. To do that, their inner speech region must become strong enough to overpower the motor impulses that are so tempting to them. This can only happen once the child's language skills are more fully developed, and that will take time. Until then, when children resist temptation to disobey rules, they do so out of fear of the adult's anger, not out of their own willpower.

Most young children are eager to develop their language skills and find countless opportunities to do so. The dialogues we often overhear between children during pretend play are a perfect example. Those conversations may sound like social speech, but the inner speech region is heavily involved as they work to stay in character. In finding the words to improvise their parts, they are drawing on the same brain mechanisms used by the finest poets. By age four, most children finally have strong enough language skills to launch their motor off switches and to begin practicing impulse control. Now they have the tools to live in harmony with one another.

THE YOUNG CHILD'S DESTINY
Perils and Promise

Free the child's potential, and you will transform him into the world.
The child is both a hope and a promise for mankind.

MARIA MONTESSORI

These eloquent words by Maria Montessori about the promise in a child's future are counterbalanced by the deep concerns of Dr. Bruce Perry for the very absence of promise facing far too many unfortunate children today. He directed the Child Trauma Program at Texas Children's Hospital of Baylor College of Medicine from 1992 to 1998, during which time he studied the neurological impacts of trauma and neglect on the developing brains of children.

As he researched the scale of the problem, he encountered the following statistics. Each year three million children in the US alone are victims of intentional trauma. Another one million will witness or experience accidents, injuries, and other catastrophic events in the same year. And of this combined four million children, at least one million of them will succumb to post-traumatic stress disorder and join the ranks of those unable to navigate the social and academic world of their peers.

Dr. Perry found that these traumatized children would soon begin to manifest one of two basic response patterns. Those who were able to fight back or flee would go on to become hypervigilant and show signs of acting-out behaviors, low attention span, poor impulse control, anxiety, and panic behaviors. Those who could not fight or flee would choose the freeze response instead. They would disconnect from what was happening around them and either hide or surrender.

Later this would lead to an inability to think, to a high risk of becoming victimized and bullied, and to severe depression. As these children continued to endure trauma, it would gradually alter the biochemistry and even the anatomy of their brains, making it much harder for them to recover.

You are to be commended for being open to the poignant information contained in this chapter. Bearing witness to the incredible suffering of these vast numbers of young children is challenging. However, we know from past research that it is much easier to acknowledge the existence of problems once we know there are solutions.

Therefore, we will end this chapter with the following gentle coaching strategies for the four basic controls we have learned about. These are the basic controls young children need to develop. We have the opportunity to keep refining these controls throughout life and will require well-developed controls if we want to enjoy the full range of our mind's brilliance. We will end each segment with a review of the strategies you first encountered when you took your personal balance inventory.

Learning to Calm

The first control is the ability to self-calm, to turn off the incoming stimulation from the world. Here are a few recommendations for helping young children create this sensory off switch.

- *Protect the senses from overload.* Overly stressed children startle easily at loud or sudden noises. Then their ears shift from listening to the meaning of words to listening for "twig snaps" and other signs of danger. When they feel unsafe, their eyes also shift from the focal vision needed to explore what interests them to peripheral vision, so they can be vigilant and scan for danger more easily.
- *Create time and spaces for resting.* Many children go home to high-energy households where rest and relaxation rarely happen. They need to learn how to do this in your setting.
- *Become a model of peace.* Most children clearly know how to escalate the emotional potential in every situation. What

they haven't seen is a role model for approaching problems calmly and peacefully. This requires some inner preparation from you as a caregiver. Essentially, you must *be peace to teach peace,* and that's not always easy in these stressful times. Your first obligation may be to stop more often, rest more often, and rediscover what truly nourishes you so you can model inner peace.

If this quality is weak for you right now, here are some things you can do to strengthen it:

- Do relaxation practices: stretching, yoga, a minute or two of deep breathing, or meditating.
- Watch the flow of nature: clouds, streams, birds, or even aquarium fish.
- Take one-minute breaks: soften your eyes, relax your face, tongue, throat, and shoulders.
- Give yourself face rubs, gently rub your closed eyes, massage your hands.
- Add half an hour of sleep per night.

Learning to Enjoy Stimulation

The second control is the ability to build a sensory on switch to handle increasing amounts of stimulation without overloading. Once children know how to self-calm, you can help them work on handling stimulation well.

- *Slow down to meet them.* The inner tempo of children is very slow, regardless of how speedy they may seem outwardly. As an example, Jimmy had been expelled from preschool for being a "child intimidator." In the past six months his behavior had become increasingly unworkable. His mother had high energy and moved quickly. After the evaluators assessed her son, they asked if she could possibly slow down with him. Then it dawned on her. They had been taking slow walks every day with an old man in the neighborhood, but he died six months ago. Now, since no one would slow down to meet Jimmy, he was trying his best to speed up to meet everyone else and it just wasn't working.

• *Encourage absorption but not addiction.* When children are engaged for long periods of time with one activity, is that healthy or not? If you hear them give a sigh of satisfaction when they are done, you can rejoice. But if they seem hooked on the activity and never want to quit, as they might with computer games, this is a problem. They are getting locked into cycling stimulation patterns that will not serve them well.

• *Become a model of absorption.* As you move about, do so with full attention. Focus deeply on each task, create artistic touches, arrange flowers, garden, sweep, set the table in a way they can easily absorb and then imitate.

If this quality is weak for you right now, here are some things you can do to strengthen it:

• Practice an "attitude of gratitude," noticing small bits of beauty and kindness each day.

• Be well rested (an unmet need for calmness will keep you from enjoying enrichment).

• Pet furry animals, get a massage, wear more lotion.

• Take up a hobby, anything from drawing to woodworking to a new style of cooking.

• Sing out loud at least five minutes a day (even privately— in the shower or in the car).

Learning to Engage with the World

The third control is the motor on switch. It is the ability to engage with the world and includes motor activity and language skills. Here are some ways you can help them take this third important step.

• *Provide more order and less surprise.* While we might find repetition boring, young children thrive on it. Daily routines, ways to handle certain toys, familiar songs and stories all help guide the young child's behavior. Children with more chaotic home lives may not recognize order easily. For their sake, make the order obvious. You are teaching them that in some settings life can be predictable. At first, order-deprived children may choose to do the same activities every day just to savor the predictability. Let them; it is very healing. Soon they will be ready to explore their environment with calm interest.

• *Make language special.* Many young children arrive in day care and school settings with minimal language skills. Some were neglected or poorly coached while others were struggling with abuse and just wanted to stay invisible. Still others were simply slow to develop the listening skills needed to guide their speech. They need to fall in love with language and discover the joy of naming their universe. In your safe setting, they can have that opportunity. Speak warmly, savor special new words, repeat them often and talk slowly so they can begin to imitate you. Never scare them with a raised or angry tone.

• *Listen deeply when they speak.* As they practice talking to you, be very patient. It takes time for them to retrieve the words they want and to make choices or answer your questions. If you wait calmly, they will often honor you with a response. You may also have more success if you avoid looking at them while they search. Many young children cannot coordinate their eyes with their ears yet, so it is hard for them to look at you while they listen or search for words to say.

If this quality is weak for you right now, here are some things you can do to strengthen it:

• Interrupt your habits and do an ordinary task in a new way, try something new, go somewhere new.
• Give and get more hugs.
• Give a small gift to someone—something you know they'll like.
• Make a list of things you want to accomplish, choose one, and begin it.

- Volunteer your time on a project that helps others.
- Organize and carry out a small event for family or friends (a party, a movie, a picnic, a hike).

Learning to Control Impulses

The fourth and final control is called the motor off switch and brings with it the ability to learn self-control. Once developed, children can learn to resist temptations, control strong emotions, stick with challenging tasks, and use language to solve problems. Here are a few useful coaching strategies to help them.

- *Guard against scarcity.* Children growing up in environments with scarce resources—food, attention, comfort, warmth, and joy—have no reason to develop impulse control. They learn to act quickly or what they want will be gone. They need to discover that in some settings delayed gratification really can pay off. Be sure there are plenty of snacks to go around. Create safe places for them to store their possessions. If they need to wait for a turn with a toy, a book, or a swing, be sure they really do get that turn. It will take time and consistency to lay down these important new patterns.
- *Provide quick emotional repairs.* Many children have been shamed too often and comforted too little. They must learn limits in a much gentler way. When they make mistakes, spill or damage things, or even lash out toward others, meet these behaviors calmly and consistently with remedies. They must learn to link negative behaviors with a way to *solve* them or make amends. If they fail to learn this, they may not recover from their early shame experiences. Instead, they may develop lifelong rage patterns that erupt whenever they feel slighted or humiliated.
- *Talk to yourself out loud.* You model inner speech when you do this, and it helps the children learn to use speech to guide their behaviors. This is especially important for those children who weren't coached to develop good language skills earlier. Rejoice

when they engage in pretend role-playing or talk out loud to themselves. They are beginning to build true impulse control!

If this quality is weak for you right now, here are some things you can do to strengthen it:

- Save up for a major purchase instead of using a credit card to buy now and pay later.
- Resist the urge to quit an endurance task, by continuing "just a few minutes longer."
- Relax your hands and shoulders and take three deep nose breaths to dissolve anger surges.
- Practice compromising—"I want this but I'll settle for that."
- Stop stressing over lost time in traffic jams or long lines— use this time to relax your muscles and breathe more deeply.

This completes our study of the four practices of enlightened activity. If we can help children master them, we will have changed their destiny, giving them a greater measure of freedom to live into their true natures. And as we continue to work with them, our own lives will be enriched as well.

THE ROAD NOT TAKEN

Lessons from
Orality-Based Cultures

UNLESS YOU HAVE ties to an orality-based tradition, the unique ways of knowing in these cultures will likely be new to you. By living with nature instead of books, orality-based peoples developed skills that those of us who were early readers never had the opportunity to cultivate.

You will find that this chapter has a different rhythm than the others. The sections seem more like a bouquet of impressions than a logical, linear stream. Let it flow like that. It will help you drop your attachment to logic and guide you into the story-based, present-moment mindset of the orality-based cultures. These unusual and often delightful skills can play an important part in your quest to uncover your natural brilliance.

PREPARING TO RECEIVE UNUSUAL TEACHINGS

We are about to enter an amazing cognitive realm occupied by most young children and brought to a mastery level by many orality-based cultures. From them, we can discover new ways to sense our surroundings, to observe in great detail, to recognize what is sacred, to learn from direct experience instead of theories, and to expand our relationship to time and space.

But first there is an obstacle that must be overcome. You are *reading* these words—you are literate. Your guides in this territory, however, are not—and many of their incredible skills and perceptual gifts are very hard to awaken or rekindle once the mind has become literate. Once again, preparatory steps must be taken before you can go further. The first two steps involve *respect* and *reverence*.

Maintaining Respect

Your primary teachers for this chapter will either be younger than you, children, or they will be unschooled adults, members of nonliterate cultures. In order to learn what they have to teach, you will need to *respect* them even though it can be tempting to feel superior to them. To learn from children, it is important to listen deeply to them and to enter their world. If you have not yet taken the silent walk with a young child, as was suggested in chapter 1, this might be a good time to do so.

In preparing to learn from nonliterate peoples, it is important to respect their choice to continue living as a nonliterate culture and to protect that choice. When we succumb to seeing them as inferior and in need of moving on against their will, we will also lose some of our most important teachers of the nearly lost set of gifts only they can teach us. You will be reading the words of teachers from various nonliterate cultures. Many of those cultures have since become literate, either by choice or from the pressure of the outside world. Therefore, after each quoted comment, there will be a date documenting when that comment was made.

I am taking great liberties even in selecting which words to bring to you, let alone suggesting that I fully understand the meaning of those words. Let me take a moment to express my apologies to these wise teachers for any and all of my errors or limitations in understanding them and my deep appreciation to them for what they are trying to teach. I have carefully avoided including the interpretations of the anthropologists who often recorded these comments, because the field is very conflicted about how to view these interpretations.

Awakening Reverence

The second preparatory step is to awaken a state of *reverence,* not to place these teachers on a high pedestal, but to alter your internal mental state and make it easier to understand their teachings.

Dr. Manfred Clynes, who has a rich background as a concert pianist, a bioengineer, and a neurophysiologist, discovered that people actually have fast and slow emotions, and the slowest of these is reverence. In the 1970s, after figuring out how to read brain waves well enough to create the first CAT scanner, he went on to create a device to read the output of emotion through measuring finger pressure while a subject activated various feelings. He then conducted some remarkable research into the wave properties and even the breath patterns of seven key emotions—anger, hate, joy, sex, love, grief, and reverence. Dr. Clynes found that the patterns, which he called *sentic forms,* remained surprisingly similar across all the literate and nonliterate cultures he tested and that anger was consistently the easiest emotion to access and reverence the most difficult. Part of the reason exists in the length of time it takes to initiate each emotion. Look at this pattern:

Emotion	Time needed to initiate the emotion
Anger	4.8 seconds
Sex	4.9 seconds
Joy	5.2 seconds
Hate	5.3 seconds
Love	7.4 seconds
Grief	8.2 seconds
Reverence	9.8 seconds

It takes more than twice as long to access reverence (9.8 seconds) as it does to access anger (4.8 seconds). And if someone is sad, look how much faster it is to initiate a response of anger or hate than a response of grief. As our technologically driven world speeds up, the slow emotions become harder and harder to access. We are simply responding too quickly. To paraphrase a Chinese idiom, we find ourselves trying to smell the flowers on horseback. To enter the world of the nonliterate mind, it is essential to slow way down. Practicing the state of reverence is an elegant way to do this.

Here's how Dr. Clynes describes the process.

> Reverence . . . is not meant as reverence for a particular person but as reverence for nature, God, or something larger than oneself. . . . For reverence, breathing is quite slow and will tend to stand still at the end of each deep inspiration. It is the opposite of sighing.

And in his book, *Sentics: The Touch of Emotions,* he says the following about reverence:

> Its course . . . begins with very low acceleration. It is accompanied by a minimum of tension of any kind. There is no abdominal tension and very little tension of the diaphragm. Respiration is slowed down to a very slow rate, slower than in any of the other sentic forms considered. There tends to be a respiratory pause at the end of inspiration. . . . Heart rate and oxygen consumption tend to be lowered considerably. Head position and gaze are often slightly upward.

Try using this way of breathing to awaken a sense of reverence as you reflect on the stories and quotes in this chapter. These words and stories are likely to make a great deal more sense when regarded from this state of mind.

Reading Out Loud

There are two final preparatory steps, *reading out loud* and *setting aside your schooled mind.* You have probably been reading silently so far, and even if you are reading every word, your inner speech is still talking quite fast. In this chapter, it is important to shift from this mental fast talk to a much slower pace. You need to digest each word and phrase, gathering the sense behind it and discovering how to match with those speakers, to sense how they see, where they are coming from, and what is the truth in what they are saying. Only then can you reclaim for yourself the skills they describe.

While you can't go back to being nonliterate, you can go back to being an out-loud beginning reader, and this will help. Read the following pieces *out loud* slowly, and reread every word, phrase, and sentence that isn't clear yet, or that you like the sound of and want to hear again. If reading out loud will bother those around you, you can at least go back to "sub-vocalizing." Remember the whispered speech you did around third grade before you became a completely silent reader? Your lips still moved, but you tried to be quiet about it. At least do this much as you read the remaining pieces in this chapter.

Setting Aside Your Schooled Mind

The last preparatory step may be the hardest of all. You need to *set aside your schooled mind's thinking patterns.* These are not the thinking strategies of young children and nonliterate peoples, and they will not help you to learn their skills. Your schooled mind loves to challenge, to analyze, to compare, to evaluate, to interpret, to have hunches and hypotheses, to think in ideas, and to use logic. We can call this *getting mental,* and when you feel yourself pulling away from connecting with the people or situations you are reading about or trying to analyze rather than match, it is time to take a break. The skills and practices of these people are likely quite foreign to you, and it can get exhausting to take in too much at one time.

If you can take these four steps *(maintaining respect, awakening reverence, reading out loud,* and *setting aside your schooled mind),* you are ready to enter a fascinating world. Enjoy harvesting many wonderful skills, some that you may have discarded long ago when you became literate and others that you never had the opportunity to develop.

THE GIFTS OF A DEEPLY FAMILIAR LIFE

A certain power of boredom is essential to a happy life.

BERTRAND RUSSELL
The Conquest of Happiness

A strange kind of repetition sets in with deep familiarity. At first glance it may seem dreadfully boring, especially if you live a life filled with novelty and change. But below the sameness and the seeming threat of boredom, a new possibility arises. No two repetitions are *exactly* the same. Subtle nuances of difference emerge with each repetition. Farmers working the same piece of land for many years almost caress it each spring, revisiting all the familiar mounds, rocks, ravines, patches of thistle, sections of barren and fertile soil, making note of how the land weathered the winter. Over time, a deep bond with nature takes form, grounding those who work the land, who fish the waters, who herd the sheep, who weave the wool, as well as those who roam familiar land, hunting and gathering to meet their needs. To those who are used to moving to new locations for work or school or in search of freshness, this intimate connection to nature may seem puzzling. That deeply familiar way of life would look to them like grinding repetition, and the teachings that arise out of such regularity would escape them.

To appreciate these teachings, we will need to make friends with repetition and learn to push through the initial boredom into a deep rhythmic practice. Imitation and repetition are the primary learning strategies of young children and remain critical to the way of life of many nonliterate cultures around the world. Most of us will never achieve the spiritual attunement of a weaver like Grace Henderson Nez, but we can learn to appreciate her mastery. Grace was born in 1913 and has spent over seventy years of her life living in the same hogan at the base of Ganado Mesa on the Navajo Reservation in Arizona. Her work reflects such a level of artistry and detail, and such a commitment to the traditional values and spiritual concentration on her craft, that in 2005, at age ninety-three, she was honored as a National Heritage Fellow. When asked about the joys of her work, she replied, "it soothes me spiritually, emotionally, and psychologically." And the challenges? They included "sustaining the desire to weave every day," and handling "the physical challenges [of] the repetitive motion and the aches and pains of sitting for long periods of time." She was clear about what has sustained and inspired her through the years. "My children, grandchildren, and my great-grandchildren are my inspiration for weaving. And weaving is my occupation, livelihood, and my life" (spoken in 2005).

We will be considering two groups of strategies, those that develop the refined observation skills needed to learn the practices of daily life and to prepare for apprenticeships, and those used to take in the oral teachings of the culture. We begin by exploring the learning and memory strategies that strengthen observation skills.

THE ART OF PAYING ATTENTION

The most basic learning strategy for young children and for members of nonliterate cultures doesn't need reclaiming. You still use it often in your life and developed it in much the same way they have. It is what we referred to in the opening chapter as *matching*. In matching, we watch others perform the activities of daily life, then copy those movements inwardly and practice them outwardly. As children, our muscles learned to obey our eyes and ears and to imitate what we noticed with increasing precision. Each time those muscles carried out the motion paths of bathing and grooming, handling tools or musical instruments, gathering materials, preparing food, or organizing the dwelling spaces, our skills improved. In nonliterate cultures, this kind of matching is a vital practice. By making closer and closer approximations, they become more skillful in these ordinary activities of their family or their culture so they can become valued members as they mature.

By the time a child reaches about age seven, practicing these skills by imitation becomes more challenging. *If the imitation becomes habitual, the skill ceases to grow.* It must be coupled with deep interest or else the subtle improvements that lead to real mastery will not occur. Grace Nez refers to the challenge of *sustaining the desire* to continue practicing her weaving skills, and the child faces the same challenge. In nonliterate cultures this transition from ordinary practicing to moving deeply into a particular skill or role in the culture depends heavily on apprenticeship. With nonliterate cultures having no way of documenting their skills, art forms, and traditions, the survival of these practices that are so important to their way of life has depended on these apprentices. Any details they failed to notice and incorporate would likely be lost forever. The masters, like Grace Henderson Nez, accepted their responsibility to teach, agreeing to transmit their skills, their focus, and their intention to any committed apprentices. Meanwhile, the apprentices did their part, learning to sustain their passion and their interest; overcoming boredom, distraction, and discomfort; and finally, entering what we might call the cognitive zone of a true apprentice.

Both the arts and the trades continue to rely heavily on this master-apprentice relationship in mainstream society today. Plumbers and electricians move from being apprentices to journeymen to masters in their fields. In the arts, master classes play an important part in helping the young musicians, artists, actors, and dancers refine their skills. In athletics, master coaches serve the same subtle function. However, in literate cultures, only those who are drawn to a particular skill or body of lore and who are supported in their pursuits are likely to transform their early practicing into such a deep commitment.

With support and the presence of master teachers, these fortunate children learn to harness their will forces to move from practicing to having a practice. The distinction is dramatic. These are the people who can't stay away from their activity without feeling a sense of longing. When my son was twelve, we took a long vacation, and he took a break from practicing piano. I was wondering where he was on the continuum between practicing and having a practice when we visited the Smithsonian Museum. As we stood outside the ropes surrounding an elegant grand piano, he suddenly lamented, "Why won't they let you *play* it?" In that moment I knew he had a practice. Twenty years later, he continues that practice as a professional musician.

Sometimes in the arts, one's extremities can even take on a mind of their own after many years of practice. Naropa University has a tradition of calling on faculty members at its fall convocation each year to generate a spontaneous poem. For many years, Laurie Doctor, a master artist and calligrapher, would capture that eight-line poem in calligraphy, writing each line that the audience offered as they spoke it. When it was over, she had created a work of art that was then displayed in the halls of the school. When asked how she could design such beauty so quickly, she explained that she didn't have to think about it at all, saying, "At this point, the dharma is in my hands." (*Dharma* is a Buddhist term, roughly translated as "practice.") A very similar comment was made by two great, retired tap dancers who were watching movie clips of their peers from the Cotton Club era in Harlem. They had praise for each of them, and finally came to one dancer for whom none of those praises was enough. Finally, they said, "That man had thinking feet!"

You might even find elements of this *mastery by imitation* arising in your own life. Are there family recipes that almost died out but were saved because some grandchild took the time to learn from the grandmother? Are there practices you carry out with greater care than most people? Perhaps you oil down blades and shovels for the winter, knit or sew well, keep family customs alive, organize drawers and workbenches, send handwritten thank-you notes—activities that remind you of your own masters, those who showed you how to do these things with such care.

With many nonliterate cultures, the master-apprentice relationship does not end when these elders die. While the elders are their main teachers, it is also common for the ultimate elders, the ancestors, to participate in the transmissions as well. Sometimes the teaching conversations arise in dreams, sometimes in awake moments—but the ancestors are always with them. Living on the land where their ancestors are buried helps them keep this connection alive and is one of the reasons they grieve so intensely when forced to leave that land.

Members of literate cultures who move frequently and approach death with a sense of finality can find it hard to imagine having such deep ties to a particular piece of land, much less communicating directly with their ancestors. It becomes more believable as you listen to the eloquent statements of the following two spokesmen from orality-based cultures.

Roy Sesana, head of the Botswana Bushmen pressure group that had been seeking permission to return to their ancestral lands in the Kalahari

Desert, expressed his joy at winning the case in court by saying first in English, "My heart today is nice!" and then adding, through an interpreter: "I'm very, very much happy at the outcome. I'm going to greet my ancestors at home. My ancestors told me I was going to win" (spoken in December 2006). (Note: Sadly, this joy was short-lived. Their struggles continue. In June 2010, they returned to court, pleading to reopen their borehole to obtain much needed water, and were turned down in spite of the government's approval of boreholes to serve the animals in the reserve as well as a tourist camp.)

The second quotation is from commentary in 1853 by the great chief of the Suquamish and Duwamish tribes, Chief Seattle. He was responding to a speech by Governor Steven who had just explained how the town of Seattle would be platted out as part of the Washington Territory. Chief Seattle's eloquent response, explaining how this would impact his people, was given in the Duwamish language and written down on the spot by a gifted translator, Dr. Henry Smith. At one point in his remarks, he said, "Your dead cease to love you and the land of their nativity as soon as they pass the portals of the tomb and wander way beyond the stars. They are soon forgotten and never return. Our dead never forget the beautiful world that gave them being, and ever yearn in tender, fond affection over the lonely-hearted living, and often return from the Happy Hunting Ground to visit, guide, console, and comfort them."

When we talk about sacred objects in a later section, we will realize that Chief Seattle wasn't completely correct about literate peoples. We do have practices and objects that keep our connections alive. And many of us still experience quiet visitations, conversations, and exchanges with our ancestors, which we tend not to broadcast since these experiences are not currently recognized as a possibility.

NOTICING EMERGENT PATTERNS

Go to the pine if you want to learn about the pine, or to the
bamboo if you want to learn about the bamboo. And in doing so,
you leave behind your subjective preoccupation with yourself.

Advice of the great Japanese Haiku poet BASHO

If we heed Basho's advice, we may be able to reclaim the ability to spot emergent patterns. First, we need to leave ourselves "behind" and fully experience the scene in front of us. Here are a few practices to get you started. Next time you see a flock of birds, shift from focusing on a single bird to taking in the flock and then soften your gaze to experience the inward sensation of rising as they lift up in unison to fly away. If you see a field of grain you can try this. Shift your eyes from regarding the shafts of grain to seeing the whole field to softening the gaze enough to join the traces of wind skirting across the top of the field. Even a glass of iced coffee can be experienced in this way. There are the ice cubes and the glass as a whole, and then there's the invitation to relax into riding the downward swirls as the cream descends.

Sometimes it takes patient waiting, without thinking, before a pattern arises. And often you are waiting for some form of movement to occur. Without movement, it is very hard for the eye to register objects in the visual field. Those who can spot the quiet rabbit in the grass or the deer on the hillside are often picking up on extremely subtle movements. But sometimes the objects are not providing the movement; your eyes are. It is their constant movement that finally allows the four-leaf clover to unexpectedly stand out or the vines that seemed to be picked clean to reveal a few more peapods. Even when you think your eyes are perfectly still, if you ask someone to watch you, they'll report that your eyes dart about almost constantly just to stay alert.

Often this capacity to see emergent patterns exists in highly focused scientists. In 1896, Robert Lauterborn published a massive and classic tome entitled *Treatise on Paulinella Chromatophora*. A current researcher who is studying the same cell type expressed his amazement at Lauterborn's observation skills, all accomplished while using the simple light microscope of his day. "He clearly shows objects in the cell that are theoretically below the resolution of the light microscope, but we know they are there because we have looked at the same cells with the electron microscope, and his drawings are absolutely correct. . . . I was astonished at how much he saw, in perfect detail!"

By attending to emergent patterns, you can even begin to notice what's missing. Have you ever been to a reunion and suddenly realized that a favorite person wasn't there? You didn't take attendance or count the group to figure this out. You simply knew, rather like this nonliterate young goatherd whose interview was in a book about Sicily in the 1950s. "I can't count, but even when I was a long way away, I could see if one of my goats was missing. I knew every goat in my herd—it was a big herd, but I could tell every one of them apart. I could tell what kid belonged to what mother. The master used to count them to see if they were all there, but I knew they were all there without counting them."

Against a background of deep familiarity, these small deviations stand out easily. Either the herd was the same as it always was, or it was not the same and that was the signal to scan for who's not there. The theme of same versus not same will arise again later in the book and will prove to be an important clue in understanding the thinking strategies of nonliterate people and young children.

This art of spotting small deviations can also arise with literate individuals who become deeply familiar with some aspect of their work. By deepening their practices through countless repetitions, they begin attending to the small deviations. In the April 1990 issue of *The New Yorker* magazine, John McPhee's article "Looking for a Ship, Part 2" describes a ship captain with such a refined skill. Captain Washburn was quoted as saying, "When you get close to a big storm, you can feel it. For some reason, the ship takes on almost a little uncertainty. She's almost like a live thing—like they say animals can sense bad weather coming. Sometimes I almost believe a ship can. I know that doesn't make sense, because she's steel and wood and metal, but she picks up a little uncertainty, probably something that is being transmitted through the water. It's hard to define. It's just a tiny little different motion, a little hesitancy, a little tremble from time to time" (spoken in approximately 1989).

More recently, the head driller in the successful Chilean mine rescue had this conversation with CNN interviewer Anderson Cooper after his team completed thirty-three days of drilling, through over two thousand feet of rock, to reach the miners. First Cooper asked, "I read that you said this was the most difficult drilling project you've worked on . . . why was this one so tough?"

The driller, Jeff Hart, explained that in addition to lives being at stake, "the geology and the strata here is very difficult to drill. It's very abrasive, extremely hard. It's got very broken parts in it and soil just—it eats up bits. We had a hard time with the angle, keeping the bushing in the bits."

Cooper said, "These drills are amazing, but you actually have to stand on your feet while you're drilling. I read [that's] because you actually kind of sensed things through your feet. Tell me about that."

Jeff Hart replied, "Absolutely. If you're a good driller, you're always standing on your feet, kind of feeling what's going on. And you can tell a lot by your gauges, but the real feel is what the drill's doing. So you're noticing whether it's good torque or bad torque. So you know whether it's time to pull a bit, or whether it's just something else in the hole that's holding you up."

You probably experience remnants of this skill of attending to very small changes. For example, when a houseguest prepares to leave, it is always easier for you to do a final walkthrough to spot items they may be leaving behind than it is for them. Only those items that aren't familiar will stand out for you, while they would have to look at everything. Imagine how much you could notice if you could see all of your surroundings in this deeply familiar way. In our rapidly changing world, this is nearly impossible but it was expected from members of nonliterate cultures.

This Native American example from the plains of Montana was given to me by Dr. Anne Forrest Ketchin, an anthropologist and a friend of the woman in the story. She passes on the story like this:

A friend, a woman who was raised non-Indian, but whose mother was a tribal member, reported to me the first time she went to the reservation and spent time with an old man who had been raised "traditional." She was hoping to learn about and participate in tribal ceremonies and activities, despite living off reservation. She wanted to connect with her heritage.

The old man insisted she and her husband take him for a ride around the reservation, a long ride. This woman's husband was driving, and she sat in the passenger seat in the front, the old man between them (an old style pickup with bench seats). To hear her tell it, the old man harassed her continually about the detail of the land they were passing through. What had she seen? Heard? Smelled? What animals, in what patterns? Where were the cottonwoods? Where were the shrubs? Near what butte or shack? She could not report any detail, even only a moment after passing something, only the grand sweep of the landscape as a vista, and even at that she did not remember how one butte related to another, or to a hollow, or a cabin. Soon she came to tears, and then the old man explained that she had to develop her ability to perceive and remember detail of the land even better than a child's face. Not just the overview, but the detail, and not just the visual, but all senses at once, including the sense of space she might experience between one sound and another. The whole, and in detail.

She realized then that she could not really describe her child's face, or her child as a whole in the way he meant, despite her love and devotion for this child. Not even the visual, much less the changing smells and sounds, though these were familiar once she got back to her child and checked in on them. But they were not imprinted on her the way he meant (the elder was speaking to her in approximately 1982).

The following two sections are devoted to a remarkable two-year research project by led by Alexander Luria, one of Russia's greatest neuropsychologists, and a small group of colleagues. They interviewed members of a peasant culture that was on the brink of moving into literacy. As you will discover, they were able to capture in amazing detail the thinking patterns before and after that change.

AN INCREDIBLE EXPEDITION

[Luria's] general purpose was to show the sociohistorical
roots of all basic cognitive processes;
the structure of thought depends upon the structure of
the dominant types of activity in different cultures.

MICHAEL COLE

foreword to *Cognitive Development: Its Cultural and Social Foundations*, by A. R. Luria

The year was 1924, three years after the Russian revolution had drawn to a close, when the intellectual chemistry of a small group of neuro-psychologists in Moscow brought that same revolutionary spark to the field of psychology. The catalyst and intellectual leader of this group was a young man named Lev Vygotsky, who had just joined Alexander Luria and his colleague, A. N. Leontiev, on the faculty of the Institute of Psychology in Moscow. They began meeting weekly to share their ideas and their research and soon invited a small circle of students to join them. In his autobiography, *The Making of Mind*, Luria tried to describe the great enthusiasm running through that group. "The entire group gave almost all of its waking hours to our grand plan for the reconstruction of psychology. When Vygotsky went on a trip, the students wrote poems in honor of his journey. When he gave a lecture in Moscow, everyone came to hear him." Vygotsky would commonly lecture for three to five hours at a stretch, with no notes, and it was up to stenographers to capture his teachings.

The group read widely in many languages, and among the authors they studied was Jean Piaget, a great Swiss psychologist who had just published his first major book that year, *The Thought and Language of the Child*. While they challenged some of his ideas, they were very interested in his idea of cognitive stages and his clinical methods. Piaget presented well-designed and very structured tasks to many subjects of different ages and then carefully studied the exact language of their responses. The group suspected that socio-cultural influences might affect which Piagetian stage a culture used, and seven years later they saw the opportunity to test their hypothesis. This resulted in the extraordinary research we are about to study.

In 1931 and 1932, collectivization was being introduced into Uzbekistan. The practice of farming independently was being replaced by a new business model that involved a division of labor. Some farmers were beginning to work on collective farms, some young women were being taught to teach kindergarten while others attended secondary schools, and farm organizers were trained to keep records, organize the workers, and monitor the production of crops. Meanwhile, in the nearby mountains of Kyrgystan, nothing had changed yet. The farmers still farmed in their traditional ways, and because the people were Muslim, the married women lived in separate women's quarters called *ichkari* and were shielded from the culture around them. Led by Luria, a small team of researchers began to make trips to the region to carry out their investigation.

They assumed that when farming was approached in a more holistic, patterned, repetitive, and intuitive way, a practical thinking style (what Piaget would call *preoperational thinking*) should serve them best. However, when collective farming and literacy were needed, they assumed that language would play a greater role and a more abstract or verbal/logical thinking style (what Piaget would call *concrete thinking*) would be necessary. They expected those subjects would become much more precise with language and use more abstract thinking strategies. Their findings strongly supported both assumptions.

However, because this research seemed to suggest that farmers who were not collectivized were being held back in their thinking, the government was alarmed. They simply could not afford to reach all the farmers at once so they refused to let these findings be published at the time. Fortunately, Luria held onto all of their work, and forty years later, after all of Russia was introduced to literacy and concrete thinking, the research was finally allowed to be published by Moscow University Press in 1974 and two years later by Harvard University Press in the United States under the title *Cognitive Development: Its Cultural and Social Foundations.*

You are about to read a number of conversations and it would be best if you could read them aloud. In that way you will be more able to match with the minds of the speakers, who often think very differently from you. Whenever I explored this research in my college classes, we brought many of these dialogues to life by conducting a readers' theater. The students paired up to present each conversation, with one taking the part of the investigator and the other speaking as the subject. You will only be reading a small sampling of these conversations, but if you want to read more you will find them in both of the Luria books mentioned above.

The researchers took the time to get to know the subjects, and in several visits over a two-year period were able to interview between fifty and eighty subjects on each task they prepared. Some conversations took place in the village tea house after the farming day was over, some were conducted by female interviewers in the women's quarters of the mountain villages (since men were not allowed to have any contact with those women), and other interviews would arise more spontaneously in both the mountain villages and the villages undergoing collectivization. When the conversations arose spontaneously, they were gradually brought around to one of the structured tasks, and while one investigator continued to converse, the others quietly took exact notes of the conversations.

The subjects in these interviews were from one of five different groups: (1) the ichkari women in the mountain villages, (2) the nonliterate farmers from those villages, (3) young women who had attended short courses in the teaching of kindergarteners but still had no literacy training, (4) collective farm workers and organizers, all of whom had taken short courses but were still barely literate and (5) women students enrolled in a teachers' school who had finished two or three years of study and were now literate.

The first two tasks involved the naming and grouping of colors. Subjects were presented with skeins of silk or wool of various colors and shades of those colors.

The female students and collective farmers used category names for colors the way urban school children would, although some of the farmers knew few color words. One explained, "Men don't know colors and call them all *blue*." However, most of these groups had no difficulty grouping the colors by category.

The dramatic difference came with interviews of the ichkari women who worked with color extensively in their embroidery and handwork.

However, their names for the colors were all related to objects that bore those colors—peach, liver, iris, spoiled cotton, and so on. And when they were asked to group them, they were completely confused and protested, "It can't be done. None of them are the same; you can't put them together." If they were pressured into grouping them, they might arrange the lighter hues together in one group and the bold colors in another. If pushed still further, about half of them could reluctantly group them the way the investigator wished, but they still didn't agree with it. The others staunchly maintained it couldn't be done. Clearly the visual appearance of each color was much more important to them than any vocabulary words that might cluster them together.

The next two tasks involved naming and grouping geometrical shapes. Subjects were shown drawings of circles, triangles, rectangles, a trapezoid, horizontal lines, and incomplete circles and triangles.

The fifth group, the teachers' school students, named and grouped all the figures by their shape name, whether they were dark or light, drawn with dotted or completely filled-in lines. The other groups, with the exception of the ichkari women, used shape names for most drawings, but might fill in a confusing one with an object name based on what it most resembled to them. The ichkari women had no categorical names and gave each drawing an object name, from plate, sieve, or bucket to naming the incomplete circle and triangle a bracelet and a stirrup. When asked to group them, they again protested that it couldn't be done. When pressed, they tried to make connections between a few of them.

For example, for a dotted square and a rectangle, "These are alike—this is a bird cage, and that's a feeding trough in a cage." For a square and a trapezoid, "This is a small bucket for sour milk, and that's a pan for cream."

The ichkari women used their visual skills to picture real-life situations that could connect the objects, and resisted using words as sorting tools. This resistance showed up with the nonliterate peasants as well once the tasks became more challenging, but not with those who were becoming literate.

Here are two examples, the first with a nonliterate peasant and the next with a barely literate one. You will note that the interviewer's notes are included in the two transcripts as well. In this task, the subject was shown four picture cards (a hammer, a saw, a log, and a hatchet) and was asked, "Which of these things could you call by one word?" The conversation with the nonliterate peasant from a remote village went like this:

"How's that? If you call all three of them a hammer, *that won't be right either."*

Rejects use of general term.

"But one fellow picked three things—the hammer, the saw, and hatchet—and said they were alike."

"A saw, a hammer, and a hatchet all have to work together. But the log has to be there, too!"

Reverts to situational thinking.

"Why do you think he picked these three things and not the log?"

"Probably he's got a lot of firewood, but if we'll be left without firewood, we won't be able to do anything."

Explains selection in strictly practical terms.

"True, but a hammer, a saw, and a hatchet are all tools."

"Yes, but even if we have tools, we still need wood—otherwise, we can't build anything."

The conversation with a barely literate twenty-year-old living in the town of Tashkent was very different and went like this:

"Which of these things doesn't fit?"

"The wood doesn't fit here. Wood just lies on the ground, whereas the other three are used for different kinds of work."

Classifies categorically though fails to use categorical term.

"Yet, some people say the hammer doesn't fit here."

"I don't know whether that's right or not. This is a log, and this is a hatchet. If the hatchet doesn't cut through, you can use the hammer to beat on it."

Reverts to situational thinking.

"What one word could you use for these three things?"

"You could call them tools."

"Name some other tools."

"Plane, shovel, scissors, knife."

"Can you call a log a tool?"

"No, it's wood."

The researchers found that while only one nonliterate peasant out of the twenty-six tested could be prompted to classify objects by category, 70 percent of the barely literate collective farm workers could do so with some prompting, and all of those with one or more years of schooling classified objects by category without prompting. For them, the tendency to think by connecting all the elements together into a single story had faded away.

They were no longer *thinking by association*. More importantly, they were beginning to identify similarities among objects that were not exactly alike. They had shifted from having two groupings—same and not same, or alike and different—to three groupings—same, *similar*, and different. This seemingly simple shift will have a profound impact on their imagination, as we shall discover in the next piece.

IMAGINATION ROOTED IN MEMORY

Luria's research team administered two final sets of tasks to the Uzbek and Kashgari people, one attempting to force subjects to deal with similarities and the other revealing how even their use of imagination was about to change.

The final similarities task involved presenting two objects that didn't bear any visual resemblance to one another and weren't likely to be used in the same practical situations. Since visual cues were clearly not going to be helpful, they wanted to see if the nonliterate subjects would finally resort to using categorical words to link the two items together. They remained steadfastly committed to their visual thinking strategies and usually ended up talking only about how the two items were different.

This interview with a thirty-eight-year-old nonliterate peasant who worked in the countryside was a good example. The interviewer's notes are again included in the transcript.

"What do a chicken and a dog have in common?"

"They're not alike. A chicken has two legs; a dog has four. A chicken has wings but a dog doesn't. A dog has big ears and a chicken's are small."

Describes differences rather than similarities.

"You told me what is different about them. How are they alike?"

"They're not alike at all."

"Is there one word you could use for them both?"

"No, of course not."

"What word fits both a chicken and a dog?"

"I don't know."

"Would the word animal fit?"

"Yes."

Accepts term of generalization.

The last task involved logical statements called *syllogisms,* which have obvious answers as long as you approach them as word problems and not visual ones. This task proved impossible for nonliterate subjects but was quite easy for even the barely literate subjects.

One syllogism presented was: "In the Far North, where there is snow, all bears are white. Novaya Zemlya is in the Far North and there is always snow there. What color are the bears there?"

One thirty-seven-year-old nonliterate peasant from a remote village responded in this fashion:

"There are different sorts of bears."

Failure to infer from syllogism.

Hearing the syllogism for the second time, he added, "I don't know; I've seen a black bear. I've never seen any others. Each locality has its own animals; if it's white, they will be white; if it's yellow, they will be yellow."

Appeals only to personal, graphic experience.

"But what kind of bears are there in Novaya Zemlya?"

"We always speak only of what we see; we don't talk about what we haven't seen."

The same.

"But what do my words imply?" The syllogism is repeated.

"Well, it's like this: our tsar isn't like yours, and yours isn't like ours. Your words can be answered only by someone who was there, and if a person wasn't there, he can't say anything on the basis of your words."

The same.

"But on the basis of my words—In the north, where there is always snow, the bears are white—can you gather what kind of bears there are in Novaya Zemlya?"

"If a man was sixty or eighty and had seen a white bear and had told about it, he could be believed, but I've never seen one, and hence I can't say. That's my last word. Those who saw can tell, and those who didn't see can't say anything!"

Luria's research team drew an interesting distinction between two kinds of imagination as they reflected on these findings. They referred to the preliteracy, precollectivization kind of imagination as a *reproductive imagination*. The subjects relied almost entirely on what they had seen in their ordinary lives and would make no speculations about things they had not experienced, as we have just learned. This limited them to thinking about the past and the present but not about the uncertain future. The strategy seemed to serve them well for remembering what they had seen, however. Later, as we explore storytelling, we will discover that this reproductive imagination was also powerful at recalling what was heard.

The newly literate subjects were willing to speculate about places they had never seen and make predictions based on verbal information. The team referred to this as a reliance on *constructive imagination,* using imagination to go beyond their lived and practical experiences. However, while Luria's research was amazingly thorough, they never assessed the way literacy would impact the capacity to memorize.

Reproductive imagination has a reduced role in literate cultures, often regarded as nothing more than a rote memory tool, a mechanism for recalling the past, and remembering what we have experienced, seen, or heard. Meanwhile, we prize constructive imagination, equating it with creativity, skillful planning, inventiveness, improvisation, and the ability to anticipate future events. Unfortunately, as our reproductive imaginations weaken, we tend to fill in with our seemingly more advanced constructive imaginations. The result has often been problematic.

For example, research into the accuracy of eyewitness accounts has begun to show that our reproductive memories are heavily influenced by a surprising number of variables ranging from comments by lawyers or police who set up lineups for the witness to scan to photographs of crime scenes and the comments of other witnesses. Since we don't really like uncertainty, it is a small step to go from a weak reproductive imagination's picture to filling in the gaps in that picture with various constructions until we are quite sure we have correctly identified a suspect or recalled an incident.

Students who try to rely on their reproductive memories to study are encountering very similar problems, finding it hard to trust the accuracy of their recollections. An observation by Vygotsky explains their dilemma. He had noticed that the young child used reproductive imagination while the adolescent had shifted to using constructive imagination. He expressed this idea eloquently in his book *Mind in Society,* saying, "For the young child, to think means to recall; but for the adolescent, to recall means to think." We see evidence of that in our daily lives. Ask a young child what happened in school today and they are likely to say "nothing." However, later something might trigger their memory and we are treated to a very detailed account of some aspect of that day. Now try to "remember" what you were doing last Thursday. Unless it was a very special day, you probably used logic to reconstruct what you were most likely doing that day. Likewise the struggling student is at the mercy of a constructive imagination that tries to reconstruct what the book or the lecturer most likely said. Only those students who have succeeded in rekindling their reproductive imaginations are likely to enjoy accurate memories.

With our current memory limitations in mind, we can now revisit the reproductive imaginations of nonliterate people with more respect and discover the powerful gifts we gave up when we began relying on words instead of direct experiences to organize our understanding of the world. In the next section, we will turn to other nonliterate cultures for insights into their incredible memory skills and explore ways we might rekindle those skills in ourselves. Following that, we will explore several other realms Luria's team overlooked, including the nature of sacred objects and spaces, and the ability to perceive seemingly invisible aspects of the environment.

AN UNEXPECTED TEACHER

One afternoon in the spring of 1982, when I least expected it, I was given a brilliant thirty-minute crash course on orality-based learning and memory strategies. I was called in as a consultant to meet with a ninth-grade girl who had been floundering in school all spring. She had done well enough before that with the help of her resource teacher, Mrs. Sanchez. But in the second semester, Mrs. Sanchez had been asked to take over the ESL (English as a second language) class, and this girl had a new teacher. "Why won't they let me stay in Mrs. Sanchez's class? I can learn anything she teaches," the girl lamented. There were six of us in the room: the occupational therapist and language therapist who had invited me, the girl's mother, the girl herself, and a friend of the family, Mr. Walter Littlemoon. All of them lived in the Denver area and were Native American, members of the Lakota tribe of South Dakota. At one point in our cognitive assessment, we realized that the girl was ambidextrous, and it wasn't clear whether she was primarily left- or right-handed. That's when my training course began.

Mr. Littlemoon suggested that perhaps she thought like a "left-handed Indian." He was left-handed, and since I was too, he directed his comments to me. What he said next remains a vivid memory, so I will share the conversation with you nearly verbatim. Then we can discuss it.

"Maybe she thinks like a left-handed Indian."

"How is that then?"

"For instance, I do a lot of things backward, like buttoning my shirt from the bottom up and reading a book from the back to the front."

"And in the classroom?"

"Well, in grade school it really helped that they never washed the windows, . . . [pause] and there was a lot of wood on the walls . . . [pause] and then of course there were those letters above the blackboard."

If I understood him so far, he would have to answer my next question with no. "Well, did that work in high school?"

"No, then I had to use my pictures."

"What kind of pictures?"

"Well, you know. You might look over there and see a chicken and some cattle, and that isn't really important, but then in the distance you see a horse running down a ravine just so. That was a picture to remember . . . [pause] I have a lot of those pictures."

"And how did you handle tests in high school?"

"I cheated."

"What would you do?"

"Well, the teachers all had plants on their desks, so when no one was look-ing, I would turn the teacher's plant a quarter turn before I sat down to take a test."

"Actually, that was OK. It wasn't cheating."

"But no one else did it."

"I know, but that's just because they didn't realize it could help them."

At this point, the conversation was harder to recall. I needed to check with him to be sure I knew what he meant by each strategy. While he couldn't quite see why I needed to do that, he was very patient with me, and I found that I had understood him quite well.

Now let's unpack these unusual strategies to learn how he used them. Each of them relied on strong visual-thinking skills and an insistence that two things needed to be exactly the same, or they were not con-sidered a match. He was drawing on his highly developed reproductive memory and avoiding any temptations to be pulled out of the present moment or into settling for similarities rather than exact matches. He found ways to resist the future thinking that distracts most students and didn't try to use what we think of as imagination at all. He only used those exact images he had actually experienced or those he had harvested from the teacher's stories.

Let's begin with the backward activities. You might say that starting by reading the end of a book ruins the surprises. You no longer are car-ried along in anticipation of how it will turn out. But this anticipation is also pulling you out of the present moment into continuous speculation about the future as you read. He found a way to stop that anticipatory feeling by knowing the outcome ahead of time. And the shirt buttons? Try it yourself sometime. There is a slight feeling of anticipation when we start at the top. You always wonder if the buttons are aligned cor-rectly or not. But if you start at the bottom, that removes all concern. Of course they will be aligned.

Why was he so glad to have those dirty windows? That meant the whole room was filled with swirl patterns, from the wood grain to the alphabet shapes to those streaks of dust on the windows. They formed a perfect template on which to embed the images arising from the teacher's stories. He was such a gifted visualizer that he could store all the lessons in plain sight, ready to be called forth when needed.

So, why wouldn't this continue to work in high school? Think about how very visual the lessons in grade school are. They are what we will later consider "concrete" or able to be seen easily. But in high school the lessons become more abstract. What does *x* look like in algebra, and what image is exactly the same as the idea of revolutions or economic conditions or chemistry formulas? To store these ideas, he turned to his remembered "pictures," to the elegant natural metaphors he had discovered and collected over time by being deeply attentive to how nature behaves. The pictures served as truth detectors. If an idea could be mapped perfectly onto the elements in one of the pictures, then it must be true because nature was like that too. If not, he could raise questions about the areas that didn't fit.

I know of one person who was able to use this same approach in reverse. She would *create* nature pictures to represent an idea. She, too, was a gifted visualizer and taught blind and visually handicapped children. At the end of every year she had to write a report about each child, conveying all the child's gifts, obstacles, and possibilities and the special support that child would need from next year's teacher. Her reports were brilliant—clear, poetic, and inspiring. The reader came away with a vivid sense of the child and how to proceed in the fall. Few people realized how much work she put into creating them, however. It could take hours. She would revisit all she knew about the child, all her impressions and understandings of the hidden potential within the child and all the qualities she wanted to awaken in next year's teacher. Then she began her inward search, asking herself what could possibly be like that. Finally, she said, a picture would emerge and she would be ready to write. When I asked once what kind of picture, her response was a lot like Mr. Littlemoon's: "You know," she said, "like a man going into the desert to paint and sitting down against a warm boulder. But he didn't have any water for the watercolors and sand kept getting into his oil paints. That kind of picture." That particular report was about a five-year-old girl, and the report never mentioned the man, the desert, or the idea of painting. But once she had that picture, she knew how to proceed with the report. Each element in the picture represented some element she wanted to include, and now she knew how to connect them and bring them to life for the reader.

Can this gift be reclaimed? The most critical rule is to insist on exact sameness. You experience a remnant of that when you find the perfect present. You say it is exactly right for your friend; it simply *is* them. There is an intuitive matching that ties the gift to the person, almost recognizing the person in that gift. That same art of matching is used by the real estate agent who senses the perfect house for a client, the poet who searches for the perfect metaphor to describe a feeling, and the matchmaker who pairs couples perfectly.

This leaves one final strategy to unpack, the turning of the plant. Have you ever had a time when you studied really well, felt completely prepared, and in that moment felt you could answer any question perfectly? If you could just freeze that moment and return to it at will throughout the test, you would do very well. Sadly, test anxiety often arises, evaporating your confidence and scrambling all the great information you knew when you sat down to take the test. Your state of mind has shifted from the prepared-mind state in which all the information was easily available to a state of confusion and anxiety. Mr. Littlemoon found a way to hold onto the prepared-mind state—*the state he was in when he turned the teacher's plant.* All he had to do during the test was to look back at the plant any time he couldn't retrieve an answer. That would snap him back to the moment when he turned the plant, when his prepared mind was fully available. He had discovered a way to awaken what researchers now call *state-specific memory.* You probably use this principle naturally when you find you have forgotten why you came into a particular room. You meant to get or do something but you simply cannot remember, so you go back to where you were standing when you had the impulse to go there. You recreate the setting and that recreates the state that held the impulse in the first place. When you lose your train of thought in a conversation, it is natural for the listener to offer prompts, key words from what you have just said, hoping to recreate the strands of your thoughts for you. But these are mere remnants of the powerful memory capacities of those in orality-based cultures.

MEMORY AND THE ORAL TRADITION

For hundreds of years, orality-based cultures have survived because of the astounding memories of their members. They recognize sameness and re-create the stories, songs, ceremonial rituals, and practical lore of daily life with an exactness rarely seen in literate cultures. There are no books, so these are the vessels that carry the wisdom of the culture, and they must be remembered exactly. There is no room for improvisation since every detail that is deleted or changed diminishes the cultural memory and weakens the culture. The same exactitude is required of the priests who perform important ceremonies.

Ruth Benedict, a renowned anthropologist, describes the responsibilities of the western Pueblo priests and assistants in this way in her book *Patterns of Culture:* "No field of activity competes with ritual for foremost place in their attention. . . . It requires the memorizing of an amount of word-perfect ritual that our less trained minds find staggering." This observation was echoed in the introduction to the book *Indian Oratory* as follows: "Ritual prayers, often lasting for hours, had to be recited without error or the omission of a single syllable. The slightest deviation would interfere with the results sought through the ritual and . . . might have a far-reaching effect upon the health, crops, hunting, and welfare of the people of the tribe." This book offers an amazing compilation of the speeches of chieftains spanning more than 150 years and makes note of "the amazing memory of the speaker and the ability of the listener to remember what was said."

Usually white traders or settlers would make notes as they heard these speeches and then translate their notes into English. However, on one occasion in 1890 the Sioux Chief, Kicking Bear, delivered a speech to a council of his people at which no outsider was present. And yet that speech was in the collection! Major James McLaughlin, who made a practice of copying down and then translating important speeches, was able to retrieve it. He had simply asked one of the attendees who was known for his fine memory to tell him the speech later. While we might try to reconstruct a speech using phrases like "and then he said" or "he talked about" and admitting to whole chunks that we couldn't recall at all, Short Bull simply recited the fifteen-hundred-word speech verbatim without any side comments. To give you some idea of his feat, each section in this book runs about fifteen hundred words, and he had only heard the speech once.

This quality of immersion in the moment is aided by living in a culture that doesn't spend time addressing what hasn't happened yet. Our preoccupation with the future permeates our mental chatter, pulling us away from the present moment. In Alaska, Ron and Suzanne Scollon have devoted their careers to the study of the native Athabaskan culture and to addressing the interethnic communication difficulties between them and the English (their term for nonnative Alaskans). The Athabaskans reported being quite puzzled by several tendencies of the English. "They always talk about what's going to happen later," and "They think they can predict the future." Even though these speakers are quite literate, their cognitive practices still remain grounded in their orality-culture roots with its adherence to the present moment.

While many of our memories seem sketchy and tend to fade over time, we usually have a few that remain as vivid as the day they occurred. When we recall them, we seem to experience those moments all over again. They activate several senses and hold precise details—where we were, who was there, the smells, tastes, and sounds of the moment, perhaps even what we were wearing. Consider making a list of some of your vivid positive memories, the heartwarming and humorous incidents that bring laughter and affection when you recall them and the ones that bring back moments of joy and excitement. Revisit this list to uplift your spirits whenever you have a frustrating or depressing day. Reliving these moments will even improve your body chemistry for a few minutes.

You may find that some of these positive memories are stored as short movie clips while most negative memories come back only as snapshots. That is simply a protective measure your brain takes to reduce the trauma memories as much as possible while still retaining at least one "wanted poster" to protect you from future harm. Have you noticed the full-bodied sensations that accompany your especially vivid positive memories? This is the natural state of awareness for orality-based cultures, and it explains, in part, why they have such powerful reproductive memories.

As we follow our mind into literacy, we will watch our focus on reproductive memory fade. These storage networks will start being used for creating new connections instead, and our mind must then find ways to compensate for progressively weaker reproductive memories. Never again will the capacity to appreciate and register sameness be so easily engaged as it was for the young child or carried to the great heights as it was in nonliterate cultures.

GATHERING KNOWLEDGE IN TRADITIONAL WAYS

Literate cultures have many sources of knowledge, from books and schools to media and the Web, and must weigh the accuracy of each source. Often it turns out that what appeared to be new knowledge is actually a distortion of the facts and the learner is faced with the task of unlearning that information. These half-truths also have a way of spreading throughout the culture and influencing behavior in problematic ways.

Orality-based cultures depend on accurate transmissions of information and cannot afford to contaminate their lore with such errors. To safeguard against that, they choose their teachers very carefully and anchor all new learning to their lived experience. Speculations about the future, descriptions of phenomena they haven't seen for themselves, and the words of strangers are all unacceptable knowledge sources. Much of their knowledge is passed on by two sources still shared by literate cultures: the teachings of respected elders in their community and apprenticeship relationships. However, they also draw from a number of other very important sources rarely used by literate cultures.

They often turn to their ancestors for information, comfort, and advice. In the mid-1960s, researchers were trying to test the ability of nonliterate tribal members in and around Kenya to visualize images clearly. They weren't expecting the additional information these subjects volunteered. The Kamba, Masai, and Swahili tribes of Kenya all explained to the examiners that they could also see the dead. Speaking of his parents and relatives, one young Swahili man said, "[Sometimes] they come into my mind and tell me something very important. . . .

I can see them properly, my father or mother or one of my relatives, I can see him clearly in front of my eyes" (spoken in approximately 1965).

Among the Aboriginal Australians, many of the cultural teachings are stored in songs that are held by certain members of the tribe, called *song men*. By the time these song men become elders, they may carry the teachings of up to a thousand songs. While many of the songs have been passed down to them and carefully learned, new songs also arise from other realms. In his book *The Man Who Sold His Dreaming*, author Roland Robinson quoted one song man explaining the source of new songs in this way: "I don't make up these songs and dances . . . the spirits give them to me. Sometimes when I am out hunting, I come to a certain place. Something in that place tells me to keep quiet. By and by I see the spirits come out and start singing and dancing. They are painted up, and they are beating the song sticks together. I keep quiet. I catch that song. I catch that dance. I catch that painting. I come back to the camp and give this song, this dance, this painting to my people" (spoken in approximately 1960).

For many with orality-based roots, even literacy will not displace this source of knowledge. Galomphete Gakelekgolele, a twenty-six-year-old Aboriginal college graduate, has two wishes: to find a good job in town and to live inside the reserve where he spent his childhood. He explained that he wanted to live "where my forefathers are buried" so that "if maybe I am sick, I can say a little prayer in their graveyard and then collect certain herbs, boil them, and drink them, and my problems will be gone" (spoken in 2010).

Some teachings have been passed down for so many generations that when asked about the origins, members would dismiss such questions with "legend has it" or, as the Trobrianders would typically say, "It was ordained of old" (spoken in the 1930s). One such teaching involves a way of combining seeds that tribes from eastern Canada down through the southwest United States all call the *three sisters*. The tribes have varied ancestral stories explaining why these particular seeds should be planted together but in each case corn, squash, and beans are grouped together as companion crops. Agricultural scientists now realize what a brilliant idea that is. The corn stalk provides the pole for the beans, the squash's primary leaves shade the new seedlings, the beans add the nitrogen to the soil that the corn will be taking out, and the three plants combine to create a completely balanced diet for the people. But their practice predated this scientific understanding by hundreds of years. How they knew to do this mystifies the researchers.

A similar mystery involves the consumption of yams in Africa. For the past two thousand years, yams have been the staple food of western Africa. Throughout the region, from Nigeria to Liberia, yams are at their best during the rainy season. However, all the tribes in that region have strict taboos against eating any yams until the rainy malaria season ends. They fear that breaking this taboo will bring great harm to their communities, so they choose to endure a three- to four-month period of hunger instead, celebrating its end with annual yam-harvest celebrations. While their behaviors are based on ancient rituals, modern scientists have discovered a powerful health reason to avoid the yams during those months as well.

Many who live in this region have inherited a chronic condition called sickle cell anemia, which is seen as a serious health problem with no benefit to those living in other parts of the world. However, for those at risk of the even more deadly malaria, it does have a benefit: It causes the blood cells to curl, or sickle, killing any malaria parasites that try to occupy those cells. Then when the danger of malaria passes, adding yams back into the diet throws the sickle cell anemia back into remission. While these orality-based cultures had no way of knowing this scientifically, they were able to arrive at the same amazing strategies.

Few nonliterate cultures live uninterrupted lives today. Just beyond their geographic boundaries, most of them are surrounded by literate cultures that may want to introduce them to new knowledge or encourage them to change certain behaviors.

Sometimes this transition can be handled brilliantly as it was in the northern forest region of India. There the Indian Institute of Forest Management has been observing and learning from the various nonliterate villages located deep within the mountainous northern forests. These people could easily see and work with the nature spirits, and often the village medicine man would share what he knew with visitors from the institute. "Don't cast shade on this herb before cutting a bit off or it will lose its potency," he might say, and sure enough their research would later show that the plant's alkaloid level drops in the shade, lowering its medicinal properties.

The land occupied by these villagers was too hilly to farm, so they subsisted on the nuts and berries they gathered from the nearby trees and shrubs and the fish that lived in their mountain lakes. They had one other valuable product, the gum they tapped from their gum trees each year. Each family had its own gum tree that was treated as an important member of the family. Weddings, funerals, and special occasions were always held next to the family tree so it could be included. Since these trees could never survive being tapped more than once every four years, the villagers formed cooperative groups of four families each and would take turns sharing in the income from a single tree's production each year.

The institute observers grew concerned because increasing poverty was threatening to force the villagers to tap their trees more often, and that would soon bring about their destruction. Every year they sold their gum to a trader who would visit each village, bringing them their primary source of income. However, they had no idea where the trader came from or where he took the harvest. About ten years ago, one professor from the institute, Prodyut Bhattacharya, had an inspired idea. He knew he couldn't simply tell them what was happening without disrupting their way of life, so he invented a board game and showed them how to play it. In the game there was a trader, there were villagers with their quantities of gum, and there was something called a *market* where the trader could sell the gum for much more than he paid the villagers. At first it was just an interesting game to them, but then he gathered an elder from each of several villages and brought them out of the forest for the first time in their lives to see this *market* for themselves. When they returned to their respective villages, they told their people that the board game was real. At the time of the next harvest, they formed a cooperative and sent their own delegate out to the market to sell the gum directly at a much higher profit, thereby saving their beloved trees. This important change was carried out so sensitively that the indigenous ways in those villages remained intact.

SENSING SACRED OBJECTS

"When a child loves you for a long, long time, not just to play
with, but REALLY loves you, then you become Real. . . .
It doesn't happen all at once," said the Skin
Horse. "You become. It takes a long time."

MARGERY WILLIAMS BIANCO
The Velveteen Rabbit

How does an object become sacred? The Skin Horse is correct; time and love *can* do it, and children are especially gifted at infusing their most cherished objects with sacredness in this way. Every parent who tires of searching when such an object gets lost and tries to give up by saying, "It's OK. We'll buy you a new one," quickly discovers what a profoundly unacceptable idea that is. Reluctantly, most of them join the community of parents the world over who are forced to cultivate the strangely intuitive ability to find lost objects!

We never really outgrow our attachment to sacred objects. They become the things we would grab first if we were forced to evacuate our homes. Invariably there are the photographs, since our weak reproductive memories need help remembering our lives and our ancestors. Next might be some important papers, but if there is time, our heirlooms will also be saved. These are the pieces that keep our memories of special people, places, and events alive. They seem to radiate a special energy that makes them stand out from all the other objects on the shelf or in the drawer. We can even spot them in each other's homes and, if we ask about them, we often receive the gift of stories from their owner revealing what has made them special.

While most of what we own is replaceable, these special pieces are not, and we would grieve their loss. Looked at this way, we can now sympathize more deeply with the two greatest laments of Indigenous Peoples who have been forcibly uprooted from their homes. Their first lament is that they no longer live on the land of their birth and of their ancestor's remains. We have already learned to appreciate what that means to them. But their second lament is the tragedy of having no *pieces*—no vessels, necklaces, cloth, carvings, tools that their ancestors had imbued with their essences. They, too, had lost their heirlooms.

Sacred objects can also be infused with increasing energy by being used ceremonially. You may be creating them without realizing it, whether it is a piece of jewelry or a hat that gets worn for special occasions or an object that you still use in family traditions, a star for the top of the tree, or the best dishes that are brought out for special guests. The more they are used, the more precious they become. You may find yourself physically drawn to them, actually sensing their energy. Some refer to this as *felt sensing*. With practice, you can refine your capacity to sense the energy in these special objects.

You might even want to gather a few trusted friends or family members together and create a mini-showing of those cherished pieces that can best represent you. Listening to each other tell your stories can be a powerful way to connect more fully with one another. Every fall, seniors in the psychology program at Naropa University would be assigned to small senior-project groups designed to support each other in their work. This activity of sharing important pieces quickly became a cherished tradition, helping them deepen their connections with one another as they began their journey together.

While frequent use of special objects can increase their energetic properties, you may have discovered, without realizing it, that this energy can gradually fade over time as well. If you have ever been faced with the daunting task of handling the estate of a deceased friend or well-loved family member, you may have found it overwhelming to simply clear out their possessions. While others who weren't as close to the person or couldn't feel the energy in objects could do this, you might have had to release the possessions more gradually, almost in layers. The first items to go were those with no charge. Then came the ones that seemed to slowly lose that charge. What remained became the "keepers" that would become tomorrow's pieces, special objects to pass on to others, to hand down through the family, or to keep for yourself.

So far, we have been considering the sacredness of ordinary objects in our daily lives. However, some objects have earned the title of *sacred* for more spiritual reasons. The sacred objects of orality-based cultures hold far more than the memories of their lived experiences. They hold a spiritual energy that is easily sensed by all of their members and is of vital importance to their ceremonial lives. Often the creation of these objects becomes a conscious practice in reverence to those who create them.

In 1980, Kashiwaya Sensei, an aikido master and then director of Rocky Mountain Ki Society, gave a public talk describing the energetic and mindful nature of ki, the life force at the heart of Aikido practice. In describing its far-ranging powers, he gave the example of wood carvers creating statues of the Buddha and commented, "If you carve a Buddha without ki, it will not sell. It will not attract a buyer." In other words, the energetic focus and intention of the carver is critical. The carvers of saints, called *Santeros,* of the southwest United States would agree with him. Felix Lopez of Espanola, New Mexico, is a renowned Santero who is literate and has been a high school teacher, but is very committed to the traditional ways of his Spanish Catholic heritage. He spoke eloquently of his practice in a video interview in approximately 1990: "When you carve a *santo,* you have to be in the right frame of mind, because it's actually like a form of prayer. At the end, you are tired, but you feel very good about what you've accomplished. This is the greatest feeling." He concludes the interview by saying, "For me, being a Santero has been a calling, a vocation from God. And I'm very thankful to Him for giving me this opportunity to create spiritual images that can help people in their spiritual lives or simply can be enjoyed by anyone if they only see it as a work of art."

His last comment makes an important distinction between those who can sense the spiritual energy in sacred objects and those who only see the outer artistic form. Very recently, the Smithsonian Institute returned a large collection of sacred objects to the Yurok Indian tribe of Northern California. At the museum, they were viewed as works of art, but the Yuroks received them as living objects, "much like welcoming home prisoners of war" explained Thomas O'Rourke, the tribe's chairman. "They are key to our existence, to carrying on our traditions and our culture—dances that we have taken part in since time immemorial." Asked what they will do with these objects, he replied, "We'll sing songs, we'll pray, we'll talk. And we will wake them up because in two weeks our renewal dances start, so we will prepare the items to dance. So they will dance this year" (spoken in an interview, August 2010).

Next time you view a traveling museum exhibit displaying the sacred objects of living indigenous cultures or the irreplaceable ancient objects preserved for generations by their now-literate descendants, you will understand what it means to these people to allow their pieces to leave home. They are placing incredible trust in the curators to protect and care for these remarkable objects until they are returned home, in the hopes that the viewers can appreciate their sacredness. These objects live in the secret realm that was mentioned in the preface. We can only understand a fragment of their reality through words and images. But they come to life in the felt sensations of those who truly know them.

SENSING THE SPACES AROUND US

What would the world be, once bereft
Of wet and of wildness? Let them be left,
O let them be left, wildness and wet;
Long live the weeds and the wilderness yet.

GERARD MANLEY HOPKINS
Inversnaid

The felt sense arising from different spaces comes to us naturally. As members of literate cultures, this energy from our surroundings often registers below our consciousness, and we ignore it the way a fish ignores the water in which it swims. However, those whose livelihoods still draw them into daily connections with the land and the waters and those who strive to reconnect with the earth in sustainable ways bring this awareness to consciousness in a manner reminiscent of the Indigenous Peoples of the world. We have been using the terms *orality-based cultures* and *nonliterate peoples* interchangeably, but for this section we need to be more specific. We want to learn from those people whose ancestors and whose entire way of life has been tied to particular lands. These are the original people of that land, whose identity is entwined with it and who call themselves the *indigenous ones.*

When a family farm goes up for auction, it is usually a time of great sorrow. A way of life, dating back many generations, has had to surrender to economic realities. And when those impacted by the Gulf of Mexico oil spill insisted that they had lost more than their livelihoods, they spoke of the generations in their families who had worked those waters. They, too, were at risk of losing a cherished way of life and a special tie to their ancestors.

It is in this spirit that we can begin to appreciate the lament of Indigenous Peoples who speak of hundreds of years of continuous, conscious relationship to their land. In an interview at the Working Group on Indigenous Peoples gathering at the United Nations in Geneva in 2005, Les Malezer, a native Australian and president of the Foundation for Aboriginal and Islander Research Action, spoke eloquently about this relationship: "I believe there is a common bond between Indigenous Peoples," he said. "It is an attachment to the land, but to a spiritual land . . . we are those who must look after this land. . . . This is the common vision of all Native Peoples of the world. . . . We are the keepers of the land."

Malezer's reference to a *spiritual land* aligns with the way these people speak of their most revered locations. And almost invariably, these are precisely the locations that also attract the mining and oil companies, wanting to excavate newfound ores, process oil or uranium, or lay pipelines. The Indigenous Peoples are responding by becoming more protective, raising their voices in defense of the land with increasing success. The New Prosperity mine in British Columbia needed a tailings pond and planned to drain Fish Lake, a sacred location on land granted to the Tsilhqot'in people. Their chief, Bernie Elkins, spoke of his people's historical relationship to that lake and the land around it, adding, "It is more than a lake to us—it is an integral part of Tsilhqot'in culture and vital to our cultural continuity and survival." Their protests drew the attention of the federal environment minister who stopped the project in November 2010, explaining, "there would be the loss of all the associated wetlands and a number of streams. Really, it was the loss of the whole ecosystem."

Similar protests have been occurring in Nevada resisting the expansion of the Barrick Cortez Gold Mine. Their actions included peaceful group protests by Shoshone grandmothers whose spokeswoman, Carrie Dann, explained to the mine company and the reporters, "We are the keepers of the land, and the keepers of the land is asking in a nice way to quit." That polite request has been paired with strong legal language in the courts as well. For now, the operations have been placed on hold, forcing the mining company to address the significant impacts that have been presented. The courts have noted that the project's extensive removal of groundwater is expected to have serious consequences, stating, "At least fifteen springs are not expected to recover within a hundred years. These are significant environmental harms." This case remains an uphill battle, but it exemplifies the efforts currently being made around the world by these keepers of the land.

What can we learn from these people about relating to the spaces that surround us? They have been relating to vast spaces, while our lives are more contained. It is easy to wake up and sense the spaces around us when we spend time in nature. The real challenge comes when we try to bring that same awakeness to our everyday lives. We do our hunting and gathering in stores, we come together socially in homes, theaters, restaurants, and sports arenas, and our ceremonial life often involves indoor places of worship. We can become more conscious of space, however, if we bring our attention to the smaller details, to the nuances of sensation arising from these ordinary spaces. Reawakening this felt sense can be a powerful practice. As we heighten our sense of the *space* we are now in, thoughts of where we've been and where we are going tend to fall away, restoring balance to our *time*-driven, sequenced lives. And in those moments we come close to experiencing space in the manner of indigenous cultures.

You can begin by noticing the space you are in right now. Are there elements you would like to adjust—more light or some touch of beauty, perhaps a flower, a more comfortable chair, fresh air, less clutter? Each of these adjustments can appeal to you, not only outwardly but also energetically, helping to shape the overall felt sense of your space.

Some peoples' spaces can feel so chaotic and overwhelming that you want to leave as soon as possible. When extreme hoarders are asked to draw maps of their homes, they often unwittingly leave out whole rooms—the ones that are completely filled. That seems to be their way of reducing the feeling of chaos around them. On the other hand, some spaces are so uplifting and inviting that you can feel your breath relax as you enter. These spaces belong to individuals who are keenly sensitive to the energy aspects of their homes, apartments, rooms, and offices. To them, clutter can feel like energy congestion, keeping those spaces from radiating balance and harmony.

Good realtors have discovered how to fine-tune this sense of space, not only getting a clear feel for all the new listings they visit in their Monday morning walk-throughs, but then matching those qualities to the needs and desires of particular clients. They know how to stage a house so it will appeal to a buyer more easily and are gifted at identifying those small adjustments that can make the biggest shift in a house's energy.

Certain spaces seem especially able to shape the cognitive states of occupants as well. At Naropa University the classrooms were incredibly varied, ranging from a former meditation hall (every faculty person's favorite place to teach) to quaint bungalows. Occasionally a room would get remodeled into classroom space for the first time, and some of the veteran teachers would usually volunteer to break it in or "tame" it that first semester so it could hold the focus of a class more easily, becoming groomed as a space for thinking.

Many public buildings were built with two ideas in mind. They needed to serve their basic function, and they needed to hold a particular kind of energy for the visitors. Libraries were built to house books and reference materials, but they were also carefully designed to support the concentration of the patrons. Banks varied over the years as the public changed its outlook. They used to look like fortresses conveying their ability to safeguard the money in their keeping. Then they became more inviting to put customers at ease for a few decades. Today they are striving to convey more trustworthiness once again. Athletic fields and arenas are designed to handle the noise and high activity of physical contests, and theaters and performance halls are designed with careful acoustics and seating so viewers can attend to the artistic nuances of the performers.

Notice the way all the buildings you enter each day impact you. How do they affect your mood and attention? Perhaps the most calculated environment in your ordinary day is the supermarket. The music, the temperature, the lighting, the produce displays, the placement of every item on the shelves have all been chosen to orchestrate your attention, your mood, and your shopping behavior. The only way you can protect yourself from the subtle influences of all these advertising devices is to become conscious of how staff are arranging those spaces.

The roads you travel can also influence you. City planners are well aware that some roads can feel frenzied, and others can relax the drivers. Often the key variable is the combination of the speed limit and the complexity of the cityscape next to the road. The same view that would be enriching at forty-five miles per hour can become highly distracting at sixty-five miles per hour, so an intricate urban housing project with porches, wrought iron gates, and multicolored exteriors might be required to have a very plain retaining wall facing the highway to hide all those attractive details.

Then there are the sacred spaces—the places of worship, cemeteries, and memorial sites—all carefully chosen, constructed, and cared for to protect the states of grief and reverence they were designed to embrace. As an example, one of the most powerful sacred spaces in the United States today is the Vietnam Memorial in Washington, DC. It is almost impossible to approach those long black walls without sensing the energy emanating from them. The space began evoking a state of reverence in the visitors almost from the day it was unveiled and has become a pilgrimage for many who come to pay respects, to grieve, and to leave intimate notes in the grooves near a special name.

Most literate territories throughout the world are dotted with historic sites and markers, each offering a glimpse into the past by telling the story of what happened at that spot. Next time you stand in one of those spots to read the bit of history recorded there, take a moment to actually *feel* the space and allow that story to come to life. You might also want to think back to special spaces you cherished in your past, to places that naturally call forth your own stories each time you visit them.

As your awareness of the designed and constructed spaces in your daily life grows, begin to include the outdoor spaces, from the streets and alleys, to the cultivated yards, gardens, and parks and finally to the harder-to-find remaining wilderness areas. Soon you will have rekindled the sensitivity that you once had as a child, the sensitivity that still lives in the nonliterate cultures we have been visiting. And if you are fortunate enough to have young children in your life, be sure to enjoy these spaces with them. Slow down to watch a few roly-poly bugs, toss some pebbles into the water, tie streamers to a stick and wave it in the wind, watch the antics of a squirrel and the flight path of a bird. And finally, let them show you the things *they* notice that you *still* aren't seeing yet.

SEEING INVISIBLE REALMS

As we've explored the road not taken in this chapter, we have encountered many examples of the wisdom and skills of orality-based cultures. However, now we come to one of the most overlooked and extraordinary capacities of all, the ability to see an invisible world. We saw hints of this in young children, but many orality-based peoples have carried it to greater heights. When they try to explain these perceptions to anthropologists, however, their comments are usually interpreted instead as beliefs or imaginings. As you read the following stories, consider the distinct possibility that they really did see things the anthropologists could not see.

I still can't see what they see, but I seem to be perched on a threshold between only seeing ordinary things and seeing invisible things. Occasionally, I glimpse auras or spot a magical place in nature that delights a child, but that's about all so far. I suspect a hazy inner seeing might be developing ever so slowly.

This slow pace limits my ability to coach you in developing this skill, but I remain committed to growing these capacities the old-fashioned way—with practice, humility, and awe, and without the benefit of any hallucinogens or exotic practices. I also remain committed to protecting you as the reader. The practice possibilities in this section are just as harmless as all the others have been—simple invitations to expand your *ordinary* reality. We will leave it to others to explore drug experiences, psychedelic states, and shamanic ceremonial practices.

Past sections introduced many examples of orality-based peoples' ability to perceive the invisible world. In Africa, the Swahili man explained about seeing and talking with his ancestors, as did the Botswana Bushman after winning his court case. The forest people of northern India shared with Dr. Bhattacharya what the nature spirits were teaching them. The Australian aboriginal song man explained how the spirit teachers gave him new songs and dances, and the chief of the Northern California Yurok tribe spoke of the sacred objects being returned to his tribe as being alive. In each case, these people were describing their perceptions, not just their beliefs.

I want to devote the remainder of this section to recapturing a remarkable conversation I had with two Fijians that could only occur because I acknowledged their perceptual capacities. The conversation took place in May 1987, but first, I need to introduce two bits of background.

At that time there was an influx of Hmong refugees whose children were entering the schools, and the teachers were being taught how to respect their culture. One cardinal rule was never to touch their heads, because, it was explained, the Hmong *believed* the head was sacred since that was where the spirit entered the body. The Hmong were an oral culture with all the cognitive gifts and differences that background suggests. Their language had only been converted into written form thirty years earlier, and most of the parents were still nonliterate. No one ever told the teachers that most of the Hmong could actually *see* the light entering the body.

The second bit of background involved a question by one of my Naropa University colleagues, the late Dr. Frances Harwood. She was an anthropology professor who had done field work some years earlier among the people of the Solomon Islands, not too far from Fiji. We were discussing the nature of holograms in my class the day she chose to sit in, and it triggered this question. She had noticed that as these people walked along the sand they could tell who had passed that way some time earlier, simply by looking at their footprints. She had always wondered how they did that and asked if it could possibly have something to do with holograms. I said I thought it might be possible if they were able to see the wave pattern directly and then somehow convert it to an image. I thought no more about this until two years later when the following conversations took place.

I had been invited by friends to a private performance put on by a dance troupe of six Fijian men who were in this country to promote tourism for

Fiji. In addition to speaking a blended Fijian dialect and Hindustani, they all spoke English fluently. After the performance, two of the men mingled with the audience, and one of them joined the small group I was in, giving me a chance to ask my questions. One of the dances acted out a fight over a headdress being knocked off of one dancer's head. I remembered the Hmong and described their taboo against touching the head, especially of children. "Oh, yes," he replied. "That's where the light enters, and touching that sacred spot interferes with that." I asked if he could see the light entering, and he said in a matter-of-fact way, "Yes, all Fijians can."

"And do you think any of the Europeans living on your islands can see the lights?"

He got very polite and said, "Perhaps . . . a few of them . . . once in a while . . . if they've lived there a long time," but he seemed doubtful.

Then I remembered my Naropa colleague's question and asked, "If someone from your village had passed by and left footprints in the sand, you could tell whose footprints they were, right?"

"Sure," he replied.

And then I asked, "What is it that you can see?"

He quickly responded, "You can see the form and structure rising above the footprints, and you can tell from that who it must have been."

I've often wondered what he would have said if I had only asked, "How do you do that?" By asking what he was *seeing,* I think he was more candid.

He left the room shortly after that, and I got to talk to a second dancer. Just to be sure about the lights, I asked him as well if all Fijians could see the lights around people, and he agreed they could. Then I asked how long his people had been literate. "Two hundred years," he said.

"Then why can you still see the lights?" I asked.

And he explained, "It's because we all have our village life, and we go back all the time." Without that, he was sure they would all lose those skills.

Opportunities to have these priceless conversations are fading rapidly, as more and more cultures relinquish their traditional ways. Perhaps, though, when you least expect it, you may still meet someone with ties to an orality-based culture. If so, listen carefully with the understanding that perhaps they have skills you have yet to acquire and with the hope that they will teach you a bit about their skills and practices.

THE IMPORTANCE OF STORIES

Orality-based cultures rely on stories for many functions. There are special stories that only certain initiates know and are keep secret until it is time to train new apprentices. These are the stories that guide the initiates as they carry out ceremonies, healings, and sacred rituals. But the stories of more interest to us as we bring this chapter to a close are those that are shared with all of the members, those that pass on the history of their culture and guide the behavior of their members. Storytellers approach the elements of these tales much as an impressionist painter approaches a canvas. Rough outlines are given, and important parts are revisited many times as more details get added. There is no set order to these elements, as long as each one is addressed, embellished if it seems important and touched on only briefly if not. The story unfolds spatially, as if it were laid out on the ground. The end result is a layering, with mounded spots holding the main features and sketchy valleys holding the minor details. The longer the storyteller goes on, the clearer the emerging landscape of the story becomes.

There is an art to telling such stories and an art to listening to them. The storyteller needs a long stretch of relaxed time and a willing audience. If you want to really experience these stories, you must also become very relaxed. First you must slow down and drop the chatter of your mind. Let go of all unrelated distractions, and then let go of the desire to create "back stories" to what you hear—no musing about the storyteller, possible hidden meanings behind the story, judgments about the details or the wording of the story. Finally, in normal conversations we keep our larynx "idling" so it's ready to respond or add comments at a moment's notice. In listening to traditional oral storytellers, it is important to drop that urge. Rest your tongue on the floor of your mouth and open the back of your throat as if you were preparing to swallow a drink of water. When young children listen, you'll see them even dropping their mouths open so they can really take the story in.

These oral tales have three potent ingredients that help them speak directly to the heart. They contain very *special words,* they use extremely *accurate metaphors or pictures,* and they have been told so often that the *culture holds the story,* making it much easier to remember.

When Indigenous Peoples name their sacred locations, they do so with great care. One area may belong to a rock they call a jaguar, another area may have a sacred lake with a special name, and a third area may be governed by a mesa, a canyon, or even a clearing. The names they give these locations are carefully chosen to express their true nature. We come very close to this when we choose our children's names. We seem drawn to certain sounds, often searching in a less-than-conscious way, until we finally settle on the perfect name. These stories are filled with such words, each carrying a special charge when spoken.

The next ingredient, the accurate metaphor or picture, also seems to arise out of the lived experiences of the storytellers and their ancestors. Most metaphors are only partial matches for the situation they describe and tend to fall apart on closer inspection. Some metaphors, however, seem to have a timeless accuracy about them. Folk tales, legends, great poetic images, and the images found in the stories of orality-based cultures often have a fundamental sameness with the idea they are representing, as if they are simply lifting this sameness to a higher level. These metaphors seem able to represent spiritual and cultural truths that are not as likely to fall apart over time. We have a special word for that kind of metaphor; we call it an *allegory.* Among these people who are so sensitive to what constitutes true sameness, most of the metaphors, names of sacred locations, and teaching stories seem to possess this allegorical quality.

The third ingredient is the power of familiar stories to live in the culture. The Western Apache of Cibecue, Arizona, drew on this power to offer moral guidance as they practiced what they called *speaking with names.* The anthropologist Keith Basso recorded a clear example of this in 1988. A village member came with her friend to seek advice about a problem her younger brother had. After she explained the situation briefly, the wise elder woman she had come to see spoke up, offering two different place names for her, and her friend offered a third one. These comments were offered slowly, with pauses, giving the distressed woman time to reflect. The conversation was in Apache, but here is the English translation for what transpired:

"It happened at *line of white rocks extends upward and out,* at this very place!"

After a pause, her friend added, "Yes. It happened at *whiteness spreads out descending to water,* at this very place!"

And finally, the wise elder concluded the counseling with, "Truly. It happened at *trail extends across a long red ridge with alder trees,* at this very place!" after which the sister laughed softly.

These long phrases are simply names of places on the reservation where events had occurred in the past. Since everyone had heard these stories many times, it wasn't necessary to repeat them, only to name the places where they had happened. These three morality tales had been just what she needed to hear.

In some situations, stories can even be used to heal very traumatized individuals in both orality-based and literate cultures. After the Bosnian Civil War ended in 1995, thousands of seriously traumatized children and adults struggled to recover. A number of therapists from the United States went over in teams to offer their services. One talented trauma therapist used picture stories to help several groups of children haunted by their war memories. Her approach was simple and brilliantly effective.

The children were each given paper and colored pencils and asked to create four drawings in all. The first assignment was to draw a picture of their lives before the war, showing what was safe and peaceful about that time in their lives. After inviting them to talk about their pictures, she introduced the second assignment. This time they were to draw a picture about the war in general and how it started. Again there was a debriefing time to talk about these pictures. Their third assignment was to draw a picture of their worst memories of the war. Had they not already recorded what peace looked like and then reflected on what caused these painful events, this third assignment would only have retraumatized them. The real healing came, though, with the fourth assignment, drawing a picture of their hopes for the future and what it could look like. She had found a way for them to *bracket* their traumatic experience, limiting it to the past and to conditions that were no longer happening, thus using the power of stories to touch and begin to heal the hearts of these young children.

This basic approach was also used in Sierra Leone in 1999 with children in displaced-persons camps who had lived through an extremely brutal war and hadn't been able to recover enough to handle school. After four weeks of trauma healing interventions, they were finally able to sleep well, concentrate, learn, and get along with their peers once again. These storytelling strategies continue to be included in therapy programs for rescued child soldiers in the Congo and Uganda as well.

Bessel van der Kolk, one of the country's leading trauma researchers, describes the power of stories in this way: "One of the great mysteries of the processing of traumatic experience is that, as long as the trauma is experienced as speechless terror, the body continues to keep score and reacts to conditional stimuli as a return of the trauma. However, when the mind is able to create symbolic representation of these experiences, there often seems to be a taming of the terror, a de-somatization of experience."

Now let's revisit the three potent ingredients of these stories as we look at the stories we offer young children in literate societies. Do they also contain *special words?* Do their stories use extremely *accurate metaphors or pictures,* and have they been told so often that their *culture holds the story* too?

Even young children recognize special words when they hear them. Magical words in stories and nursery rhymes and before that, their own names, all have a charged energy when spoken. They are also more easily remembered. Some fascinating experiments may show why that is, but to understand them you will need a bit of background.

In 1981 Rupert Sheldrake, a very respected English plant physiologist, published a book called *A New Science of Life,* which received very mixed reviews. One major English journal, *New Scientist,* offered the praise ". . . the science in his ideas is good. To absorb what he says involves what Thomas Kuhn termed a 'paradigm shift' which means putting aside our assumptions on how the world works." At the same time, a rival journal, *Nature,* was outraged, saying his book "is the best candidate for burning there has been for many years." Essentially, Sheldrake proposed a theory about how living systems come into form. He looked at the genetic information and concluded that it wasn't sufficient to create that form by itself. The forming *(morpho)* aspect of the genes *(genesis)* needed some kind of information field to guide the genetic material to take its proper form. He called this a *morphogenetic field.*

New Scientist journal and the Tarrytown Group in the United States soon posted competitions with prizes for anyone who could demonstrate that such a field existed. Three years later, three projects were chosen as winners, and the top two won for demonstrating that these fields existed around *words!* One study used eighty words from the Hebrew Bible. Twenty were used over five hundred times in the Bible, another twenty occurred less than twenty-four times, and the remaining forty words were actually scrambled letters. When college students who knew no Hebrew were asked to guess at the meaning of each word and rate how confident they were about their guess, they proved to be twice as confident about the frequent words as the rare ones and least confident about the scrambled ones. The second design involved the use of real and nonsense Persian words, which were written in calligraphy. College undergraduates who knew no Persian were shown each word and then asked to draw its calligraphy from memory. The students' memories for the look of the real words were significantly greater than for the nonsense ones.

These experiments hint at how special words that are repeated over and over in rhymes and stories are more easily remembered. It isn't much of a stretch then to suspect that classically worded rhymes and tales themselves might live in the culture as well, held together by their own morphogenetic fields.

This brings us to our final consideration about story. How do we choose the stories to share with young children? Do we change the complex words so they can understand it better, or can they pick up on the *sense* of those words long before they know the literal *meaning* of them? Do we soften the harshest language and say the old woman in the shoe "kissed them all gently and sent them to bed" rather than the original version where she "whipped them all soundly and put them to bed"? The traditionalists change nothing, maintaining that these stories are merely metaphors for the odd and disturbing behaviors children see in the adults around them, while reformers see them as emotional stories that might shock a young child and choose to soften them. So do we make changes or preserve the rhyme's or story's morphogenetic field? Is there a right answer?

We find we are faced with a paradox. These stories touch the heart, and may seem filled with emotion to us, but they weren't told to stir the emotions. They were meant as subtle teaching stories and need to be offered in that way. Ranging from whimsy to wisdom, from nuanced details to powerful deeds, each involves ordinary to absurd to larger-than-life characters. But the telling of these stories should be done in the relaxed tone of voice of an elder or a grandparent, not with the energy of a dramatic, emotional performer. That voice will have a role once the child is older, but not now. Told in this gentle way, most children's stories will engage the child without shocking them. Furthermore, they aren't likely to ask for stories that disturb them. So, by all means, read to them!

Let the rest of the world slow down to where there is just you, the child, and a familiar book of the child's own choosing. Those moments are priceless, creating deeply cherished memories of warmth and peace to nourish them as they prepare to move on with their journey. On this note, our own journey along this *road not taken* is finally complete.

It is time to say to this chapter, in true storytelling form, "The End."

THE ADVENT
OF LITERACY

We should note the force, effect, and consequences of
inventions which are nowhere more conspicuous than in
those three which were unknown to the ancients, namely,
printing, gunpowder, and the compass. For these three
have changed the appearance and state of the whole world.

FRANCIS BACON
Novum Organum, Aphorism 129

WE ARE ABOUT to discover the transforming power of one of the
three inventions mentioned above, that of printing. Our brains are ready
to begin reading by mid-childhood, just as they were for members of
cultures several thousands years before books were ever available. But,
unlike learning to speak, literacy doesn't automatically happen. Something has to motivate us, and it had to motivate whole cultures as well.
As we trace the driving forces that propelled whole cultures to move into
literacy and transformed them in the process, we can begin to appreciate
how profoundly it has transformed us as well.

This chapter follows the slowly building momentum that culminated
when books finally swept through cultures, transforming science, the
arts, and decision-making patterns. It is an amazing story and one well

worth telling, so let your imagination help you breathe life into the steps highlighted in the next three sections. Along the way you will encounter several valuable practices to help you harvest their teachings.

INVENTORIES, LAWS, AND SACRED TEXTS

The progression from inventories to laws was the first step and began as far back as 5,500 years ago in Egypt, Mesopotamia, and the Indus Valley of western India when people began migrating into city-states. Trade flourished, and economic development became a driving force creating a need for written records. Archeologists are finding remnants of these trade records carved into rock and engraved on clay tablets. This record keeping slowly evolved from simple inventories to legal documents describing trade agreements and then to broad sets of laws written down by scribes, who served the various kings and pharaohs of each region. This provided a new measure of stability to the fluctuating empires. The codes of laws grew over time, as each leader incorporated the best of what had gone before. One of the most famous and elaborate of these, the Code of Hammurabi, was written 3,700 years ago and contained 182 laws that formed the basis for the Old Babylonian Empire. Wanting the document to live beyond his reign, King Hammurabi had it carved onto an eight-foot-tall pillar of black stone. This pillar remained in place for six hundred years, until it was taken as plunder by a king from a northern region within present-day Iran, where it was rediscovered in 1901. It is now on display in the Louvre in Paris, one of the museum's most prized possessions.

Libraries and sacred texts were the next step. This phase originated between two thousand and three thousand years ago and called on scribes to become copiers of sacred and inspired literary texts. Great stories like *The Iliad, The Odyssey,* and *The Epic of Gilgamesh,* all of which had been held in the oral tradition, finally began to be written down. The I Ching and many portions of the Old Testament in the Bible were also recorded during this time. Libraries sprang up to house these expanding collections, often forming schools that invited a growing class of scholars.

Now imagine you are looking inside one of these libraries. There are no compact, bound books. In one area there might be a large set of clay tablets, in another perhaps carved wood blocks. Several rooms will be filled with rolled scrolls of papyrus, a fragile material made of woven reeds. And if the library is fairly modern, it might also contain sturdier books, written on leather parchment sheets. These sheets were typically folded down the middle, nested together in bundles of five sheets, and stitched along the center seam to create ten pages that can then be written upon on both sides. These bundles, called *quires*, are stored between covers as a folio, rather than a bound book. A sizeable manuscript might contain sixty or more quires, calling for the skins of fifty to seventy sheep and taking well over a year to scribe. The great library complex at Alexandria was said to have housed at least forty thousand of these texts, gathered from all over the known world.

Try to picture the grateful scholars in this library who would have traveled hundreds of miles just to read these rare books. There were no "quiet" signs, because no one knew how to read silently yet, so it would be rather noisy as groups of listeners gathered around various readers. Off to the side, there would be a special room, a scriptorium, filled with scribes faithfully creating new copies of the more fragile texts.

The work of a scribe can feel much more real if you do a bit of *scribing* yourself, either now or at least after you have read the incredible history that follows. You will need a single piece of handmade paper, which you can probably purchase in an art store. Then think of some words that are so special that you would like to scribe them onto this precious paper. Perhaps it is a poem for a child or a carefully worded note of appreciation for a friend. Now you must choose the pen to use and perhaps even the ink. Knowing you have this one rare piece of paper and can't simply throw it away if you make a mistake, you will want to take great care with the lettering. And when you are done, you will have created a very special gift for someone. For that brief period you will have sampled the life of a scribe, writing on special paper almost as rare and valuable as the materials on which they wrote.

The golden age of scholars was the next powerful step and began as early as 2,700 years ago in India. Takshashila University, widely recognized to have been the oldest university in the world, was attracting over 10,000 students to India from many countries. At about the same time, an era that would be called *The Hundred Schools of Thought* began taking form in China, and many books reflecting varied philosophies were created there. Midway through this Golden Age of Chinese philosophy, in 427 BC, the famous Nalanda University began in northwest India. Shortly after that, in the third century BC, the great Library of Alexandria in Egypt opened its doors to scholars.

A similar literary impulse was developing in Greece with Pythagoras's school in about 550 BC and then with Socrates and Plato's school a hundred years later. Socrates is credited with introducing the practice of presenting one's ideas based on reason and logic, breaking with the long Greek tradition of persuasion based on poetic oratory and metaphors. He could have spared his students the great effort of committing these thoughts to memory by allowing them to write their arguments down, but he refused.

Ironically, the only way the teachings of Socrates were preserved was through the faithful scribing of his main student and fellow philosopher, Plato. Plato recalled Socrates's prophetic warnings about the perils of writing in his book *Phaedrus*.

> It will introduce forgetfulness into the soul of those who learn it: they will not practice using their memory because they will put their trust in writing, which is external and depends on signs that belong to others, instead of trying to remember from the inside, completely on their own . . . you provide your students with the appearance of wisdom, not with its reality. Your invention will enable them to hear many things without being properly taught, and they will imagine that they have come to know much while for the most part they will know nothing. (Recalled by Plato and written down in approximately 370 BC, twenty years after the death of Socrates.)

While Plato would have penned his words onto papyrus scrolls, they were eventually scribed onto parchment in various libraries as finances allowed. Historians know, however, that many of the great books of this early period, including perhaps the majority of Aristotle's works, were lost forever as the original papyrus scrolls disintegrated before money could be found to make new copies.

This remarkable period of scholarship and philosophy, of libraries and scribes, lasted for nearly a thousand years before it was brought to an end by a series of sieges from 700 BC to 213 BC, destroying all but one of the ancient libraries. That last library, the Imperial Library in Constantinople, lasted for another nine hundred years before it too was destroyed, but the golden period of scholarly initiatives in the ancient world had come to an end.

The next profound step in this journey toward literacy was the invention of paper in 105 AD. The Han Dynasty in China contributed this stunning invention that would help to bring literacy to the masses 1,400 years later. They invented a form of paper that didn't rely on reeds like papyrus or animal skins like parchment. Rather, it was made from rags, soaked and beaten into a pulp, and then drawn out into long sheets to dry. While the preferred writing material would remain parchment for the coming one thousand years of the Middle Ages, the art of papermaking would travel first to Korea, then on to Japan by 610 AD, where tree bark replaced rags as the preferred ingredient. From there it traveled quickly through Tibet to India and on to the Arab world where a scarcity of wood again made rags the preferred ingredient and a very high quality of paper was developed. As we will discover later, paper was now poised to play its vital role when the print revolution helped to bring the Middle Ages to an end in the late 1400s.

For the remaining one thousand years leading up to that change, it fell to the scribes to keep these cherished books alive. They labored in medieval monasteries and in scattered schools that began to form, reviving the commitment to scholarship. These scribes approached their duties as spiritual practices, often committing themselves to copying the works of a single philosopher or sacred text. They sought out ancient texts, carefully copied them, and at times even translated important ones from their original languages into Latin. A steady stream of more recent manuscripts that were seen to hold enlightened teachings were also copied and made available to the priests, monks, and other scholars visiting their libraries.

To understand the depth of commitment of medieval scribes, we need to reverse our thinking about the nature of books. If you had to choose between an original edition of a college text and a revised version, you would expect the more accurate information to be in the revision. Furthermore, if you studied drawings in one copy of a book, you would assume all the other copies would be identical and that no information had been lost or distorted.

But the reverse would be true with scribal manuscripts. Each rendition was one step further from the enlightened original. If copy errors were made, they would get recopied into the succeeding versions, making it even harder to understand the original intentions of the author. Drawings and illustrations suffered the same fate, becoming more obscure and less accurate with each new copy.

Scribing was not a mental task at all. It was an act of attunement to the original writer, a commitment to sense the line of transmission back to its purest form, back to the light of inspiration, the radiance that was given to the author. While modern scholars would gravitate toward the light of reason, this era sought to preserve the light of wisdom, painfully aware that each new copy inevitably dimmed that light a little more.

If you would like to experience in a small way the powerful attunement these scribes felt, try creating a copy of an old document that means a great deal to you. Perhaps you have an original letter from a friend or family member or even from one of your ancestors. After choosing paper similar to your original letter and perhaps even selecting the kind of pen the writer used, read the letter several times as you work to embody the writer. Once you can feel their words flowing through you, proceed to write their words down for the second time. You will find that this kind of writing is completely dedicated to drawing the past into the present in the same manner as the devoted medieval scribe. You may find that this activity has deepened your understanding of the letter writer you have chosen as well.

The next set of steps on this historical journey into literacy will trace how these early ripples of literacy altered the minds of those it touched, while reflecting on the thinking patterns of the vast majority of peasant farmers whose lives would remain unchanged until the print revolution transformed their world.

A NEW LENS BEGINS TO FORM

The next major step toward the cultural transformation into literacy was the medieval period or Middle Ages. It began around 500 AD and would continue for one thousand years. Before 500 AD, only two broad groups of people had been touched by literacy—the merchants and the monastics. Literacy had a way of pulling both of these groups away from a life lived only in the present moment. It drew the scribes, clerics, and scholars into the past and enriched their inner lives, while it drew the merchants, kings, and pharaohs into the outer, material world and toward future thinking.

This is a dramatic shift from the pattern that still prevailed among the vast peasant populations during this period. For the peasants, a sense of enoughness and sustainability shaped their lives. As long as the land these people tended remained free, their lives could continue uninterrupted. Soon, however, the empire leaders began promising the right to various parcels of land to warriors to buy their protection and to favored friends to buy their loyalty. The peasants were caught in these shifting decrees, but their long history of bending to the ways of nature gave them a resiliency to tolerate the increasing hardships that were to come.

On first glance, when the leaders moved from sustainability to growth, that might not have seemed too significant, but it actually involved a radical shift in the driving forces of the mind. Some aspects of our lives are best served by periods of ongoing forward motion, where each step forward is reinforced and calls forth another forward step. We nourish our children so their bodies can grow taller and stronger. Each meal leads to more progress, and a call for more food. Unfortunately, for many of us, when that growth phase tapers off and we want to simply sustain our fully developed bodies, it is hard to change "drivers." We have been following what scholars of systems patterns would call a *positive* or *reinforcing* feedback loop. And when that driver runs away with us, we can slip into an addictive cycle where each action leads to a desire for more of the same.

The early merchants and empire builders were caught up in their own version of this cycle. Each increase in goods expanded their markets, which then drove them to seek new trade routes to build still greater inventories. They would even hide their route maps from other merchants so their paths could remain secret. There never seemed to be a stopping point, a point where they felt they now had enough.

The challenge for those merchants and leaders when their businesses and empires grew to excessive size and for us whenever addiction looms is to shift to a different driver, one that satiates, that turns off when it senses it has reached a state of enoughness. That driver is often called a *negative* or *balancing* feedback loop. Once a system reaches maturity, it can sustain itself best by the self-correcting nature of this balancing driver. Our bodies use balancing feedback loops to regulate many functions, from body temperature, balance, and hunger, to breathing, heart rate, and sleep-wake cycles. We are also able to override many of these automatic balance mechanisms if we choose. For example, we can alter our breathing patterns, and as we all know, it is remarkably easy to override our hunger signals, continuing to eat long after the body signals "enough."

The lives of the medieval peasants were remarkably immune to positive feedback drivers. As long as they could sustain themselves, they felt that was enough. Most indigenous cultures also remained committed to sustainability and shared wealth until the hardships from the outside world became insurmountable centuries later.

Migrations and linear time marked the next cognitive step and occurred around 1100 AD as people began to move from the peasant and indigenous life on the land to an urban life in the growing city-states. There they served the wealthy, worked for the merchants, or developed a trade. They lost the sense of cyclical time they had learned from nature and were more easily shocked by unexpected upheavals and disasters. As peasants, they had accepted these tragedies and reversals as natural aspects of life, taken time to grieve, and then set about restoring their world, but they felt less resilient and more fearful in their urban circumstances. Their minds were caught between two kinds of time. The familiarity with nature's cyclical time that would have prepared them to accept these events had faded from their minds, but the sense of linear time that took its place was of little help to them. Their minds could now focus on future time, but without any new tools to handle the unknown, it was often a source of stress. It would be centuries before the rise of modern science could provide the predictive skills and control tools to help people cope with these upheavals.

We can harvest many useful practices from exploring how they coped with adversity. These urban poor were suffering from what we now call *learned helplessness*. It is typically brought on by shock and can lead to anxiety, depression, or both. A major negative event or a series of unexpected smaller ones can create anxiety as the person worries about when or whether they might happen again. The feared event might be a natural disaster, health crises, abuses at work or in the home, or concerns for the well-being of loved ones. Each situation calls for enormous resiliency. Without it, the stress of never knowing when it might happen again, of being unable to *predict,* leads to a state of anxious learned helplessness.

While failure to predict negative events triggers chronic anxiety, some events are quite predictable but seem impossible to endure or to change. When the person is faced with inescapable negative events and feels helpless to change them, this lack of *control* leads to depressed learned helplessness. Medieval times brought great hardships and upheavals to city dwellers and peasants alike. However, anxiety and depression added to the burden of the urban poor, while the more resilient rural peasants often avoided these pitfalls in spite of equally harsh conditions. We can see the same stunning resilience in largely nonliterate farming and fishing villages today after hurricanes, floods, or earthquakes strike them. We marvel at their ability to somehow pick up the pieces and rebuild their lives while their urban counterparts seem more devastated and overwhelmed.

If we can rebuild our sense of sustainability or enoughness and cultivate increasing resilience in the face of an unknown future, we will have taken two significant steps toward rebuilding the indigenous outlook we lost when we became literate. Consider creating a practice for yourself based on one of the following ideas.

The first practice involves living more sustainably and becoming more able to live with less. Being bombarded with seductive advertising makes it hard to override our impulses. Learning to distinguish between wants and needs is an important step toward embracing enoughness. With big purchases, try sleeping on the idea for three nights before acting. If the urge has faded, it suggests you may have *wanted* the item, but you hadn't *needed* it. With small urges for treats, accessories, or gadgets that catch your eye, try savoring them with your imagination and feel the surge, the waning interest, and the growing willpower to walk away from each invitation. Rejoice each time you succeed. Finally, notice the nagging fear of scarcity that frequently drives the urge to keep shopping or hoarding and shine a light on it.

Begin regarding the act of being frugal as a positive quality. Keep using that chipped mixing bowl, repair an old tool, reglue a broken chair, mend a favorite old shirt. Let each act serve as a proud symbol of your ability to make do with what you have. Try softening any hoarding urges by giving away things you no longer need. You could even sell the more valuable items to begin funding your own small savings portfolio. Today young children are often coached to create money jars labeled for saving, for spending, and for sharing. As adults, we too can save up for major purchases, afford small pleasures, and help others. As the fund for helping others grows, it subtly alters the way we listen to problems in the news. No longer do news stories trigger a sense of overwhelm and futility; instead they become opportunities for donation from the sharing fund.

Finally, let's consider ways to strengthen resiliency so the uncertain future is less intimidating. Life is full of small irritations and discomforts that we weren't expecting. However, they don't always need to be fixed. Learn to say, "I'm not enjoying this," while relaxing with the irritation. Shift your response to a buzzing fly or a glass that breaks or a flat tire from a "Why Me?" complaint to a chance to practice acceptance. We tend to respond with adrenaline far too often in situations where calmness would be more helpful.

Even with major events, take time to assess the *workability* of it before scrambling to make it go away. One of the best solutions for learned helplessness builds on this awareness. The person is asked to bracket a negative experience in *time* by noticing that it is only happening now, not always, and bracket it in *space* by noticing that it only affects certain aspects of their life, not their whole life.

Some situations truly cannot be changed and must be endured. Once again, calmness can allow us to meet the challenge as a *forced practice* rather than a tragedy. It is nothing we would have chosen, but since it has chosen us, at least we can make friends with it and let it teach us something. One young man who was diagnosed with type 1 diabetes at age fifteen was able to say two years later that he wasn't sure which he would choose between having to have it the rest of his life or never having had it at all. When asked why that was, his amazing answer was, "Because it teaches me so much about balance and harmony, and that's what I'm all about." It had clearly become a forced practice for him, and he had befriended it.

THE TRANSFORMING POWER OF THE PRESS

A growing population of literates arose between about 1100 AD and 1400 AD, marking the next critical step in our historical journey. Increasing numbers of scholars and clerics entered universities throughout Europe in these closing centuries of the medieval era.

This growing population of literates stood out from the peasants and nonliterate city dwellers not only in their ability to read, but in their sense of reality itself. They now lived in two worlds—in the world of lived experiences, or *primary reality*, that they shared with the nonliterate population and in a world that is often called a *secondary reality*, the world of written knowledge that comes from books rather than from life experience. Their exposure to written stories began to reshape the filing system used by their memories and enhanced their ability to plan for the future. Their cognitive lens was becoming much more similar to the lens our schooled minds use today. These pioneering scholars would soon be joined by countless others as this leisurely pace of development began to change.

The passion to read was beginning to stir by 1400 AD, and within three hundred years, an accelerating chain of events would not only bring literacy to the masses throughout Europe, it would transform religion, science, and the arts in its wake. Only the indigenous communities living in isolated pockets throughout the world would avoid this shift for another five hundred years.

For the great masses of people, however, the progress toward literacy continued to build up speed. The events of early modern Europe led the way and revealed the incredible power of literacy to alter the course of entire cultures. The tipping point, ironically, was a book that was forbidden to the masses, the Bible. Originally written in Hebrew, Aramaic, and Greek, it was the fourth-century Latin translation that was studied by monks and priests and then interpreted through sermons to the populace. By the 1300s, the Catholic Church had amassed great wealth and land holdings and had hit a low point in its conduct. Indulgences and other fees were regularly extracted from the poor, outraging increasing numbers of priests throughout Europe. One by one they began to speak up, often at the expense of their lives.

The next step, the construction of the first German paper mill in 1390, further accelerated this race toward literacy. It was built in Nuremberg, where just sixty years later the second and final great invention was created—the famous Gutenberg press with its moveable type. This would transform the availability of books forever. No longer would books require costly scribes and parchment, restricting literacy to the wealthy and the scholarly elite. They could now be printed quickly and cheaply on this newly invented paper. However, to this day some vital documents are still hand-copied on leather parchment, from the "sheepskins" of some diplomas to the Hebrew Torahs, the British Acts of Parliament, and the three founding documents of the United States: the Declaration of Independence, the Constitution, and the Bill of Rights.

As the unrest among many Catholic clergy grew, the printing presses fanned the movement toward reform. Between 1450 and 1500, nearly ten million books and pamphlets were printed, many of them religious and most of those in Latin. Then the second wave of reform erupted as the Dutch religious scholar Erasmus created a new dual translation of the Bible into both Greek and Latin. Copies of his book spread rapidly, inspiring John Tyndale to create the first print version of the Bible in English and Martin Luther to create the first translation into German. The Catholic Church worked strenuously to stop this spread of common-language Bibles, to no avail. When presses were afraid to print the English Bible in England, it was printed in Germany and smuggled back into the country in bales of cloth. The tensions grew rapidly throughout Europe, and regional wars broke out as ruling lords and monarchs switched back and forth from Catholic to Protestant rule, throwing reformers into peril during one period and liberation the next, culminating in the Thirty Years War involving most of Europe. Much of the fighting took place on German soil, eventually claiming the lives of an estimated 30 percent of the German population before coming to an end in 1648.

Once the printing presses made the Bible widely available, the general population responded with great interest. In spite of the wars, the Black Plague, and political upheavals, the masses took their first giant step toward literacy. They *learned to read*. Soon another cultural shift would occur, guiding them to take a second step. They would begin *reading to learn*.

We have now reached the mid-1600s, heralding a new era called the *Enlightenment* or the *Age of Reason*. No longer was the newly literate population content with simply reading the words on a page. Now they were beginning to question that information. While the Bible first invited them to read, it was the development of the encyclopedia with its vast collection of knowledge that would inspire them to use reading to learn.

In spite of the religious turmoil, science made important advances. Now that printing could maintain the accuracy of the charts, tables, and drawings, true research could begin. Galileo published his telescope measurements, launching the field of data-based astronomy. A similar burst of research began documenting the plant kingdom, with accurate drawings that couldn't be distorted by careless scribes. It heralded a flood of amateur naturalists, all investigating, drawing, and then printing their findings. Censorship continued to set limits on scientific freedom, however. When Galileo published his *Dialogue Concerning The Two Chief World Systems* proposing that Earth revolved around the sun, the Church tried him, forced him to recant, and held him under house arrest the remainder of his life, forbidding him to do any more writing. Nevertheless, he secretly wrote a second work, *Discourses and Mathematical Demonstrations Relating to Two New Sciences,* smuggling the manuscript out of Italy to Elsevier Press in Holland where it was then published. His works and those of his predecessor, Copernicus, along with the common-language Bibles and the works of several other philosophers, all joined a list of books banned by the Church. Printers happily posted this list throughout Europe, knowing it would only serve to increase sales.

Soon the thinking strategies of this newly literate population grew more abstract. They began applying reason to everything they read or thought. Philosophers began to apply reasoning to religious beliefs. Whole systems of thought arose in philosophy, in politics, and even in the arts, analyzing the nature of everything. In politics, the divine right of kings to treat their subjects unreasonably was questioned and would eventually contribute to both the French and American revolutions. This confidence that reason could organize all aspects of the world reached a high point when Isaac Newton wove Greek geometry and Arabic algebra into a calculus that could solve scientific problems, thus establishing mathematics as the model for all knowledge.

While science, religious reform, and the publishing that supported those movements were increasingly unwelcome in Italy, the arts found a true home there during this turmoil. The economy was shaken from the aftermath of a devastating European plague that had wiped away a third of the population, but the poor who survived easily found employment, and the wealthy families were left with surplus money. In Italy this situation invited imaginations to flourish, giving rise to a remarkably creative array of artists, all in need of patrons just when both the Church and many of the leading wealthy families were in a position to sponsor them. Their willingness to embrace these gifted sculptors, painters, architects, poets, musicians, and writers gave birth to the Italian Renaissance.

The printing press played a key role in awakening this burst of creativity. These artists were given two great gifts: the security of a patronage to free them from financial concerns and the liberation of their memories. Before literacy, learning depended entirely on a strong reproductive memory. There was no room for innovation, for straying from what was already known. Those times called for a high degree of what we now call *fixed intelligence,* and even in the arts, traditional styles were followed. But with the coming of books, memory could fade and the important information could be captured in print, inviting a new *fluid intelligence* to emerge among the literate population, driving the imagination, challenging tradition, and helping to fuel the renaissance.

We can appreciate the scale of this shift by looking at the impact literacy had on story itself. In cultures based on oral traditions, storytellers held the wisdom of the culture and transmitted it to the entire community in an artfully sculpted way. The story became a spatial experience even though it was unfolding through time. Now look at what happens when that story is written down. First, the redundancies are removed. "You said that already, so there is no need to repeat it," the scribe might say. Then the remaining elements are reorganized according to what happened first. The story has now moved from a spatial pattern to a sequence laid down in time.

Storytelling cultures used their precise reproductive memories and their deep cultural connection with the storyteller to mirror the speaker and virtually map the story onto their bodies. This kinesthetic or body-based strategy fell away once stories took on a written form. Then a new memory strategy called *sequential memory* arose to help them construct meaning out of the words on the page. The oral tales held together naturally so we could say they were *coherent,* but words on paper are passive. It is up to the reader to breathe life into them, organize them, and make them meaningful. In other words, the reader has to provide the mental glue to piece the story together and create the coherence the writer intended. You have had to do that as well, just to breathe life into these words. You have actually been using your brain differently than a nonliterate person would.

A remarkable research opportunity arose in Colombia in the first decade of this century to show that the act of learning to read actually alters the anatomy of the brain in critical ways. As decades of warfare died down in that Latin American country, most of the guerilla fighters began to leave the jungle and rejoin the rest of the culture. They had missed out on schooling and were nonliterate, so they were embarking on literacy training to learn reading as adults. Manuel Carreiras, a neuroscience researcher from Spain, entered at just the right time to measure the impact of literacy on this rare group of modern-day nonliterate adults as they were about to change. It resembled the situation Alexander Luria and his colleagues encountered seventy years earlier when they studied the impact of collectivization and literacy on the peasants of Uzbekistan.

But now science had advanced to the point where Carreiras was able to study the *anatomical* changes brought on by reading. One group of twenty had already been through a literacy training program and a matched group of twenty-two others had yet to enroll in the program. All of them agreed to let Carreiras conduct brain scans on them. The findings were dramatic. A key language area of the brain and the connective fibers connecting the left and right hemispheres in that region were significantly larger in the newly literate group. The nonliterate subjects had brain patterns very similar to those of dyslexics, suggesting that those regions were not causing the dyslexia, but were simply a symptom of dyslexia. Since the dyslexic had yet to learn to read, those changes had not been laid down yet. These findings shed even more light on the impact literacy had historically on cultures as it spread throughout the population.

Once the majority of the population in a culture possessed the ability to derive meaning from the printed page, to apply this new information in their lives, and to use reason to reflect and form their own thoughts, that culture became a literate society. This was the path most cultures followed in becoming literate. The Indigenous Peoples of the world experienced this wave of literacy very differently, as we will discover next.

THE PRICE OF LITERACY

There is only one way in which one can endure man's
inhumanity to man, and that is to try in one's own
life to exemplify man's humanity to man.

ALAN PATON, South African social activist
Cry, The Beloved Country

Now our attention must turn to the indigenous cultures throughout the world that came to literacy in a radically different way. They often occupied lands that required complex practices in order to yield the food, water, clothing, and shelter needed to survive, and this was their focus. For these close-knit groups, the need for written records and the desire to write and read those records never arose. Their oral teachings were quite sufficient. Nevertheless, by the 1800s, indigenous cultures around the world began to be pressured by religious and political groups to become literate.

In this period when reasoning and literacy were held in such high regard, the zeal to convert and educate these people was relentless. The literate cultures saw themselves as bringing an unquestioned gift to the Indigenous Peoples, a gift that would somehow "civilize" them. The indigenous cultures' shared relationship to land clashed with the view of the majority culture that land could now be privately owned. Often the land occupied by various Indigenous Peoples began to be sought after by governments and entrepreneurs. Encroaching industries wanted these people to become a literate labor force. Missionaries wanted to convert them to Christianity. Overall their tribal lives were seen as primitive, uncivilized, and interfering with progress.

The early projects were aimed at fostering adult literacy and were often carried out by missionaries. Their efforts rarely succeeded. If they began by trying to teach the adults to read, they couldn't explain why it was important. If they started by converting them to this new religion, they still had the obstacles of teaching them to speak and read in the language of their Bibles. They usually concluded that either the adults were too old to learn or that their cultural beliefs were preventing them from making the adjustment. By then, the literate cultures were feeling increasingly uneasy with their indigenous neighbors and began rationalizing that it was imperative to "civilize" them, to replace their traditions with the ways of the literate world. They decided that it would be necessary to work with the children instead, often taking them to boarding schools far from home. Thus began a tragic and brutal chapter in the history of the Indigenous Peoples and a shameful one in the history of literate societies.

In 2007, the United Nations called for a report on Indigenous Peoples and boarding schools, and two years later an extensive comparative study under that title was presented to the United Nations Permanent Forum on Indigenous Issues, documenting the many atrocities that were carried out in the name of literacy. This painful history needs to be told, and I ask you to join me in bearing witness to samplings from that report and to a few of their stories.

The history of indigenous boarding schools began in the mid- to late 1800s targeting children in New Zealand, Australia, Canada, the United States, and the nomadic tribes of the Middle East and the Scandinavian countries. Later the Russian Federation and China would also begin creating boarding schools, while poverty kept much of Africa and Latin America from participating in this practice.

Only the Maori of New Zealand would succeed in resisting the settlers' efforts to remove their children and deprive them of their cultural training. All the other indigenous cultures were severely outnumbered and forced to yield to the will of the authorities. These school authorities would round up all of the children from three or four years of age onward, transporting them to boarding schools far from their home villages. Some boarding schools brought the children home for vacations once or twice a year, but there were some schools in the United States and Russia where the children would not see their families again until they were in their teens. Once in these boarding schools, the children were always forbidden to use their native languages, wear their native dress, and practice any native customs. Having lost out on their tribal teachings and traditions, these children usually found it very difficult to reintegrate or survive on their native lands once they did return home.

Bob Randall, an Australian Aboriginal, was one of countless such children to be impacted. At age seven, he was abducted by the school authorities and taken away in chains to a church-run boarding school thousands of miles from home. He was rarely allowed to see his family after that. Both his family life and his tribal life were taken away from him. Looking back on it, he explains the impact this abduction had on him as a member of this *stolen generation*.

Teachings are done at time of ceremony, you know, when
the kids are taken away into the bush camps and then taught
through the stories, through the songs, through the art form,
and through the dances, how to survive in this country. And
if you miss out on those three like what I did, being taken in
an institution like I did, being one of the stolen generation
folks, you miss all that. You have no deed or title to your land.

Everything was taken away—my title to my land was taken away, my language was taken away, my ceremonies was taken away.

Sadly, this barely touches the surface of the traumas these children endured. The UN report stated that the boarding-school treatment in Canada, Australia, and the United States was

particularly brutal. Thousands of children did not survive these schools, either through neglect, inadequate medical care, inadequate food, or even in some cases, murder and torture. Countless children were also sexually, physically, and emotionally abused. These abuses continue to have intergenerational impacts on indigenous families as these patterns of abuse are then passed down from boarding school survivors to their children.

Both Canada and Australia are finally acknowledging this tragic legacy. The Australian Parliament passed a motion apologizing to all Aborigines for laws and policies, including boarding-school abuses and forced removal of indigenous children, that have "inflicted profound grief, suffering and loss." They have yet to offer any compensation or support services, however. Meanwhile Canada has gone a step further in instituting a Truth Commission to begin documenting and apologizing for the abuses and has established an Indian Residential Schools Settlement Agreement that is taking first steps toward compensating some of the victims. The UN report goes on to state, however, "Unlike Canada, the United States has made no attempt to address the legacies of boarding school abuses."

As the indigenous cultures and individuals struggle to heal from this long and painful ordeal, several tribes in the United States have created a national Boarding School Healing Project to document abuses as a first step toward healing and restoring their dignity. This journey back from the psychological damage of the boarding-school years to a sense of identity and self-worth is long and arduous.

One powerful documentation of that journey is a book entitled *They Called Me Uncivilized: The Memoir of an Everyday Lakota Man from*

Wounded Knee. The author is Walter Littlemoon, the same wise teacher you read about earlier. With his incredible awareness of how his mind works, he eloquently describes what it means to be so brutally dismantled, "Our ability to feel and be human had been taken away." Later in his memoir he describes the slow process involved in reclaiming his life:

> I had to slow way down in my thinking to sort out negative
> things I had learned and to attempt to get rid of them. I wish I
> could say it happened quickly, but it has taken me thirty years
> of remembering, applying common sense, and struggling from
> that day to reach this point of understanding what it means to
> be Lakota, to be a human being, and to accept myself and find
> some peace.

There are many other remarkable signs of recovery around the world today as well. Many indigenous languages are being brought back from the edge of extinction. In Mongolia, Russia, and New Zealand, the public schools are now instructing in native languages. Tribally run schools in the United States are often teaching Native languages and emphasizing Native cultural traditions as well. The UN report sums up this trend by describing some indigenous groups as "developing alternative indigenous models of education that try to work outside the mandatory mainstream models. They are experimenting with a variety of forms to provide the skills necessary to survive in the dominant society without erasing their own cultures and languages."

This resurgence of indigenous wisdom is beginning to extend beyond restoring their language and customs. It is awakening their voices, and they are finding ways to speak to the majority culture about important matters. As they work toward defending their indigenous rights, as more of them go on to college and become social activists, lawyers, and environmentalists, they are reclaiming their role as keepers of the land around the world. Mining projects, deforestation plans, dams that impact agriculture and affect whole ecosystems are being challenged in court like never before. By bringing political reasoning, law, and scientific knowledge together with the wisdom embedded in their cultures and even in their languages, this new wave of individuals with indigenous roots is demonstrating that it is possible to live in both worlds and to incorporate both the indigenous and the literate lenses. Now that we recognize this, it frees us to consider developing other lenses of our own. This new generation of indigenous pioneers is showing us that it is possible to embrace one another's realities, inviting us to cultivate their lens as they have cultivated ours. We can learn to see the natural world through their eyes and to let nature nourish our lives more deeply. We can even join them as keepers of the land and become inspired to champion environmental causes we might have overlooked before. If we have any trouble finding worthy causes, all we have to do is ask the children. Their environmental awareness is becoming quite acute, and they long to help protect their futures.

REVISITING THE
SCHOOLED MIND

What's past is prologue.
WILLIAM SHAKESPEARE
The Tempest

Strange, what brings these past things
so vividly back to us, sometimes!
HARRIET BEECHER STOWE
Uncle Tom's Cabin

BEFORE OUR JOURNEY ends, we will soar beyond the boundaries of our schooled mind, but first we need to revisit our years of schooling and understand how they have shaped our present mind. We can then keep schooling's gifts as building blocks for tomorrow and let go of its limitations, freeing us to move on. If your years from first grade through high school were relatively enjoyable, this chapter's portion of the journey will serve as an interesting refresher course, helping you reclaim the cognitive skills you might have forgotten. If those years were unpleasant and less successful, this could be a healing process for you, allowing you to receive those teachings more easily now. Both your thinking strategies and your brain itself went through a series of transformations during those years. As you moved from first through twelfth grade, your brain progressed in spurts and plateaus, driven sometimes by a change in its chemistry and at other times by alterations in its structure. Many other variables paired up with these brain changes to determine which pathways would be laid down strongly and which ones might even miss their opportunity entirely.

The following sections invite you to examine your own cognitive skills in detail and to gather many new skills as well. As you read about the obstacles facing many children today, your understanding about poverty, schools, and societal problems may deepen and shift in some ways. As usual, read slowly so the ideas can settle well, inviting fresh mind skills to arise.

ENTERING THE CULTURE OF SCHOOL

Around the world, cultures conduct rites of passage for their children when they reach six or seven years of age. Traditionally, orality-based cultures would choose this age to introduce new life skills and give new responsibilities to their children. In many literacy-based cultures, the age of seven has been heralded as the age of reason, a time to begin formal schooling and the age when a child is even recognized by common law as old enough to testify in court.

There is a good reason for this particular age to be marked in such a ceremonial way. We already learned about how chemical changes at age two paved the way for language acquisition to begin. Now researchers have discovered another chemical change at age six that heralds a two-year-long brain growth spurt in the frontal areas of the brain. These changes will make it much easier to exercise impulse control and practice simple reasoning and sequential thinking. New neural connections grow rapidly during this period with the aid of DHEA, a chemical compound that is starting to be produced by the adrenal glands. This growth calls forth new blood vessels to serve the increasing brain pathways, enlarging the brain mass until it finally pushes against the skull, forcing it to expand before the spurt finally slows down. As we mature, the brain and body often take turns growing, and ages six to eight are very clearly the brain's turn. The skull will be forced to stretch one more time during a brain spurt around age twelve, before reaching its final size. The skull is designed to handle this stretching, though, since its plates are linked together like the metal teeth on bridges that expand in the summer heat.

Now let's turn our attention to the young children approaching school for the first time. They must enter a culture where time seems terribly important; where paying attention to the teacher, waiting, and taking turns are required; where standard English is the language of the land; and where they are expected to discover how to crack codes, especially the phonics code, which will reveal the secret behind learning to read. For many of these children, it is an exciting time, and the new rules and procedures all seem to make sense. They come from homes where the language was the same, where the phrases "It's time to . . ." and "It's time for . . ." mapped out their days, where they learned to share, and where they were often rewarded for waiting. But if all of this bears little similarity to their cultural ways or their home life, sparks can fly unless the school helps these children overcome their culture shock and find success in this strange new world.

Imagine what it would be like to listen to your native language being spoken differently, or even more challenging, to listen to a foreign language that you barely know at all. How confusing it must be to be shown something new and just begin to get interested in it only to have the teacher announce, "It's time to put it away." That makes little sense to a child whose home life flows along without imposed forms, where there are no set times for anything. And if food and toys were scarce, it never made sense to wait for a turn either. You learned to take what you wanted when you had the chance. Unfortunately, this would not work at school, and before long you would end up labeled as unruly, unfriendly, and unable to follow instructions.

While most children *prefer* to use one channel at a time, either looking or listening, to avoid information overload, some of them *require* it. For children who are easily overwhelmed by all the new information and rules, research is showing that teachers must either show *or* tell when they teach. If they want to talk, they need to stand still. If they want to model how to do a task, they need to do it in silence and talk afterward. Otherwise these children may fail to take in the new learning, and they will start falling behind. Soon they may begin to dread new learning, get tired of feeling confused and ashamed, and begin down the path of school alienation.

The importance of gifted first-grade teachers, who are working with six- and seven-year-olds, cannot be overemphasized. If they can intervene and help the more vulnerable children in their classes begin to succeed, they will have changed the course of these children's lives.

Children usually enter first grade with their *magical* thinking skills intact. It has been their primary way of making sense of the world around them. They would never call their style magical, but it is such a departure from the reasoning-based thinking of the adults around them that it can seem magical. They make their connections based almost entirely on what they have experienced directly, often sharing insights that the reasoning mind would never have considered. And if their world was threatening, they also learned to be extremely vigilant at all times. Now they enter this calm, safe world of extreme order, where there seems to be a time and place for everything and a predictable sequence as well. Even for those who were exposed to an orderly home life, their brains aren't quite ready to make the leap into making logical predictions. The idea that if this is so, then that will happen, or if you do this, it will always lead to that is transformative. This power to predict, to plan, and to have a new measure of control in one's life diminishes the need for magical thinking. For most children, therefore, magical thinking begins to fade at this point. However, with some effort, we can reclaim that gift. Picasso spoke eloquently of the effort involved when he said, "It took me four years to paint like Raphael, but a lifetime to paint like a child." If you long to increase your artistic skills and your creative imagination, this pre-reasoning mind state is definitely worth cultivating.

While six- to eight-year-old children work to create order and make logical sense of their surroundings, you can move in the other direction. Begin to notice how tightly ordered some parts of your life have become—the route to work; your daily routines; even the order in which you dress, left sock then right sock; or how you brush your teeth, in what order and with which hand. Now intercept a few of those routines and do them a different way. When you do this, you are *deconstructing* habitual order. This is a great first step to regaining that magical, nonlogical, spontaneous quality of mind you probably gave up back in first and second grade.

You may be the exception, however. Perhaps you never did really embrace order after all. If those first two school years are extremely chaotic and unpredictable at home, some children decide nothing makes real sense, and they continue to be spontaneous, fairly impulsive, and weak in reasoning skills. When they grow up, they may find niches that tap their creative and colorful ways without requiring a great deal of order. Or they may need to rely on others to handle the organizational side of life for them. If this describes you, then you might want to work on claiming the mind skill you missed, that of creating order.

You can begin anywhere, but start small. Tackle one drawer, or set up one routine like bill paying. Try planning a few meals ahead of time and then getting the ingredients that you'll need in one shopping trip. Or simply try making a grocery list before going to the store and then insist on sticking with what is on that list. It could also be that predictability is a challenge for you—missing appointments, being late for meetings, agreeing to do something and then forgetting about it. If this sounds familiar, then choose a few simple things to remedy at a time. Try showing up five minutes early to all appointments for one week or creating a system for making note of tasks you agree to do. You may not enjoy high-tech cell phones and computer-based reminder systems, but perhaps a simple day timer would be worth trying out.

MAKING PAPER TALK

The transition from the oral world of the young child to the private, interior world of the accomplished reader occurs gradually. If you learned to read in a traditional school, you probably remember the little reading groups, where you took turns reading passages around the circle. That was a brilliant way to begin. It built on social engagement. The connections between the letter symbols and their sounds were constantly getting reinforced as you listened to your peers and followed along in your own book. It was a gentle bridge between the storytelling of young childhood and the silent reading that would be expected of you in a few short years.

Moving into literacy is actually done in many ways, with many different timelines. Some children are drawn to explore reading as early as three or four, while many others wait to make the transition until their brain enters its next growth spurt sometime between six and eight years of age. Still other children may be so dreamy and imaginative that they continue to resist giving up their somewhat magical, experience-based thinking to begin the kind of reasoning reading requires. It so, they may hold out till nine years of age. One special condition bears mentioning, however. If a child has reached age nine and continues to be unable to understand letter symbols, often reversing their shapes when trying to copy them, showing little sign of associating sounds with letters, and unable to recognize simple words, he or she may have a neurological condition called *dyslexia*. The eyes and ears of children with dyslexia don't process the sights and sounds on the page in the same way as their peers, making reading extremely difficult. For them, early identification and consistent coaching are keys to creating reading breakthroughs. On the bright side, they often excel in careers like cooking, architecture, performing arts, athletics, sculpture, art therapy, and working in nature and with animals, all fields that rely less on reading than on refined attention to the sensory world.

On the opposite end of the continuum are those children who successfully tackle reading at a very young age. They tend to approach reading either as a visual memory task, building up sight words and "word calling" in order to read, or as an auditory memory task, remembering the story as if it were lines in a play, then performing it, page by page. Eventually, however, these early readers will convert to becoming code crackers because it is so much more efficient once they can grasp the idea of reversibility, where letters stand for sounds and sounds can be written down as letters. First they discover, for instance, that the letter *P* can be decoded into the sound "puh," and the sound "puh" can be put into code by using the letter *P.* From there it is a fairly simple step to begin hooking sounds together to create words. The brain naturally gravitates toward this process if it can because it uses so much less storage space this way, freeing the visual and auditory memory systems to work on other aspects of learning.

We can be tempted to equate earlier reading with superior intellect, but research shows that early readers simply have a faster developmental timetable than the dreamier child. By fifth or sixth grade, these differences fade and most nondyslexic children have become comfortable with the world of reading and are performing at grade-level. There are exceptions, however. With some children and in some schools, we see very different patterns.

Over the years I have worked with many children who struggle to stay engaged. They seem sleepy, but they aren't sleep-deprived. They are often the ones who have allergies. They become mouth-breathers during the fall and spring months if their problem involves pollen and air-borne irritants, and are year-round mouth-breathers if the problem is persistent or involves foods or household dust. Try mouth-breathing for half an hour, and you'll discover just how tiring that can be! So I have encouraged them to get up, run errands, work standing up, work in teams so they can be socially engaged, carry water bottles and stay hydrated, suck on cinnamon candies or peppermints, and sit on the edge of their chair so their knees are lower than their hips and they can wiggle around more easily. But every so often there is a child for whom none of this seems to work. It tends to drive such children further into withdrawal, and their numbers are increasing significantly. What is happening?

Trauma research describes a freeze response that may explain the problem. A child who is overwhelmed and who cannot fight or flee from the situation will resort to shutting down. This shutdown is related to the resignation in a prey animal once caught or the immobilized fear of the quail or rabbit who can sit without moving for long periods of time in an effort stay invisible to the predator. It doesn't necessarily mean that the child is suffering from what we typically consider abuse. It can simply be that they are new to the class, their home life has been disrupted suddenly, they are biologically predisposed to shyness and are being given far too much attention, or their teacher speaks too boldly, and it frightens them.

If the under-aroused child is actually in a freeze state, none of the ordinary interventions will work. They don't feel at all safe, and their hope is not to be noticed at all. For these children, the goal is to create *much* more safety. They need less pressure, more time to do things, and very safe seating in the room. They can barely follow the teacher's voice when in a freeze mode so they will need visual demonstrations of the learning tasks. Ideally, even those demonstrations won't be presented directly to them but to a child near them so they can watch inconspicuously. As classroom ceremonies and routines become familiar and predictable, they may relax enough to learn. To do this, however, they must have a teacher who possesses a great inner calmness and peace.

This addresses some of the needs of low-energy children, but what about the ones with exuberant high energy? Many of them are very capable students. Even though their energy level may be hard on the teacher, these children may be quite skilled at initiating, staying focused, and completing their work. If so, they really don't have an attention problem. They just require a high-energy parent or teacher to keep up with them and appreciate their style. However, there are other children who are so delighted with novelty that they fail to complete anything. They can't continue to attend to the teacher's voice if a more interesting voice competes with it. They may notice twice as much in a science lab as their peers but can't remember which details they were asked to notice. They can't seem to harness their overly alert minds. Wise parents and teachers can coach them to control their focus and begin bracketing their visual or auditory world so they can be more successful. Choosing a seat with less visual distractions and sitting next to quieter classmates can be very helpful.

But what if we add high stress levels to the picture? Suppose that the child in question is far from exuberant and is instead hypervigilant and agitated. Now trauma research again becomes relevant. The signs are easy to spot. Such a child will startle easily, will very likely be sensitive to touch, will find it hard to relax, and will respond more to noises than to voices. They will have poor impulse control once they get upset because under stress whatever inner speech they might have shuts down, and they can't redirect their actions. If we could test their body chemistry when they are in this state, we would find it flooded with cortisol and adrenaline, which gives rise to a fight-or-flight impulse and shuts down higher-order thinking skills so the body can react quickly to danger. That's fine when a situation calls for quick survival responses, but it doesn't serve the child well in the classroom.

Nature has a wonderful antidote to cortisol that can be very helpful. It is oxytocin, and there are a number of things that will raise the oxytocin level in a child and calm this stress response. Anything that invites friendly social engagement: smiling, turning one's head to look at the next person in a discussion circle, singing, and engaging in conversation are all helpful. It is also helpful to activate the sucking and chewing response or to provide gentle tactile stimulation. Using a coiled straw to sip water, eating snacks, massaging one's own face or ears, stroking one's arms, petting a friendly mammal, watching fish in an aquarium are all oxytocin-raising activities. Sadly, one of the most comforting and oxytocin-inducing experiences of all—to give and receive a hug—is no longer regarded as appropriate classroom behavior in many settings.

When we see signs of visual or auditory processing difficulty, we usually assume that weak sensory integration is causing these processing issues. However, trauma research is suggesting that high stress can also be a causal factor, destabilizing a person's sensory integration and having a direct impact on vision and hearing. When a child feels the need to become hypervigilant, the eyes support that need by emphasizing the peripheral regions, much like a prey animal does. This works against the classroom demands to focus the eyes narrowly on a target for close tasks like reading. When the child tries to hold that tight focus, he or she will fatigue quickly. The child can override the intention of the eye muscles to shift into peripheral scanning for a while by squinting, but this can only work for short periods.

When the ears are called upon to become hypervigilant, the muscles in the inner ear that normally hold the eardrum taut will relax, making it very difficult for the child to attend to speech. Under stress, the body has no time for such a luxury and reverts to "twig snap" listening—only picking up on environmental sounds and alerting with extreme speed to any hint of danger, again like the prey animal. Because the ears are much faster at processing important cues than the eyes are, the body counts on this alerting mechanism for survival, making it very difficult for overly stressed children to "pay attention" to what the teacher is saying. They can override this vigilant auditory pattern briefly by raising their eyebrows, which tightens their eardrums so they can process speech for a short time, but this too is very tiring.

When the listening channel is overly stressed, it often affects children's speaking voices as well. They aren't attending to their own voices, so they fail to control the volume and intonation as they speak. These are the children teachers are always asking to quiet down, use their "inside voices," and speak more softly.

It is important to understand that these symptoms do not necessarily originate from bad parenting or intentional stressors in the classroom. This "epidemic" of learning disabilities and related conditions like asthma, allergies, migraines, and digestive disorders points to a larger problem. We must recognize the pervasiveness of heightened stress in these times and consider the strong possibility that we are expecting far too much resilience from our children. These conditions can and should serve as a reminder to breathe more warmth, calmness, and social engagement into our classrooms, our homes, and our personal exchanges with one another and most especially with our children.

TAKING ONE'S OWN COUNSEL

When he read, his eyes moved down the pages and
his heart sought out their meaning while his voice and
tongue remained silent. Often when we were present . . .
we saw him reading to himself, and never otherwise.

ST. AUGUSTINE
on watching his mentor, St. Ambrose, 397 AD, *Confessions*, Book 6

The fascinating quote above is one of the earliest recorded references to inner or silent reading. Prior to that all readers in the Western world read aloud, and most of them would continue to do so for another five hundred years. So when we ask children today to begin reading silently by third or fourth grade, we are asking them to take quite a leap in consciousness. They are moving from *learning to read* to *reading to learn,* and in so doing, they are becoming aware of their own inner voice. They no longer need to learn by social engagement, following the same stories as all their peers and discussing everything out loud with them. Now they can each read different books and begin to have their own private thoughts as well. They are beginning to develop a dramatic new mind skill as they develop this sense of individuality. They are learning to *take their own counsel.*

We can encourage this marvelous quality by modeling it ourselves. We can think aloud in front of them and honestly listen to them as they begin to talk about problems and ideas. When children are below age nine, this is fairly easy because we will usually be able to hear them talk out loud to think. We use inner speech to do all of this private thinking, but it won't become a truly inner and silent process until age nine. We already traced the origins of inner speech in earlier chapters, but it is helpful to have an overview of its path of development.

Inner speech has its own region in the left frontal area of the brain and continues to develop throughout the school years in clear steps. The first step showed up as soon the child began to speak. Most of this newfound speech was directed toward others, but occasionally children were heard talking to themselves. Rules were remembered but not obeyed yet, and plans were spoken aloud ("I'm going to get my teddy bear"). This period from age two to four causes parents great frustration. Their child understood a rule, even voiced the rule, and then proceeded to violate it anyhow. Many parents succumb to child abuse during these years because it is so hard to realize that children are not yet able to obey their own minds. The brain cells that regulate inner speech also regulate motor impulses. Until the child is about four and has developed *strong* speech skills, the speech powers of those cells just aren't capable of overriding the motor urges of those same cells.

The second step in inner speech development arises with the chemical and structural changes to the brain that we discussed in the last section. This occurs around age six or seven, giving most children the ability to override their impulses and show clear signs of self-control, just in time for school. But those children with weak language skills, who haven't been encouraged to talk during their early years, now have the additional obstacle of weak inner speech skills as they enter school. By second or third grade, when their peers are beginning to show increased signs of thinking before acting, planning ahead, and resisting the urge to lash out, these children are just beginning to develop impulse control. Once again they appear less well-behaved and more quick-tempered than their peers, adding to their school-adjustment challenges.

The third and final inner speech quality is reasoning. It has been developing all along, but becomes very important by fourth grade as the curriculum begins to stress reasoning skills and silent reading. This inner speech is now ready to become the child's key tool for organizing thought, for arranging sequences of steps in problem solving, and for bringing forth language during writing tasks. It will eventually be able to draw forth eloquent, poetic language; follow and develop complex logical arguments and explanations; discover new problems to solve; and stimulate creative thinking.

Our population of slow developers simply isn't ready for silent reading by fourth grade and would benefit a great deal from an additional year or two of out-loud reading, listening to books on tape, and increased discussion and social engagement in the classroom. Not only did they experience culture shock on entering school, many of them come from cultures that strongly favor social engagement over the highly individuated alternative of taking one's own counsel. So this means that, in addition to falling behind while adjusting to the school environment, they are now being asked to learn in ways that clash with their cultural backgrounds. Without added reading support, they rarely make the transition into silent reading, and by middle school, while the average student has read over eight hundred thousand words, these children will have read barely sixty thousand. Their reading skills remain so low that school success becomes increasingly difficult.

For most children, however, third and fourth grade are great years to focus on silent reading, on writing, and even on foreign languages. While the brain is enjoying steady maturation between two very important growth spurts, it is undergoing rapid branching in the language regions. This brain change brings about a burst of new skills that rely on improved links between the tongue and the ear. Tongue twisters become popular, and music teachers are delighted because they can finally introduce three-part rounds and harmonies without the singers derailing if the person next to them sings a different part.

Learning to write is another extremely important skill to begin developing during these years. Tracing the way writing skills unfold and develop could be a fascinating way for you to assess how far you have come, where the rough spots were, and what you might want to work on next if you wish to become a stronger writer. Make note of how many of the following steps you can recall mastering.

Before any actual writing could happen, letters had to begin making sense. If you are reading this, you clearly mastered the early steps. You learned to remember the shapes and sounds of all the letters and to control the pencil well enough to put them on paper. You learned to put spaces between words so grown-ups could follow what you were trying to say. Your writing moved from just words that came to mind to whole sentences, and finally you reached the point where you could hold just one topic in mind for all the sentences. If you were lucky, you might have had a scribe, someone who would write those sentences down for you while you thought them up. That way you wouldn't forget what you wanted to say if you weren't sure how to write one of the words.

By third grade, you began learning lots of rules for how to write. There had to be capital letters, commas, periods, and every sentence had to have a subject and a verb. It wasn't like speaking, where you could just say parts of sentences, and the other person could understand you. So far, if someone asked you what writing was, you would probably say it was putting down on paper whatever came to mind. If the topic was interesting, you might write a lot, but if it was dull, the writing would be short and dull too. It was always a record of how you saw things. That is, it was always from your perspective or point of view.

In fourth or fifth grade, the teacher might have asked you to try a new approach and put down the ideas in a form that would make sense for a reader. You had to shift the information around sometimes to make that work and had to have a plan before you started. Your teacher might have known about a really interesting trick that made it easier. It turns out that if you say what you want to write while you are facing a listener, your words will come from *your* perspective and sound like social speech, but if you sit back-to-back with the listener, your words are likely to sound like written language, arranged to make sense to the listener. Your words will have become reader-centered, and that is what this new kind of writing requires. By now you are becoming aware that the words are beginning to happen in your head before you say them. Instead of relying on social speech, you are now beginning to rely on your inner speech. This opens up some really powerful writing skills that may begin emerging in middle and high school.

If you have learned to take your own counsel, to think about ideas on your own with that inner speech, you will find you have a lot to say. You can begin drawing on these thoughts, writing them down in a way that can persuade others. With practice, a strange new skill will begin to emerge. You will find yourself being both the writer and the reader, editing your own work as you go along. It is as if you are now wearing two hats at the same time, and all that you have learned about grammar, composition, points of view, and persuasion are coming together finally.

If you were *very* lucky, there is one final skill that could have arisen, perhaps in college. It is a mind skill that makes those who experience it fall in love with writing and end up finding ways to weave it into their lives from then on. It is possible to reach the point where your inner speech no longer dictates the writing process at all. Instead, the very act of writing seems to invite thoughts to emerge on the page, and you discover them for the first time as they appear. The writing is now transforming the writer, and the thoughts you had when you began writing actually change during the act of writing. Carl Bereiter, a leading cognitive researcher and emeritus professor from the University of Toronto, has called this *epistemic writing*. He describes it as representing "the culmination of writing development, in that writing comes to be no longer merely a product of thought but becomes an integral part of thought."

Your writing is now tapping into those deep thoughts that tend to dwell below ordinary consciousness, giving them voice. It is as if you have stumbled onto a direct connection to the secret realm of your mind.

Like all aspects of this secret realm, it cannot be learned with our intellect. It has a greater chance of emerging, though, if you develop a writing practice that captures your mind as it flows most freely. Out of that openness, powerful insights are more likely to bubble up. If you are especially interested in creating the conditions for this exciting writing skill, the final section in this chapter, "Incubating and Composing: The Art of Writing" will be of great help to you.

PROTECTING THE BRAIN'S NEXT TURN

> The frontal lobes, long regarded as silent areas, are the portion of the brain most essential to biological intelligence. They are the organs of civilization—the basis of man's despair and of his hope for the future.
>
> WARD HALSTEAD, pioneer in frontal-lobes research
> *Brain and Intelligence*

We have been tracking an elegant timetable for body and brain development in children. During most periods, this timetable calls for the body and the brain to take turns undergoing changes. The period from four to six was the body's turn, followed by the brain's turn from six to eight. From eight to ten, the middle childhood years, both the body and brain advanced together. We are about to explore the next important brain turn, one that is in great jeopardy these days. Ages eleven and twelve *belong* to the frontal lobes. Finally, these incredible lobes are poised to take the lead once again and awaken some extremely valuable mind skills. In a few years, the onset of adolescence with its powerful hormonal, emotional, physical, postural, and speech changes will bring this brain turn to an end. But in some cases the adolescent body turn comes too early, causing the brain to miss its turn entirely, with significant consequences.

A century ago, this adolescent body turn occurred in the late teens. Fifty years ago it was in the midteens, but changes in our culture have been coaxing adolescence to happen at ever younger ages, and now it is threatening to encroach on the period between ages eleven and twelve.

That is a very serious matter because if adolescence kicks in during these two precious years, it simply overpowers the brain's turn, and those children will fail to develop a vital set of skills. Their brains must then wait for the next brain turn at about age fifteen or sixteen, assuming they are still the least bit interested in academics, having fallen so far behind.

For most children, however, the brain gets its full turn and proceeds to reorganize its operations, shifting from an emphasis on the visual, auditory, and motor regions in the rear areas of the brain to the frontal regions once again. The body's drive to apply sensory-integration skills in new ways drew the emphasis to the rear areas for first through fourth grades. Finally, at age eleven, bands of fibers linking the rear area to the frontal regions start to insulate, integrating the brain from front to back. One special feature in this shift is that it opens up a new pathway for learning to read. Remedial reading teachers love working with fifth graders, because they can often produce dramatic results at this age. It isn't at all uncommon for a child who was stuck at an early third-grade reading level to have a breakthrough and jump to grade-level reading in that one year. Children whose brains couldn't coordinate the visual and auditory regions well enough to master reading now seem able to use the new frontal-lobe connections to succeed.

These frontal lobes first helped us as young children to regulate our bodies, so physical excitement didn't overpower our impulse control. These same frontal lobes began to aid us with emotional issues in middle childhood, giving us the self-control needed for handling emotional excitement. This was very helpful as we learned to play with others and to express our feelings through movement games and the arts. We were developing social impulse control so our feelings wouldn't overpower us.

At eleven and twelve, these frontal lobes could finally assist us in handling *mental* excitement. The thrill of new ideas, of creative discoveries, and of learning to master challenging subjects became our mind's playground. Perhaps you can recall the first time an idea caught fire in your mind, and you felt the real joy of thinking.

We can trace this transformation by asking what I call the *spinach question*. Imagine presenting this question to different-aged children: If all boys like spinach and Jimmy is a boy, does he like spinach?

The very young child who still relies on intuition and a bit of magic will try to think about Jimmy and may say something like, "No-o-o, Jimmy doesn't like spinach." With literacy comes a reorganization of thinking processes, and the seven- or eight-year-old child is very likely to hone in on the content of the question—spinach. If that child doesn't happen to like spinach, the answer might be, "Spinach? Yuk. No boys like spinach."

But once this eleven- to twelve-year-old reorganization begins, it is no longer spinach that catches the child's attention, but the *form* of the question instead. Now the response is likely to be, "Of course. If all boys liked ziggle, and Jimmy's a boy, he'd like ziggle too."

That simple response arises because a number of changes have taken place in that child's brain. *Forms* are beginning to carry meaning so charts and graphs can make sense now. *Logic* becomes even more powerful than truth. It is used for defending one's ideas, for negotiating with others, and for creating and following the rules of law. Thinking about the future, following hunches or hypotheses in science, studying activities and processes that are impossible to see and ideas that aren't stated directly also become possible now. We call this *hypothetical thinking.*

Now the theme, which is unspoken in a story, is as easy to identify as the plot that is spelled out by the events. Now the *x* in an algebra equation begins to make sense as a placeholder, not as a fixed amount. And when physics research claims to identify the behaviors of the planets or atoms by mathematical measurements even though these behaviors remain impossible to see, the learner can accept that. These are just a few of the cognitive shifts this brain change brings about.

As we continue to explore the range of transformations that first arise during this incredible window for brain development, see if you can recall when you first discovered and began using each of the ones that follow. If you were strongly engaged in school in fifth and sixth grade, you may have awakened many of these capacities back then. But if learning wasn't exciting yet, most of these capacities probably remained dormant for several years or perhaps didn't awaken until college or even adulthood.

Whenever your brain awakened its passion for learning, these frontal-lobe skills were ready to engage and serve you. To make it easier to track these skill sets, we'll give each one a name before discussing it.

Going beyond Black and White

In fifth and sixth grade, the study of mathematics continued to embrace a high level of precision, treating the equal sign in equations seriously and converting fractions to decimals accurately. There was still a correct or incorrect, right or wrong, black or white quality about it. Later, as probabilities and more advanced mathematical operations were studied, you would begin to entertain the idea of similarities or approximations in mathematics.

In other subjects you were already exploring the idea of similarity, however. Remember those compare-and-contrast essay questions and the challenge of explaining the meaning of a poem? There simply was no right or wrong answer to fall back on, and you had to develop an ability to work with similarities. You generalized and applied ideas you learned in one situation to new situations. You might have struggled to explain these similarities until you discovered how to use metaphors. Once discovered, they quickly became very important tools for exploring this abstract world. Metaphors were able to serve as a bridge between the concrete world of events, objects, and experiences and this new world of logic, possibility, and formulas.

These metaphors became very useful for describing visual impressions, and your creative writing probably improved. When Alfred Noyes said, "The road was a ribbon of moonlight" in *The Highwayman,* he described the look of the road, but that's as far as that metaphor could go. It was neither a ribbon nor was it made up of moonlight, but it made a fine poetic image.

As science began using visual metaphors, serious problems often arose. Botanists created classifications based on appearances to cluster plants. If a newly discovered plant had enough visual characteristics in common with a class, it was declared to be part of that group. However, more recent genetic studies have found serious errors in this picture-based approach and are now challenging the traditional classification system.

Once you discovered how to use metaphors to describe functions, your brain made another cognitive leap. Now you could link events or experiences to metaphors by comparing them, using phrases like "It was as if . . ." or "It was like . . ." You could talk about everything from sports events to headaches to your feelings with a new degree of nuance.

However, even these metaphors, which we could also call analogies, usually break down eventually, as scientists realize. For example, the heart was thought to function like a pump for over a century. Accepting this metaphor kept researchers from realizing that it really operated on an entirely different principle. Single pacemaker cells were actually creating vortices of movement, shooting the blood upward from one chamber into the next. The pump analogy was so widely accepted that no one noticed just how thin the lower chamber's wall was. It was far too thin to withstand the pressure of a pumping action, and illustrators would depict it in medical texts as much thicker than it really was.

Expanding a Sense of Empathy

Fifth grade is consistently chosen as the year to introduce lessons on disability conditions, and there's a good reason for this. An important new capacity to link one's feeling life to the frontal lobes is awakening. The natural empathy that was present in the very young child has now become conscious. The ability to empathize with others and to re-create their experiences within oneself is now heightened. Often students will spend a day in a wheelchair, wearing clouded glasses, putting cotton in their ears, wearing mittens, or going through the day using only one arm to deepen their understanding of the challenges facing those who wrestle with these obstacles every day. Once they have practiced placing themselves in these situations, their empathy is aroused. The teacher often follows this exercise by inviting guest speakers who actually live with these conditions. This gives the students a chance to exercise their mirror neurons and match with these speakers to understand the condition more completely.

This sensitivity can be cultivated if children are encouraged to champion social causes, to help people who face special challenges, to fundraise for those in need, or to volunteer their time to help others. Perhaps you can recall the desire to be of service at this age as well. When a school culture takes the time to foster a strong sense of empathy among the students and creates outlets for service, it builds a climate that is much less susceptible to the bully-victim dynamics that typically arise in middle school.

Stretching Your Working Memory

Can you recall the frustration when you first tried to take notes? The teacher just kept talking, and you were expected to get that information onto paper somehow. It soon became clear that verbatim notes were not going to work. For one thing, the lecture went too fast. For another, you may have encountered trouble with your mind's "mute button." As soon as your attention went to writing down what you had just heard, you were no longer able to listen to what was now being said. Huge chunks of the presentation went missing, and soon your notes made very little sense. If you survived this initiation process, you eventually learned several tricks. First, you learned to chunk information, to distill long sentences down to succinct phrases that you could jot down quickly. Then, you may have learned an equally important trick—to keep tracking the teacher's voice while jotting down these phrases. So now you were double tracking—chunking the past words into phrases while attending to the present ones. Later, you might have gone on to become a triple tracker, finding a way to track your own thoughts and jot them down as well!

Note-taking wasn't the only way you learned to stretch your working memory. You also wrestled with having to raise your hand before speaking, with having to hold your thought until called on, and with remembering what you wanted to say once you got the floor. Schools struggle to engage the attention of these fifth and sixth graders today, and many classrooms have shifted away from lectures, notes, and the call-and-response pattern of raising hands to speak. Instead, they are relying on social engagement, group activities, and oral discussion to reach increasingly stressed students who lack the tolerance for the frustrations you endured. These same students are falling farther behind in math, science, and foreign languages, subjects that rely on the logical self-talk that arises from strong inner speech and a powerful working memory.

Perhaps you are becoming concerned about your own working-memory strength these days. If so, take heart. Our working memory is a fragile gift and very susceptible to letting us down if we are stressed or sleep deprived, overly excited, or even dehydrated! The next section will look at the many ways we can call on the body to support the mind. They are all lessons that belong in the school curriculum but are rarely mentioned.

FINE-TUNING THE BODY-MIND CONNECTIONS

Now that the frontal lobes are again leading the schooling process, a new set of strategies becomes possible. Your frontal lobes have the unique ability to track at a conscious level what is happening within your body, and this opens up a host of new body-based mind skills. This practice of thinking about the act of thinking is being called *metacognition,* and it deserves a place in today's curriculum. Early adolescence is an ideal time to introduce and begin developing these skills, since it is clearly the body's turn anyway. Nevertheless, you probably never learned any of the skills we are about to explore when you were in school. They are powerful tools for your adult mind as well, so have fun experimenting with them. See which practices benefit your mind the most, and add these to your growing collection of practices and the mind skills that result.

Because this section is so filled with ideas, it is divided into four segments to give you good stopping points. You will benefit most if you can take the time to try out the ideas in each segment before moving on.

Breath, Water, and Sleep

We spoke in an earlier chapter about the impact of mouth-breathing on the ability to think. It not only deprives our brain of its full measure of oxygen, it can keep our nasal cavity from cooling the blood leading to the frontal lobes, literally resulting in a more hot-headed mind. Optimal thinking, of course, calls for coolheadedness, so nose-breathing and relaxed or slightly smiling facial muscles are ideal.

Water also plays a major role in keeping our brains well charged for thinking. Aside from the more obvious side effects of dehydration such as headaches, general irritability, and increased distractibility, water is needed to perform critical internal functions. It assists with our breathing by lubricating the air sacs of the lungs. They need to be moist so the oxygen can dissolve and pass through into the blood. Our nasal membranes also need to be well lubricated so they can filter out airborne pollutants and allergens. Water maintains the optimal electrolytic balance within the cell membranes, and for our brain this results in both faster information processing and better access to higher-order reasoning skills. Research with children has even shown that drinking a glass of water right before taking a test leads to significantly higher test scores. A decline of as little as 2 percent of body weight in water intake can lead to serious cognitive difficulties. Memory traces won't hold, math processing becomes more difficult, new learning is harder, and the mind suffers from confusion and forgetfulness. So before you begin to suspect you have early-onset Alzheimer's, try upping your water intake and see what that can do for you.

If you are breathing well and drinking enough water but your mind still seems to perform poorly for you, it is time to explore your sleep patterns. Chronic sleep deprivation is a very common and subtle problem. It can masquerade as a number of other learning and psychological problems. If it has been going on for a long time, you may have slipped into a chronic "wired tired" state that can be hard to recognize. You no longer have the telltale signs of yawns and droopy eyelids. Your body simply kicks into overdrive and keeps going, but it also keeps getting less and less efficient at what it does. The brain suffers even more severely than the body, first losing the ability to handle details and be accurate with numbers, then becoming weaker at memory tasks, and finally even failing to reason well.

For decades researchers have been advocating later starting times for middle and high school students. The findings clearly show the connection between an added half hour of sleep each morning and improved school performance. A thorough study of three thousand high school students correlated the grade-point average to the average amount of sleep each student received on school nights and discovered that the difference between the A and B students (who got seven hours and twenty-one minutes) and the D students (who got six hours and forty-five minutes) was a mere thirty-three minutes of sleep per night. No other variable could be found to distinguish between these populations so clearly.

Sleep researchers are beginning to explore the various stages of sleep in greater detail, finding that deep sleep early in the night or at the onset of a nap is especially useful for embedding factual information. So students who are cramming lots of data are much better off sleeping for at least an hour before an exam even if they have stayed up all night studying. Otherwise, all that crammed information just might not be there when they need to retrieve it.

To anchor motor tasks, phase-two sleep that occurs farther into the night is most beneficial. For those trying to master a motor skill like gymnastics, dance steps, or piano, or trying to improve their reaction time in martial arts or mechanical tasks, it pays to sleep longer. Some researchers insist that waking at 5 A.M. makes no sense for athletes in training. They are missing the most valuable hours of REM (rapid eye movement) sleep, where rehearsal and muscle memory are occurring. And for the creative thinkers wanting to pull together the odd bits they have been wrestling with, to create coherence or the insight patterns that are so exciting, the goal is to have as much REM sleep as possible too. The field of sleep research is extremely active right now, and while athletics will likely be the first field to apply each new finding, it would be wonderful if education followed closely behind. How much sleep each of us needs, how that varies as we age, and how to restore natural sleep cycles for the chronic insomniacs are just a few of the questions being explored right now. Some things are already becoming clear, however.

Researchers have known for years that sleep deprivation takes its toll on the mind, and recent findings are suggesting it can also affect the body. Insomnia and heavy snoring can interrupt or fragment a good night's sleep. This seems to interfere with the ability to manage emotions, leading to more aggressive behaviors. A high percentage of students with behavior problems and bullying behaviors has a history of sleep disorders. A growing number of research studies are linking fragmented and insufficient sleep with obesity as well, though the reasons for that are still unclear. Infants who slept less than ten hours a night were found to be twice as likely to be overweight or obese later. Thin adults averaged two hours a week more sleep as infants than heavier adults. Some scientists speculate that more sleep may increase the production of appetite-suppressant hormones. One study is showing that subjects who sleep less than 6.5 hours a night also need 50 percent more insulin to process glucose than those getting over 7.5 hours a night. This may seem harmless enough, but scientists are wondering if it could lead to late onset diabetes in time—just one more reason to take sleep seriously!

Diet, Allergies, and Cognitive Cycles

Your brain is also very much affected by what you eat. Unfortunately, there is no magic pill or meal that will do wonders for everyone. You will have to make a study of your own mind's reaction to your eating patterns to see if there are ways you could be more supportive of yourself and increase your brain power through dietary adjustments. The following inventory will get you started:

- *Consider the special impacts of certain foods.* Which foods ground you, which ones energize you or overstimulate you, and which leave you dulled or exhausted?
- *Consider the qualities of attention that arise.* What is the quality of your attention on a full stomach, an empty stomach, on a not-quite-full stomach? (Many health practitioners advise that we stop eating just before we feel full to avoid feeling dulled.)
- *Consider allergy and food craving patterns.* When do you crave fats (nuts, oils, fried foods), sweets (soda, sugars, alcohol), salts (chips, pretzels, salted popcorn), dairy (milk, ice cream, cheese, cream), or caffeine (chocolate, coffee, colas)? Often cravings are linked to allergies so you might try eliminating a craving category for a while to see what impact it has on your thinking.

You don't give up on your body just because it varies in its vitality, its ability to endure, and its need for food. And you don't decide that your heart qualities are disappointing just because sometimes you are in the mood to be social, and other times you feel a need to be quiet or solitary. Well, your mind has very definite phases and cycles too. Some of them are quite regular and can be predicted and planned for. Others may seem to arise out of the blue. The trick is to match the task you want to do with the cognitive state your mind is in or is able to shift into at the time. Thinking problems tend to arise when we ask our mind to do the wrong kind of task at the wrong time of day or under the wrong conditions—perhaps we are too full, too warm, or too tired, or the environment may be too noisy or too cluttered.

There are no pat formulas that will work for everyone. One person may discover that creativity is greatest on an empty stomach in the morning, while another finds it is easiest at midnight following three cups of coffee. One person may tackle a long research project over a few days in four- to eight-hour sessions in the library, while another needs to take exercise breaks every hour or so and may break the task up into smaller chunks spread out over several weeks. One person wakes up ready to handle highly complex learning first thing in the morning, while another's mind wakes up gradually throughout the day and finds early morning time only suitable for mundane tasks.

One of my college students was returning to school after years in the business world. She had long thought of herself as a poor reader because she always tried reading in the evening when her mind was already packed from a full day of work or school. She shifted to reading in the morning when her mind was fresh and found she could read with ease.

Ergonomics and Clothing

Back in the 1960s, some top executives ordered custom-designed Franklin desks for their inner offices. These standing desks were quite popular with those CEOs who, like Ben Franklin, could think more clearly on their feet. Other executives purchased elaborate chairs that allowed them to make micro-adjustments of seats, backs, headrests, footrests, and armrests, all with one goal in mind. They were searching for the optimal posture for thinking. This quest to refine the relationship between workers and the work environment quickly found its name, *ergonomics*. Since then, the field of ergonomics has expanded from making refined studies of furniture for office workers to studying motion paths for factory workers and the ways we interact with technological tools.

In the 1970s, physical therapists began working with adjustable wheelchairs for children with cerebral palsy and other motor disorders. To their surprise, they discovered that altering the tilt of a child's spine and head support by a few degrees could shift that child from a stuporous state to a very alert one. Some children who were thought to be nearly vegetative were now able to become engaged and learn.

You might expect that the next population to be given ergonomic furniture would be the children in schools, but to date that has not occurred. However, some creative teachers are experimenting with using therapy balls and air cushions for chairs, allowing some students to stand at podiums and counters to study, and letting them use insulated ear-muffs to block out sounds or sit in carrels to block out visual distractions.

Try extending this exploration to your workspace—what lighting works best, what locations help you become more alert, and which ones trigger a more sluggish state? Test out your furniture choices to see which ones give you the posture that serves your brain best. You might even consider the layout of your workspace. What is at your back, where is the door, and what beauty lies in your visual field? You could also help create a home office that works well for any students who live with you. If you would like even more suggestions, check out the article called "Creating a Home Office" on the website for this book.

Your choice of clothing is also important. In the late 1800s, corsets were extremely popular but they never allowed women to take a deep breath to oxygenate their brains, while the men wore tight collars and ties that pressed on their larynxes and held their emotional responses in check. Their attire contributed significantly to the gender differences in behavior and thinking abilities in those times. In lesser ways, the clothes you choose to wear each day can affect the kinds of thinking that will be easy or difficult for you to access that day. Simply paying attention to what you are wearing can help sensitize you to this fascinating variable. Notice the fabric's texture—is it soft, coarse, crisp, or supple? How does it fit—snug, loose, layered, tight at the waist? What color have you chosen—does it affect your mood in some way? What have you chosen for your feet—tight-fitting or laced shoes, loose shoes, sandals, socks, or bare feet? Do you prefer having your feet and hands warm or cool? And what suits your neck best—a turtle-neck or tight collar, open neck area, jewelry of any sort? You are already making these choices unconsciously, but by bringing them to conscious-ness, you can heighten your mind's performance.

As an example, for a couple of years I directed a teacher-support team, and every Monday morning we met to go over the week's requests and divide up the responsibilities. For me it was the most challenging part of the week, and one Monday morning I caught myself reaching for a black outfit. Then it dawned on me—I always wore black to those meetings.

So from then on I deliberately chose bright, upbeat colors for Mondays. It changed my outlook dramatically and very likely made me more agreeable to my colleagues as well.

Postures and Stress Levels

As we think, we often slip into frozen postures without realizing it. Before long, these tense muscles cause an adrenaline build-up that interferes with our frontal lobes and impairs our comprehension and our ability to concentrate. It is easy to remedy this situation by doing the following posture and muscle checks before and during any period of intense mental activity and then releasing any tensions you discover.

- *Check your breath.* You may find you have backed off to tidal air, a thin stream of air that doesn't involve the diaphragm much. That is fine as long as you aren't holding your breath as well. In the martial arts, they suggest you should breathe like a turtle, so slowly it isn't even noticed.
- *Check your mouth.* Are you clenching your teeth? Move your lower jaw back and forth a couple of times, open your mouth wide, and then close your mouth gently. Keep your upper and lower teeth separated. If the tip of the tongue is comfortable touching the back of your front teeth, that's fine, but let the rest of the tongue relax at the bottom of your mouth. This will drop the tension but keep you alert.
- *Check your eyes.* See if you can let your eyes relax into a soft focus whenever possible. You may even discover you have been reading with such a tight focus that you are almost trying to pierce through the page. Try to back off and just look lightly at the page instead. Your eyes won't get nearly as tired that way.
- *Check your facial muscles.* Are you scowling or squinting as you think? Or perhaps your face is flaring instead, with arched eyebrows, wide eyes, and flared nostrils. In either case, it is time to relax, and the easiest way is to massage your face for a minute, first rubbing your cheeks and forehead and then drawing your fingers gently across your closed eyes.

- *Check your neck.* Often, if your facial muscles are tense, your neck is going to be tense as well. To release the tension, slowly bend your head forward until your chin touches your chest. Take your time with this, waiting for your neck muscles to soften and allow your neck to lengthen. Once your chin reaches your chest, let your shoulders drop as well, and rest in that position for a minute or two.
- *Check your fingers.* This is the final check. See if your fingers are gripping more tightly than necessary on whatever is in your hand or if you are simply making a fist without realizing it. When your hand is tight, your jaw is very likely to be tight as well. It is much harder to take in new information with a clenched jaw than with a relaxed one. To release this tension, stretch and massage your hands gently while relaxing your jaw.

The final two sections in this chapter will look at how the emerging young scholar combines all these ideas to help with the exciting cognitive transformation that can arise in high school.

THE EMERGING SCHOLAR

The last great cognitive shift to arise during the journey from kindergarten through high school is triggered by the brain's final growth spurt at fifteen to sixteen years of age. The frontal lobes are now able to handle increasing levels of complexity. Even those students who entered adolescence too early to experience the eleven- to twelve-year-old frontal-lobe growth spurt can benefit this time. These were very likely the students who led researchers to insist that adolescents are too impulsive to think ahead, anticipate consequences, control their impulses, use logic, and empathize with others. Finally, the inner speech and reasoning centers of these students are better coordinated and more able to exert control over the increased emotional impulsivity of adolescence, helping them catch up with their peers and begin to think before acting, show improved judgment and empathy, and plan ahead more skillfully.

While this is a welcome change in behavior, this growth spurt also brings the possibility of an elegant cognitive shift. Now the true scholar can finally emerge. We have lost many students along the way, but during this critical cognitive window, gifted teachers and creative programs are succeeding in rekindling the love of learning in some of these students. We hope to bring as many students through this transformation as possible because this cognitive shift paves the way for enjoying lifelong learning. If you experienced this transformation, then you can probably recall having enjoyed increasingly nuanced understandings and an ever-widening knowledge base in your favorite subjects. Even if your peers lost interest in those subjects or moved on to other topics, your curiosity stayed focused and helped you follow your early questions on to a rich intellectual quest. If it continued beyond high school, perhaps it even formed the basis of your advanced studies or your expertise in the world today.

Two words capture the essence of this last schooled-mind transformation: *complexity* and *coherence*. The simplicity of earlier learning, with its right and wrong answers, its one or two variables at a time, and its appeal to the mind's pictures and imagination gives way now to more variables, more ambiguity, and ideas that no longer lend themselves to easy metaphors.

The only hope for organizing such complexity is a dramatic increase in the mind's ability to create coherence, its ability to bring many bits and pieces together into meaningful forms that the brain can then work with. The data must be chunked into digestible clusters that are easily stored.

Let's consider the challenges facing educators today in trying to bring this transformation about. Because many middle school students remained emotion-bound learners, feeling strongly but thinking only when they absolutely must, the teachers learned to be good storytellers to reach them. By spicing up their presentations with shocking, gory, tragic, exciting, and strange bits of information, they created much of the coherence or mental glue that helped their students hold the information together. This crutch worked well enough in subjects like history, literature, and the social sciences to enable the students to use their memory skills and recall the information when needed for a test. Once that unit or course was over, the memory file was often emptied to make room for the next topic. Their learning remained fragmented and lacked the rich complexity that we want students to achieve in this final shift.

Furthermore, it would not work at all with subjects that needed to convert new learning into a foundation for the next layer. Deciding to dump the memory file on verbs so the nouns can be learned in a foreign language or deleting fractions so there is room to cram decimals simply isn't an option. We can call these subjects, along with science, *scaffolded* subjects that can only be mastered if earlier lessons form the foundation or scaffolding on which the new lessons can be placed. When we read of the poor test results of US public schools, it is in the scaffolded subjects of math, science, and foreign languages that the greatest failures occur.

Music, athletic skills, and drama are also scaffolded subjects and could be used to help these students learn to construct scaffolds. They all require a high level of mastery and build on practice and refinement, inviting learners to *play* with what they are learning. Yet these are the very subjects that get cut first in spite of research showing that students in arts-enriched schools end up performing better in all subjects.

The secret to scaffolding is to create *coherence,* to create a pattern that the brain can store and build on. This places increased demands on a cluster of frontal-lobe functions—strong working memories, clear inner speech, the ability to take one's own counsel, and the power of complex reasoning all must come together to draw forth this coherence. Most courses offered in the final years of high school include practices that invite the student's mind to reach this advanced new level of thinking. You probably recall many of them.

Early note-taking called on you as a student to write key phrases that captured what had already been said while somehow overriding the mute button, so it became possible to listen to the new information at the same time. Finally you learned to track your own thoughts while attending to the thoughts of the speaker. The same increased challenge awaited you as you read. Not only did you need to track the events or facts and the theme or ideas the author had in mind, you also had to track your own reflections about what was being written.

The expectations around writing also shifted. No longer was it enough to jot down a stream of consciousness and call it a paper. Now your paper needed to address a complex subject, and your thoughts needed to be coherent. The end result was expected to be a well-organized composition. If you were a really skilled student back then, you probably developed your own personal strategies for "meeting the muse" and producing good papers. You had discovered how to research well, to incubate your ideas, and to time your work so that the ideas were ready to come together right when you needed them. You probably set aside a block of time to do the actual writing, making sure you were well rested and able to sustain your focus long enough to capture your thoughts as they came together.

I met several times with a group of academically strong high school students, asking them to describe how they worked with their favorite scaffolded subjects. Here are some of the patterns they shared. See if you can identify with any of their strategies.

They tended to daydream consciously, rehearsing the information from each class just because they enjoyed it. They *played* with it outside of class. If it involved math concepts, they practiced and looked for new patterns the teacher hadn't mentioned yet. If it was a foreign language, they tried to speak it with each other throughout the day, to tell jokes in the new language, and use it to make comments they didn't want others to understand. If it was a science concept, they would look for those patterns everywhere, even treating them as metaphors to help organize their thinking about other aspects of their world.

They all noticed that key terms or words from those subjects kept popping up in other contexts or in other subjects. This gave them a sense that all these ideas and subjects were actually interconnected. In other words, they were constantly searching for larger and larger webs of *coherence*. Some learned to pace their enthusiasm while others would even forget to eat or sleep when they were deeply engrossed.

These gifted young thinkers had all discovered a powerful brain zone that has only recently been identified. They were entering the same zone that supports mathematical thinking and the intense pattern searches that drive good scientific research. For now we will call it a *hypercalm* state. These thinkers had to stay very calm and contain their excitement while engaging in an extremely rapid scanning behavior at the same time. Eventually, they would be forced to take a break because the excitement would overtake them, and they could no longer sustain that remarkable state. We have been exploring very advanced capacities for taking in information and playing with ideas in our minds. We can make the same detailed study of the art of incubating and then expressing those ideas in writing. This final section is devoted to that exploration.

INCUBATING AND COMPOSING
The Art of Writing

We will be talking about assignments, but you can treat that word broadly. In your life, the assignment might be an elegant cover letter for a job application, a strong letter to the editor, an important written presentation at work, or a family-history story to pass on to future generations. These practices can help bring eloquence to any piece of writing that really matters to you.

Sometimes we can say that a paper seems to "write itself" or that a musical composition or piece of choreography "composes itself." When that happens, our incubation process has occurred in a less-than-conscious way, giving rise to an organically composed piece. This is the epistemic writing we talked about in the last section. It would be nice if we could consciously practice this less-than-conscious incubation activity, but that is obviously impossible. As you probably are suspecting, it belongs to that mysterious secret realm. This means that we cannot always be sure whether we are incubating an idea or an assignment or are, instead, perhaps ignoring and dropping the task.

However, we can deliberately practice carrying out those activities that tend to support the incubation process. When we find ourselves practicing these activities in the face of assignment deadlines, the chances are we are actually busy at work incubating. These supportive activities all require an unusual amount of patience. There are two approaches we can consider and try practicing. The first approach involves passive processes, and the second uses more active ones.

The passive processes all play with turning time into space. They force us to drop our time pressure to come to completion and replace that with a highly relaxed and almost leisurely feeling of space. First you need to feed the information to your mind, and then you can begin these "digestive" activities. So, do them right after spending time focusing on the theme you wish to incubate.

- *Try dreaming.* You can either take an actual nap, or you can simply let your mind daydream about what you have just reviewed.

- *Go blank.* After reviewing the material you want to write about, let your mind drift into a dull "down time" where you have no thoughts running at all. This may seem pointless, but it is giving your less-than-conscious mind the opportunity to work with the material. If you have a meditation practice, you have already discovered the subtle benefits that build up when you give your mind this empty awake time. Everything seems to deepen, not just your understanding of what you are studying.

- *Get rhythm.* Without thinking about any new topics that could erase the writing assignment from your mind, take on some mindless rhythmic activity. Go for a walk, swim laps, shovel or rake, weed, wash a batch of spinach, or do housework that calls for repetitive motions. These rhythmic activities will keep your frontal lobes awake and engaged so they can play with and organize your thoughts.

- *Seek out quiet chaos.* While holding the writing task in your mind, work on a jigsaw puzzle, work on untangling a ball of string, or watch the movement of water in a stream. The ambiguity inherent in these tasks can help your mind become more fluid in its thinking.

- *Become obsessive.* Choose a key question that summarizes the theme you are trying to write about and just mull it over again and again. Keep asking the question as you pace about or doodle, or engage in any of the activities above but don't even try to answer the question during this time. The really elegant answer will emerge later, after a nap or in the shower, or in the middle of a conversation hours or days later when you revisit the assignment.

Now let's look at the *active processes.* They are all designed to loosen any connections and order you might already have constructed and they work to pry your conscious, ordering mind off of the content. Once you have taken in the information you want to consider, you are ready to play with it in the following, very deliberate ways.

- *Randomize the information.* As you think about the topic, try saying "whatever," "perhaps," or "maybe not" to every thought that arises. As you look at the written bits you hope to include, try plucking out the author's logical links and ignoring them. Drop the arguments that are holding the idea together and let the bits stand on their own.

- *Play with paradox.* Spot the incompatibilities among the bits—perhaps between the authors you are hoping to weave together, or between your ideas and those of one of the authors—and begin to fuss with them. Try joining some of those bits together. Create logical clashes among the bits and let them "fight it out" in your mind. See if you can discover ways in which both could be right. You'll be amazed at how easily that discovery can rearrange your whole approach to the paper.

- *Juxtapose the bits.* Now that you have backed the ideas to their original, unconnected state, begin to flip around among them and combine the bits in odd ways, just for fun.

- *Muse deeply.* Take time to fully soak up the bits or your new questions as they arise. Respond to them with an attitude of "Is that so!" Don't be discouraged by the new doubts and confusion. Be fascinated with it. Mull on it, but take no action yet. Don't analyze, and don't push for a conclusion.

- *Learn to "hold your thought before you have it."* This may sound like a strange, and even impossible, piece of advice. However, scholars do it all the time. They just haven't tried to describe it. The sensation is a bit like waiting for a sneeze. You know it is coming, but until it arises, it is only a moving, visceral sensation inside. Thoughts feel just like that if you pay close enough attention. Try savoring the choreographic sense of the idea as a visceral sensation for as long as you can before letting it come into language. Even waiting a few minutes is helpful. It will make the idea stronger and clearer when it does show up. Then you are less likely to lose it as you begin to write about it.

You are now ready to begin the composing process. There is a world of difference between grinding out a paper and inviting a paper to unfold. The process is different, and so is the end product. You already know how to force the words onto paper to plod through an assignment, and you know how disappointing that process can be. Let's talk now about how to bring forth much more elegant work. If you have been incubating the material well and have played with it creatively, you are now ready to bring the paper to life.

Remember to do all the body-based strategies you have learned. Carve out a good block of time, be rested and comfortable, and clear your mind for action. Pay special attention to which posture works best for this task. Next, take about twenty minutes to look over your notes and the source material you want to play with to rekindle your thoughts and insights. Then invite the words to arise. You are about to become a secretary to your own mind, taking down the inner speech as it flows.

You will be able to tell the difference between lifeless chatter and the flow of elegant words because, once the ideas begin to flow, it feels different. Some describe it as being in a "state of grace," being blessed by insight or being "in-formed"—that is, inwardly formed—by the discovery. The great French linguist Maurice Merleau-Ponty described the art of such writing in this way in *Consciousness and the Acquisition of Language:*

> To become a writer is to learn a personal language. The writer creates his own language and his own public. He, therefore, recommences the creation of language on a higher level.

To keep those insights alive and to keep the language flowing as you write, you can try the following techniques.

- *Revisit the visceral sensation beneath the words.* Take frequent breaks to go back to holding your thought before you have it.

There is a rough brilliance about exploring your ideas in that voiceless form that can be refined by mulling it as a picture-thought or by choreographing, rehearsing, and improving the grace of the thought's inner gesture. You can also recapture the flow by rereading what you have written so far. Do this often; it is not wasting time at all.

- *Fret over the weak spots.* Notice any flaws, bugs, warts, snags, or glitches in your writing and fret over them until it triggers further insights or transformations, and your inner speech either offers a revised version to use or collapses the pattern entirely. If it does collapse, don't panic or try to salvage the old version. Just be patient, start the process over again and allow a new pattern to present itself. This can be hard, especially if you have become attached to your old ideas, so you might enjoy reflecting on the following advice of Annie Besant about letting go:

> Can you be content with such a result? Years of labour, years of thought, and see everything crumble into dust, and nothing remain? If not, then you are working for self, and not as part of the Divine activity; and however gilded over with love of others your scheme might have been, it was your work and not God's work, and therefore you have suffered in the breaking.

- *Check over the number qualities.* From time to time, as you tease out the themes you want to weave together in your paper, take a glimpse at the number of themes you have identified and see if it matches with the qualities of that number. Don't force the issue, just look gently with the possibility that this may help you see if an element is still missing. For example, if you have three elements, does it reflect will, heart, and mind by any chance? If you have four elements, are there two pairs, and do they balance like the four directions or the Greek temperaments or Jungian archetypes perhaps? Or perhaps it is clearly a three idea but you have four elements. In that case, are two of them really two aspects of a single element? Always ask yourself if anything is missing too.

- *Know when the muse is done for the day.* Your whole paper may not arise in a single sitting. Once you find yourself forcing the words, becoming too tired to keep the inspiration alive, or losing your connection to that inner-speech voice, it may be time to take a break for a few minutes, an hour, or even a whole day. So, don't wait till the last possible day before beginning to write or else your paper will read like a lot of books do—off to a great start and then fizzling halfway through (a sure sign that the publisher has put too much pressure on a deadline or that the writer has started to compose too late to do the whole paper elegantly).

Sometimes the obstacles to awakening this wonderful facet of your natural brilliance can be as simple as your surroundings or your anxiety level. Here are a few of the discoveries my students have made over the years. Perhaps their ideas can help you find your way as well.

They had many thoughts about clean rooms and getting organized. Here are a few of the best.

- I have found that the basic routine of keeping things neat and cooking and cleaning up afterward gives my mind time to be clear and focused on something simple so that when I sit down to bigger projects, art, or school, it's easier for me to focus and not have the towel on the floor nagging my attention away.
- I am pleased to be experiencing that when I take care of things in my physical world, it definitely contributes to being more alert and alive mentally. Now I am able to see how I can be more enthused about the mental assignment simply by doing the things that prepare me to be in the space to comprehend the material.
- I began to make myself do things I did not want to. Like make food instead of telling myself I was too busy and going out to eat. I vowed to stay at home more in my mess so that my nest would become more of a priority. As a result my room got a lot

cleaner, and I actually had more time do the things I wanted to—like paint, which I wouldn't have been able to do if I was constantly avoiding my unfinished mess. It is still extremely difficult to force myself to stay home and cook or clean, not that the domesticity is hard, but it's hard to be within myself and my simple work and at the same time fight the distraction of greater projects or things that are more fun.

- If I step back before assessing a situation or before I sit to read or start a paper and just organize my thoughts, I come out with better results.

Finally, you might enjoy their thoughts on pacing themselves and coping with writing anxiety.

- In monitoring the amount of time I spend studying, I determined that two hours is the maximum for me. Then I need at least a two-hour break before I transition into another subject that requires reading or writing.
- I rewarded myself for every thirty minutes of study—food, exercise, music, a walk, phone call.
- There are times when I am writing a paper and find it difficult to come up with more information, so I'll take a break. At this time I may go for a run, do housework, or do whatever will take my mind off schoolwork. Within two hours or so when I return, my mind and body feel open, and I can usually get back into it with new ideas.
- I attempt to balance work so I am never caught in last-minute living. I know my brain will have a fit with me. It won't cooperate. Productivity gets risky. Pacing has become everything. My brain lets me have it when I create pressure or put myself in the path of a pressured dynamic. Listening slow is listening well, and that is what my mind delights in.
- When I realized how speedy I had become, I decided to add another facet to my will practices. Stopping. I tried to become aware of when I was getting crazy. When I noticed myself getting this way I would stop briefly, even for just a few

minutes, and breathe. I discovered that by stopping, I was able to "come back," so to speak. I could then approach the task at hand with a clearer mind.

In the final chapter, you will have the opportunity to uncover and develop an even more exciting array of skills and lenses. Taken together, they will provide you with the tools you need to meet life's growing complexities and bring your natural brilliance to its full potential.

IN SEARCH OF WISDOM
From Complexity to Emptiness

Do I contradict myself? Very well then I contradict myself,
I am large, I contain multitudes.

WALT WHITMAN
"Song of Myself," *Leaves of Grass*

MOST OF THE problems encountered by the schooled mind had a static quality about them. While life seemed to offer confusion, changing circumstances, and unpredictability, the problems we tackled in school were conveniently clear. For example, math problems had clear right answers, science labs were set up to reveal known outcomes, and history was usually presented as a series of logical responses to events of the period.

We must expand our ways of thinking if we wish to address the complex problems we face today, problems that refuse to hold still, what we now call *systems problems*. As we learn to recognize the systems that weave through our lives, we will be forming a powerful new set of lenses for viewing the world. We will then look at several exciting new neurological discoveries that will help us understand how our mind can possibly think in these new ways, how it ages, and how to embody some of these discoveries. The epilogue will close with the exploration of emptiness, the last practice in our quest to uncover our natural brilliance.

EXPLORING COMPLEX PROBLEMS

When we try to pick out anything by itself, we find
it hitched to everything else in the universe.

JOHN MUIR
My First Summer in the Sierra

Humankind has not woven the web of life. We are but one
thread within it. Whatever we do to the web, we do to
ourselves. All things are bound together. All things connect.

CHIEF SEATTLE, 1855

Today the network of relationships linking the human race to itself
and to the rest of the biosphere is so complex that all aspects
affect all others to an extraordinary degree. Someone should
be studying the whole system, however crudely that has to be
done, because no gluing together of partial studies of a complex
nonlinear system can give a good idea of the behavior of the whole.

MURRAY GELL-MANN, 1969 Nobel Prize winner in physics for work on subatomic particles
The Quark and the Jaguar

Some problems in our lives simply refuse to hold still. We encounter them at every level of our existence, from our relationships, our personal health, our finances and jobs, to the larger scale of the changing environment and climate patterns, changing markets, and changing political realities.

Each of these problems has a lot of moving parts, and efforts to manage or change them call for an approach to thinking beyond what we learned in school. We need to study how these moving parts relate to each other. Since they come together to form systems, we need to start *thinking in systems.* Some of the behavior patterns we will explore are also of great interest to physicists, mathematicians, biochemists, economists, neuroscientists, and philosophers, and each of these fields has developed complex theories often involving elaborate formulas, vocabulary, and research findings.

However, the saving grace of systems thinking is that it can be done with very simple language, metaphors, and stories as well, and that's what we will be doing. In fact, you probably already resort to this systems thinking in your daily life whenever you face complex challenges. Think about how your mind approaches tasks like planning a party or wedding, making vacation plans, approaching a complex repair task, or designing a garden. You may have to track many moving parts in your work life as well, needing to shift your pace, your priorities, and your roles to meet these fluctuations. It is nearly impossible to survive in the service fields without this skill. Restaurant workers, especially those in fast-food settings, health care providers, educators and support staff in schools, emergency crews, and trade workers handling construction and repairs are all dealing with highly fluctuating flow patterns. When asked how they can possibly handle such uncertainties all day long, they simply explain that each situation has "a lot of moving parts," and they have learned how to track them well.

We can learn to track the moving parts operating in living systems ranging from our bodies to nature itself and to recognize when those systems are in real trouble. We can even learn to tell when crises are brewing quickly enough to head them off or at least soften their impact. There is a freshness to this way of thinking that may be new and exciting for you. As you begin to see more and more amazing patterns, be prepared as well to notice more of the world's problems.

Many leading systems thinkers are voicing an urgency that we learn to recognize the patterns beneath humanity's large-scale environmental, economic, cultural, and political problems as quickly as we can. Two of our most respected thinkers have expressed it this way:

> We shall require a substantially new manner
> of thinking if humanity is to survive.
>
> **ALBERT EINSTEIN, 1954**

We are faced with an entirely new relationship to the universe. We
are going to have to spread our wings of intellect and fly or perish.

BUCKMINSTER FULLER, 1970

While both of these voices refer to thinking in systems as new, it is only
new to those of us with minds steeped in literacy. If you have ties to
indigenous ways of knowing or have a lineage rooted in an orality-based
culture, these ideas will already seem familiar. Then you will feel great
sympathy with this third voice asking us to use nature's systems as a lens,
an indigenous representative of the Yanomami tribes in Brazil.

Our wisdom is not useless. It is the wisdom of the Earth,
which is very important for the survival of humanity. I go out
into the world to tell people this. . . . These are my words.

DAVI KOPENAWA, Yanomami tribesman
spoken in a 2009 interview for *We Are One: A Celebration*
of Tribal Peoples by Joanna Eedy

In order to work with systems patterns, we need a much higher level
of impulse control than we may have used in the past. It takes time to
assess the true complexity of a systems pattern before responding. If we
simply react to the erupting behavior without this pause, we can end up
making matters worse. Our reaction can cause even further disturbances
in the system, creating all kinds of side effects. This "oops factor" can
lead to what gets called *collateral damage* or fallout, the price to pay, or
the accepted cost to society, to the environment, or even to one's health.

Living systems tend to have certain behavior patterns in common.
Understanding these patterns can help us improve our judgments and speed
up our response time while keeping our mistakes to a minimum. As you
strive to understand a particular system, here are a few key patterns to track.

Notice How the System Handles Fluctuations

When a system is fairly stable, it strives to maintain balance. Since it
is alive, it can't just reach a balance point and stay there, so it makes

frequent shifts to smooth things out, making course corrections to counterbalance any extremes. Our bodies do this continuously, regulating our hunger and digestion, our mental and physical activity levels, and our response to colds and other illnesses. Most of us can take this rebalancing process for granted, but if our immune system fails to handle allergens, insulin levels, or infections well, we need to take conscious control of the balancing task. In extreme cases, like insulin-regulated diabetes, our lives actually depend on our ability to intervene and regulate the highs and lows. Extreme fluctuations can be life-threatening.

With some systems, these course corrections occur over longer intervals, and it is harder to be sure whether they will rebalance on their own or will require an intervention. Will the ship withstand the stormy seas, or will it capsize; will a particular species recover from human behaviors or a natural disaster, or will it become extinct; will the organization recover from the loss of its leader, or will it collapse; will the stock market make a correction, or is it likely to crash; will an incident of civil unrest play itself out, or will it lead to a full-scale uprising? These are all the same basic question. Are we looking at a teeter-totter movement, or are we looking at a cascade? Did the movement go too far to be able to return to the center or not? The poetic image of the falcon and the falconer in William Butler Yeats's famous poem "The Second Coming" speaks to that point where the ability to return to center has snapped.

> Turning and turning in the widening gyre
> The falcon cannot hear the falconer;
> Things fall apart; the centre cannot hold.

Notice How the System Handles Growth or Acceleration

We have been looking at how systems can take information about their behaviors and feed it back to themselves in order to make course corrections. This activity is often referred to as using a balancing feedback loop or a *negative feedback loop*.

There are also situations when living systems strive to promote growth by building on the last activity and taking it further. This pattern is usually referred to as using a *positive feedback loop*. As long as this pattern maintains a moderate pace, it can work. We can understand how this works by watching the growth of small businesses in developing countries. As long as there is a smooth and moderate movement of money between the farmer, craftsperson or trader, and the buyer in village markets, prosperity exists. But if the money stops flowing well, the markets die out, and the villagers fall back into the stagnation of deep poverty. The same disaster will befall them if the money starts flowing too rapidly, causing runaway inflation. The smaller players in that kind of financial climate can't keep up, their buying power collapses, and again they fall back into stagnation.

As a rule, systems have a much harder time remaining stable with positive feedback loops. They have a tendency to keep accelerating, feeding on themselves in an endless spiral, like Yeats's runaway falcon.

Addictions are like that. They may start as an escape from some frustration. Consider teenagers who feel alienated from family or friends and turn to drugs. The drugs then diminish their coping skills, further increasing the alienation, which drives them even further into drugs. This never-ending spiral has no natural rebalancing point. It will continue until the system crashes or an outside intervention occurs.

Cancer cells behave in much the same way, growing without respect for cell boundaries or the needs of the larger system of a person's body. They lack the mechanism that tells other cells when to grow and when to stop. When we look at economics and resource management, it is easy to consider greed to be another runaway positive feedback loop that has no built-in brakes or intention to seek a balance within the larger system.

Notice How Crises Impact the System

Are you witnessing a crisis moving in slow motion? If you can see the problem inching toward a catastrophe, you may have time to intervene. A great example of this would be the spreading colony collapse disorder that threatens to destroy the bee population. By applying our systems lens, we can easily see the incredible fallout if it is allowed to continue. Without bees, pollination falls off dramatically, and we lose most of our precious nuts, fruits, and flowers. Scientists are identifying pesticides that seem to be large contributors to the situation. This means we might be able to rouse the public to demand a stop to their use in time to turn that problem around.

The sixty-one thousand residents of the fishing villages on the Marshall Islands atolls aren't so fortunate. As they watch the oceans slowly rise, salt water is already beginning to contaminate their wells and ruin their crops. As a UN-member country, they are asking for help on many levels. It is clearly too late to stop the effect of global warming on the ocean. Where will they go? Will they retain their citizenship if they lose their land? Will they still control their fishing waters, so important to their economic survival? And how can they preserve their culture when even their ancestors' graves are being washed away?

Is the crisis occurring suddenly, taking everyone by surprise? A small event like a loud noise, a crack in a snowfield, or a faint wisp of smoke can trigger a cascading response. Herds of animals startle and stampede; the shifting snow becomes an avalanche; a smoldering pile of leaves ignites a mountainside. There is no time to interrupt this kind of event, so we must attend to our survival and reorganize when the crisis has run its course.

Is a disturbance in one part of a system unexpectedly affecting a distant part of that system? A volcanic eruption on the ocean floor can trigger a tsunami hundreds of miles away. Within the global web of economics, the African rice farmer toils, unaware that rising or falling subsidy levels in distant countries are about to make his crop more valuable or nearly worthless by harvest time.

Are you witnessing actions taken without regard for the larger system, even when that system is understood? In Egypt, the threat of swine flu gave the government a rationale for destroying all the swine in the country, an estimated 250,000 to 400,000 pigs in all. In the largely Muslim country, pigs were seen as dirty, and the Muslim religion forbade living near them or eating them. The owners of these pigs were Coptic Christians, living in the Zabbaleen villages outside of Cairo. They were the unofficial garbage collectors, gathering up all the organic and recyclable waste, sorting and selling the recyclable materials, and feeding the organic matter to their pigs. These pigs, in turn, were their major source of dietary protein, and when sold to traders were an important source of income as well. Once their pigs were slaughtered, their reason for collecting the organic portion of the daily trash ceased, and the city was faced with rapidly mounting organic waste that then led to an increase in infectious diseases and rat populations. The strong bias against pigs may well have overridden the systems thinking of the governmental agency that authorized the slaughter.

How long should you wait for changes to take place? If a child isn't catching on to reading like his classmates, do you wait or seek remedial help? Will the class lessons take hold soon, or are they failing to register at all? Years ago I was part of a teacher enrichment center, and we were experimenting with creative ways to inspire the faculty. One of our members seemed reluctant to try those ideas the first year, but the following fall she was excelling at them. When a teammate said, "You sure have changed this year," her surprising response was, "Oh, I changed last year. It just shows this year!"

Parenting strategies, city-planning policies, business ventures that might have worked in time may fail needlessly because we give up too soon. In schools, perhaps the greatest challenge in this waiting game falls to the high school drama director on the days before opening night. Hardly ever is the dress rehearsal a real success, but the director just hopes that the practice was sufficient and the addition of the energy from the audience will bring the elements together at last. Miraculously, it usually does!

Now that we have developed an appreciation for the importance and behaviors of systems, we can move on to the fascinating sections ahead. They introduce valuable skills that will combine to make seeing the world of systems easy, natural, and enriching. To prepare for them, you can begin by noticing as many systems as possible in the world around you. See if you can determine how they work. Are they striving for balance, needing conscious regulation to keep that balance, moving toward growth, or developing addictive cycles? If they are falling apart, are you able to help reduce the fallout? Are they making quick changes that catch you by surprise or progressing so slowly it is hard to notice?

The next section will explore the art of seeing from multiple points of view, which makes it much easier to track the many moving parts in systems.

PLAYING WITH PERSPECTIVES

It all depends on how we look at things,
and not on how things are in themselves.
CARL JUNG

What was most significant about the lunar voyage was not that
men set foot on the moon but that they set eye on the earth.
NORMAN COUSINS

The bat hanging upside down laughs at the topsy-turvy world.
JAPANESE PROVERB

Perspective shifts can sneak up on you when you least expect them. Just when you think you are seeing the world as it is, you realize that once again you are only seeing it from your own point of view. That hit me rather dramatically one lovely summer morning. I was walking from an upscale-department-store parking lot in downtown Denver to the Brown Palace for Sunday brunch. There couldn't be a more elegant walk or destination, and I was bringing a young adult friend with me. Dawn was in her late twenties and had been one of the leaders in the school for dropouts I directed ten years earlier. She was street-smart, fearless, and had a tough veneer, covering her wise and tender heart. She saved me from countless mistakes in those years by explaining the cultural realities of her peers, and she was about to do it again.

I was reveling in the sophisticated, well-dressed folks we passed on the sidewalk and the fancy cars going by on the street when she pierced my reverie by saying, "Denver sure is a tough place."

"I suppose it is in some parts," I responded.

"No, I mean here."

"Well, perhaps at night," I said, thinking I had put that thought to rest. Her next comment woke me up.

"No, I mean now."

I looked at the passersby with fresh eyes and saw for the first time a surly, tough fellow approaching who had his eyes on her but hadn't seen me any more than I had seen him. And among the cars was one beat-up, older car with boys leaning out the window leering at her. We were one foot apart on the sidewalk, but layers of reality apart in our experience. How often was this happening in my life? How often does it happen in yours?

The next section explores ways to remove our unconscious blinders and view the dynamics of all kinds of systems from multiple perspectives.

Flipping the Question

Remember the young goatherd boy who could always tell which goats were missing? He didn't know how to count yet, but that didn't matter. He knew his herd so well that he simply noticed the *absence* rather than the *presence* of its members. When teachers work to build a sense of community in their classes by taking roll with the question, "Who's not here?" they foster this same awareness that they are members of a group and build an appreciation for missing classmates.

We can also play with a companion question: "What isn't being talked about; what aren't I hearing?"

I took an education course exploring closed-head injuries a while back, knowing I had a much stronger background than the other teachers in the class. During the first session, I was full of questions, mostly about what wasn't being studied or tried, clearly being the kind of student no instructor would want. I knew I had to change my ways, so after that I began to take voluminous notes and say very little. The instructor was relieved, and I learned so many things he could never have taught me directly. My notes were full of what I wasn't hearing, what the field was not yet doing, and what might be worth trying. I had flipped from listening to what *was* being said to what *wasn't* being said.

This same lens-flipping created miracles for the malnourished children in poor villages in Vietnam twenty years ago. That was when Jerry Steirin and his wife, Monica, accepted the invitation of the Vietnamese government to go on behalf of Save the Children and help solve the problem of childhood malnutrition among the poor. Their invitation was only to be for six months, and they would have no assistance and no budget. But at the end of that time, a very clear trend was in motion, and they were invited to continue. Within two years, the malnutrition rate had dropped between 65 and 85 percent. The secret to their success was to study those children who were *not* malnourished in each village and to engage the mothers in each village to help with the research. All the children under age three were weighed and measured. The largest and healthiest children stood out from the others, so the team interviewed their mothers. How was it that they were living in the exact same poverty conditions as the rest of the villagers but their children were thriving? What was their secret?

Once a village's team discovered the answer, these secrets were then shared among the other villagers. The secrets varied a bit from village to village but typically involved adding some kinds of food that had been seen as beneath the dignity of the other villagers until then. The special ingredients ranged from sweet-potato greens to tiny shrimps and crabs from the rice paddies. These mothers also fed their children small portions throughout the day, even if they had diarrhea, while conventional practice involved one or two meals a day, with food just put out for the child to eat if they chose, and they weren't fed if they were sick. Once a village realized that they already had the solution from among their own people, it became an idea with staying power. They would continue these positive changes on their own from then on. This approach to studying the *positive deviant* proved so successful over time that it is now used in over twenty countries throughout the developing world.

Harvesting Big-Picture Information

While most of our shifts in perspective occur as we revisit the small details, we are living in a time where a bird's-eye view of our lives is also a possibility. Satellite images of neighborhoods, of weather patterns, and even our movements and location revealed by the GPS signals on our cell phones all create a vast new body of information. They give us a new perspective on our place on the planet and a new way to relate to our surroundings.

Often sites that aren't visible on the ground are showing up with aerial photography and the help of Google Earth. These views are helping archeologists immensely in their work. The Angkor Wat Temple in Cambodia was constructed with between five and ten million bricks, some weighing as much as thirty-three hundred pounds. Earlier speculation was that those quarried blocks were floated down a canal and then rowed back up a river against the current, which didn't make much sense. With recent satellite imagery, the faint traces of hundreds of small canals linking the quarries to the temple site were finally discovered, solving the mystery.

Climatologists are now reading the vast drift patterns of the sand dunes as residual traces of ancient weather patterns that reveal a time when the winds blew from very different directions than today. The most recent puzzle captivating these researchers is thousands of ancient stone configurations they are calling *desert wheels* in the extensive desert regions throughout Jordan and neighboring countries that had remained unnoticed for millennia by land travelers. Their purpose is still unknown, but they were clearly constructed intentionally.

Finding Workability

Sometimes glimpses of the bigger picture fail to help us at all. When they reveal a chaotic scene, they can catch us off guard—the kitchen full of dishes after a dinner party, our first glimpse of a child's messy room, the need to pull together this year's tax information. Then we must shift our perspective away from this messy big picture to locate an entry point that allows us to restore order to the system.

Large-scale disasters call for a similar shift of perspective. When a rash of injuries suddenly fills the hospital with emergency cases, when fires or floods wipe out whole communities, we count on the clear thinking of emergency workers on the scene who have been trained to see the workability within the chaos. They reframe these scenes quickly, prioritizing the work to be done and then begin taking effective action almost immediately.

This same shift of perspective is needed with more chronic conditions as well. Some systems are so stagnant there seems to be no way to see them as workable, no place to intervene that could bring about better conditions. This calls for a radically new perspective, one that can show the way to transform the whole system. Therapists can reach a point where their sessions with a client seem to be going nowhere. Teachers can feel stymied by the lack of progress with a student whose behavior or learning issues seem to have them locked in a holding pattern. And families can find themselves in a state where no one is thriving, where the dynamics between them is making all of them angry, sad, frustrated, or apathetic.

Times like these call for what psychology students at Naropa University referred to as a *FLAG meeting*. It's a wonderful idea! FLAG stands for "fresh look at the ground" and involves dropping every assumption you have about the situation so you can look at it with fresh eyes. Dissolve any storyline you might be harboring about why a person's behavior is a certain way. Then begin noticing little details as if you are seeing them for the first time. Make no judgments. Just get a feel for what it is like to *be* that other person. If you long to revitalize your whole family, imagine becoming each family member in as many ways as possible. Try their arguments on for size, imagine taking on the pressures that they face, notice what pleases them, then when you feel you have honestly matched with them, think of just one small thing that would bring them joy or relief. In the following days, find a way to carry out those small gestures for each of them. Systems can often make dramatic changes with very tiny adjustments if they are the right ones.

Often seemingly intractable poverty conditions around the world can yield to interventions arising from these radically new perspectives as well. This next example is one of those inspiring interventions. Tanzania faces problems typical of coffee-growing regions in East Africa. Unstable weather offers no guarantee that food crops will make it to harvest, and with the cash crop of coffee, the market could fall, leaving farmers with an inedible crop that yields little cash. Even when the market is strong, it still leaves six lean months of low nutrition between harvests. The coffee-growing areas must also contend with coffee's by-products: mounting piles of rotting husks, leaves, and spent grounds that release large quantities of greenhouse gases and are so high in caffeine and tannin that even the cattle can't digest them.

This is all changing now, thanks to a radical shift in perspective held by ZERI (Zero Emissions Research and Initiatives) Foundation. One of their basic principles is "whatever is waste for one is a nutrient or food for another species belonging to another kingdom," so they saw this residue from the coffee harvest as an untapped resource rather than as waste. ZERI identified several varieties of edible mushrooms that would grow on beds made from these mounds of waste. As they grew, they would also consume enough caffeine and tannin to turn the remaining pulp into a rich, high-fiber feed for cattle. Furthermore, these mushrooms were high in protein and B-complex vitamins, providing important food for the farmers and a small cash crop to take to market as well.

Under the leadership of a group called Sustainable Harvest, the directors at ZERI and Equator Coffee Company from California came together to launch a pilot project called Pulp to Protein that showed fifty women from rural areas how to prepare coffee-pulp beds properly and cultivate these mushrooms. This pilot effort has proven so successful that the idea has begun spreading throughout the region and is even being tried on other continents in an effort to bring the idea *to scale*. Every breakthrough idea like this must eventually face the challenge of growing large enough to really make a difference. They call this *getting to scale*.

Strange obstacles can interrupt this growth process. One humanitarian effort found a surprising way around their roadblock. In Tamil Nadu, the southernmost state in India, correctible blindness from cataracts is extremely common. In 1976, a nonprofit organization named Aravind began treating patients. They collaborated with a social entrepreneur in the United States, David Green, and enough funds were raised to donate twenty-five thousand lenses a year. Half of their patients were able to pay for their surgery, so Aravind would use that money to help pay for the other half of their patients who had no money. They had the doctors, the patients, and the clinic settings to expand, but the bottleneck in the equation was the cost of replacement lenses, which typically cost several hundred dollars apiece. So, rather than allow that to be the limiting factor to their growth, they collaborated with Green again to create their own manufacturing company, Aurolab, and make their own lenses. Aurolab now produces nearly two million lenses a year, reducing the cost to less than ten dollars apiece. Today, Aravind operates seven hospitals and over thirty satellite centers, treating three hundred thousand patients a year. By removing that bottleneck, they succeeded in bringing their operations to scale.

Are systems in your own life failing to develop as well as you would like? Hopefully these stories have inspired you to address the obstacles and bottlenecks in your systems so they can flow better too.

ENCOUNTERING FRESH PATTERNS

Discovery consists of seeing what everyone else is
seeing, but thinking what no one else has thought.

ALBERT SZENT-GYORGYI
1937 Nobel Prize winner in physiology for discovery of vitamin C and its uses

To raise new questions, new possibilities, to regard
old problems from a new angle, requires creative
imagination and marks real advance in science.

ALBERT EINSTEIN

On November 18, 1861, Julia Ward Howe created the most inspiring song of the Union armies in the Civil War, "The Battle Hymn of the Republic." The soldiers sang it in their camps each night, and many regarded the morale boost from that song to be a critical factor in their winning the war. She didn't labor over the song, however. It formed itself in her half-conscious mind one night, as she describes in her journal:

> I went to bed that night as usual, and slept, according to my
> wont, quite soundly. I awoke in the gray of the morning twilight,
> and as I lay waiting for the dawn, the long lines of the desired
> poem began to twine themselves in my mind. Having thought
> out all the stanzas, I said to myself, "I must get up and write
> these verses down, lest I fall asleep again and forget them." So,
> with a sudden effort, I sprang out of bed, and found in the
> dimness an old stump of a pen, which I remembered to have

used the day before. I scrawled the verses almost without looking at the paper.

How often have you enjoyed aha experiences like that? It can happen in simple ways like imagining a new way to arrange the furniture or more complex ways like restructuring your finances or taking important new steps in your career or family life. But perhaps you find yourself stuck dealing with patterns that are just not good enough, with no breakthroughs on the horizon. In this section we are going to explore promising ways to refresh the mind and to bring forth new patterns of possibility. Before you go on, you might want to jot down a few of the patterns you would like to shift. Perhaps one of these strategies can help you achieve a breakthrough or two.

Revisit Old Problems from a New Angle

Many scientific breakthroughs arise when a researcher devises a new study that challenges the focus or the conclusions of older studies. You can do this too. Notice the patterns in your life that feel stuck and unworkable and then challenge them. Here are a few scientific challenges to show you how it's done.

Too much close work, like reading and computer screens, is causing increased nearsightedness in children, right? Or perhaps it is just hereditary. Maybe not. Both assumptions were challenged by researchers in two key studies. In 2007, Ohio State University researchers tracked American children with two nearsighted parents and found another variable that split the group in half. Those who spent at least two hours a day outdoors were four times less likely to become nearsighted than those who spent less than one hour a day outside The following year, other researchers compared two populations of children of Chinese ethnicity: a group living in Singapore who spent only three hours per week outdoors and a group living in Sydney, Australia, who spent nearly fourteen hours a week outside. Both groups of parents had similar levels of nearsightedness, but their children varied dramatically, depending on their time in the sun. The children in Sydney were nine times less likely to develop nearsightedness. The takeaway suggestion is to look for a new variable that could change your undesirable pattern.

After decades of searching for ways to destroy cancer cells, a new question arose: who's helping these cancer cells thrive? Why have some neighboring cells become such facilitators, and can that environment be made less inviting? This new research path became much more promising in 2003, a year after a large federal study pointed to the increased risk of breast cancer from taking a combined estrogen and progestin compound called Prempro. Breast cancer had been inching upward annually since 1945, but suddenly, in 2003, it dropped by 15 percent and has held steady. The only change that could explain this was that millions of menopausal women had heeded the warning to stop taking Prempro. Its presence in their systems had apparently been weakening the boundaries surrounding the small deposits of naturally occurring cancer cells in their breasts. This had made it much more likely that these cells could burst out of their local neighborhoods and cause damage. Its elimination allowed those boundaries to build back up. Now many researchers are searching for additional ways to reverse cancer by altering its cellular environment. The takeaway suggestion is to notice what surrounds your undesirable pattern, not just the problem itself.

Are we looking at a problem with the faucet or the drain? That answer could strongly influence the direction of Alzheimer's research. All brains manufacture beta amyloid, but with Alzheimer's patients, it is known to build up and create clumps that interfere with key regions of the brain. The research focus has been on reducing the level of beta amyloid in the brain and on trying to stop its production. But amyloid has important functions, so that might not work. For example, it serves as a nerve-cell tranquilizer of sorts. When nerve cells begin firing too intensely, they release amyloid to lower their signals back to normal. A seven-year research effort that began in 2003 has recently proven that the production of beta amyloid in Alzheimer's patients is normal, and the problem is with the drainage. They are much slower at draining it back out of the system. This finding has opened a whole new line of research, looking for ways to improve the drainage, for states of mind that don't call for as much amyloid in the first place, and for other ways to calm nerve cells so they call for less amyloid. The takeaway suggestion is to look at what might drain off its intensity instead of focusing on what is causing your undesirable pattern to build up.

Interrupt Your Brain's Logic

When we reason, we organize our thinking in step-by-step sequences so we can justify our conclusions. This leaves little room for new possibilities to sneak in. To invite your brain to think in new ways, it can help to scramble that order. Deliberately read or listen to ideas that seem unrelated to the pattern you are working on. When I was in graduate school, I would often look over the books on the reshelving cart in the library. It held a mixture of books I would never have chosen ordinarily, books that didn't seem to relate to my current research question at all. I would pick three or four of them to skim through before starting the day's research, and I would often get breakthrough ideas from stepping outside my field in this way.

Even if your challenges are less academic and more down-to-earth, you can try the same harvesting technique by reading magazines or journals about fields you have never explored or talking to people whose situations are unrelated to yours. Once you discover how they think and what patterns they have discovered, see if you can apply them to your challenges.

Borrow a Brain

Sometimes the best strategy is simply to borrow someone else's brain. You can try an experiment similar to one that my classes really enjoyed. They would break into two groups, and each group talked about the questions they seemed stuck on. Once each group settled on one question that would interest all of their members, the groups *traded questions*. Their task was to reflect on the other group's question for a week or two. Then we set aside time in class for the reflectors to sit in an inner circle to discuss their thoughts while the group who was stuck on the question sat in an outer circle listening quietly. The following week it was the other group's turn to hear their question reflected back to them.

If you try this, it helps to have at least four people join the activity. One of you can ask the other three to reflect on your question. If they answer right away, they can only give their immediate thoughts and opinions, and that is rarely satisfying. However, when they take a few days to reflect on your question, to dream over it, and to think more deeply, they will bring a much richer offering to the table. When they come together, it is extremely important for you, as the questioner, to listen without comment while they talk among themselves about what their minds did with your question. They must not talk to you directly, just to one another. By staying out of the limelight, you can almost feel your mind becoming unstuck as you eavesdrop on their conversation.

Learn to Invite *Emergent* Patterns

We have been exploring patterns that are just hidden from us. But some patterns simply weren't there when we last looked. Local products can go viral on the Web and become major trends, social uprisings can lead to new political realities, and small initiatives can spread throughout a population for the common good. When Wangari Maathai gathered a group of women together and led them to plant trees in her native Kenya, she empowered them to take back the land from a corrupt leadership and reclaim the growing desert at the same time. Her foundation ended up planting thirty million trees, but she could not have foreseen that it would inspire the United Nations to take this idea worldwide, eventually planting another eleven billion trees. Nor could she even dream that she would be chosen as the 2004 recipient of the Nobel Peace Prize for her work.

Some emergent patterns are impossible to see without the aid of massive computer systems that can process such huge amounts of information that they have earned the nickname of *big data*. The US government has established a Big Data Research and Development Initiative, connecting the powerful supercomputers in its own laboratories with research centers in universities around the country. Some of this big-data research has become controversial since it is seen as invading privacy, while other research is proving to be quite helpful. One beneficial project arose in response to the Human Genome Project. That project had found that less than 2 percent of the roughly one million DNA pairs were involved in shaping genetic inheritance. Nearly 97 percent of the remaining DNA bits seemed to have no purpose and were dismissed as *DNA junk.*

In 2003 the Encode project was launched to study this junk, leading to a nine-year collaboration among 440 scientists in thirty-two labs from around the world. Their findings are finally being released, and all contribute to the same startling discovery! Most of this junk DNA consists of *switches* that regulate the behavior of nearby genes. In a recent *New York Times* article, one project researcher, Michael Snyder of Stanford University, is quoted as saying, "Most of the changes that affect disease don't lie in the genes themselves, they lie in the switches." The implications for medical research are staggering and hold the promise of great benefit.

But the most enjoyable prospects for emergent patterns exist in our own minds. We don't always have to wait for them to happen either. We can actually learn to invite them by tapping into the back burners of our mind.

I live in the country, and a farmer's ditch runs through my back pasture. It's part of a large network of irrigation channels serving the area, but it hasn't always been there. One day I visited with Frank, the ditch rider who had been overseeing my ditch for thirty-nine years, and it turned out he was the one who organized the water conservancy district among the farmers. Farmers are notoriously independent, so I asked him how he did it. His response puzzled me at first. "I had the time," he said, but he meant much more than I thought. He explained that he visited each of the farmers in the region to explain the proposed project, but then he would shift the conversation and visit about other things for a while. Sometimes this tangent would last half an hour or more, but as he said, "I had the time." At some point each farmer would shift back to the idea of the project, saying he'd been thinking about it and had decided he'd go along with it. This thinking had been happening on the back burner while Frank deliberately visited about other topics. He was quite certain that demanding an answer right after explaining the proposal would have yielded a lot more no votes than yes ones. He instinctively knew how to work those back burners!

Sometimes you may not even realize your back burner is operating. One morning during graduate school, I awoke with my head feeling stuffed with ideas from all the courses I was taking. I longed to wash all those thoughts from my head for a while. So I went to the library, chose a small table near the wall that had a very thick book on it, and sat down. The book happened to be the titles of all the paperback books in print, and I thought it would do nicely since I had absolutely *no* interest in that. I sat there for nearly eight hours, rhythmically reading titles, authors, dates, publishers, cities, and states with no other competing thoughts. When I left that day, my mind was refreshingly empty—or so I thought. But about three days later, I began to get a sense for what was *not* being published! There was no way I could have created that awareness with my conscious mind. It had to bubble up from the back burner!

While that pattern emerged in three days, some patterns can take much longer. Perhaps you have held questions for weeks or even years, only to stumble on the answer seemingly out of the blue. You had been studying that question all along, but the bits and pieces were getting filed below your conscious mind until they were ready to surface as your own emergent pattern.

The next section describes an emergent pattern that was thirty years in the making! I think you'll enjoy it.

DISCOVERING A FIVE IDEA!

Some ideas are especially wedded to a particular number. There are "three" ideas like ground, path, and fruition or beginning, middle, and end or will, heart, and mind. The Greeks spoke of four temperaments that paired up with the four seasons. Airy spring was the sanguine. Fiery summer was the choleric. Changeable autumn was the melancholic. And watery winter was the phlegmatic. Indigenous Peoples often paid careful attention to the four directions. In modern times Carl Jung revisited the Greek pattern and developed his four styles of mind: the intuiter, the sensor, the feeler, and the thinker. And then there are "five" ideas like the Chinese five-element theory based on fire, earth, metal, water, and wood. They tend to connect to each other around a circle. What follows is a five idea.

I wish I could say it came to me all at once in a dream or from studying other five ideas, but it didn't. It brewed and incubated and accumulated over about a thirty-year period. The underlying question that drove this growing list into its final pattern was "What are the basic qualities needed to free the mind to think well?"

I discovered the first two qualities early on. I was teaching children with learning difficulties and emotional issues back in the 1960s and '70s. Some had such a low frustration tolerance that they couldn't stand any confusion without giving up. But new learning is always ambiguous at first, until you understand what is being explained. Somehow I needed to cultivate their tolerance for ambiguity or they would never be able to engage in new learning. So we worked with stretching that tolerance. I would throw out a puzzling question and ask them to mull it until the next day when we would work out the answer. We would consider issues that had more than one "right" answer, depending on one's point of view. We had a wonder board where they posted questions that had no easy answers. Why are there wars? Do fish like to play? Why do flowers come in so many shapes and colors? Gradually, their ambiguity tolerance would improve.

Those students often had a second major obstacle to learning. They couldn't tolerate repetition, calling it boring. This meant they wouldn't practice their skills, so they were failing in those subjects like math and foreign languages that built on prior learning. I decided to tackle that problem head-on. We actually practiced enduring boredom, extending the time they could stand to do simple math problems without starting to daydream or leave their desk. They progressed from two or three minutes to as long as fifteen minutes at a stretch. For years, those two tolerances—for ambiguity and for boredom—were what I noticed.

Then, in the early 1980s, I began teaching at the college level and quickly noticed an unusual trait among the arts students. There was an element of the unexpected about everything they did, and I realized that they had an extraordinary tolerance for novelty. I wondered, briefly, if this could be a "three" idea. Were boredom, ambiguity, and novelty akin to any of the "three" patterns I knew? It just didn't seem to be a fit, so I kept them as just an odd list I was creating.

I noticed the next tolerance in the late 1980s and early '90s. These years were filled with terms like "bottom line" and the conviction that everything, even chaos theory, boiled down to very simple patterns. But, to me, things just didn't look all that simple, and I kept suggesting that things were actually incredibly complex if we looked carefully enough. This was an amazingly unpopular view until the field of mathematics brought forth the complexity theory. With their "fuzzy logic," mathematicians were able to detect patterns from data that weren't quickly apparent and to create a generation of intelligent machinery that could adapt to each owner's needs. Voice-activated equipment could recognize a speaker's accent, washing machines could learn the kinds of loads the owners tended to run, and investors had a new tool for spotting trends in the market. At about the same time, Barbara McClintock was discovering the enormous complexity of genetic material. Medical researchers studying cancers and AIDS began to grapple with the labyrinth of mutating viruses and the biochemical cascades behind so many conditions that had been incomprehensible when the search was for a simple explanation. The field of deep ecology also flourished with this new tolerance for complexity. Finally, the richly complex systems in nature could be appreciated for all their dazzling interdependencies and variables.

Surely, my list of four tolerances must be a "four" idea. I worked a long time, trying to pair up ambiguity, boredom, novelty, and complexity with the temperaments or the qualities of the four directions. But it was to no avail. It was still just an odd list. I set it aside and nearly forgot about it.

In the mid 1990s, psychology began dwelling heavily on theories of attachment, narcissism, and borderline personality. It was thought that the problem was linked in some ways to poor "boundaries." These folks either had weak boundaries and were overly influenced by the energy fields around them or they only saw things as an extension of themselves, which meant they weren't open enough to experience the world for itself. It was confusing, and I kept wondering how that related to the ability to sense the energy fields in the environment and the physical, emotional, and cognitive states of other people. What was a massage therapist doing when he or she gravitated to the locus of energy imbalance? What was the friend doing who commented on the mood of another before that person had said a word about it? What was the teacher doing who listened to the question of a student and tailored the response to the way that particular student's mind worked? Were we all borderlines?

I was actively mulling my boundary question one day when a somatic-psychology student came in for an appointment. "Say something about boundaries," I said, to begin our interview. "Well," he replied, "there's the skin, of course." And then I got it. The skin is a semipermeable membrane. The issue wasn't about boundaries, really. It was about permeability! Then the diagnostic question would be whether people could *regulate* their permeability or not. If it were stuck open, they would be overly sensitive to the energy fields around them. If it were locked shut, they would be oblivious to others. But if they could expand and contract their permeability to fit the situation, they could be highly skilled in their work and in their lives.

I remembered my old list of four tolerances and cautiously added this fifth item to the list. Could this actually be a five idea? Did they have a special relationship to one another, each one having its own location around a circle, each one supporting or enhancing the one that followed? If one of the elements is blocked or missing, is there an interruption in the flow of energy? This actually seems to be the case! Here's how they seem to sit around their circle.

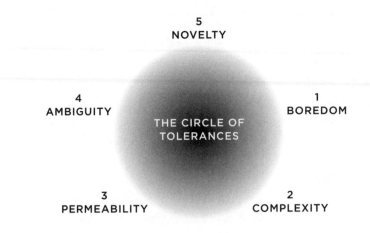

5
NOVELTY

4
AMBIGUITY

1
BOREDOM

THE CIRCLE OF
TOLERANCES

3
PERMEABILITY

2
COMPLEXITY

We can follow them around the circle this way.

1. *Boredom* (or stillness) creates the calmness to cope with
   increasing complexity. Too much boredom tolerance, on the
   other hand, leads to incredible procrastination, and nothing
   can get accomplished.

2. *Complexity* tolerance allows the mind to stretch and feel at
   home in an increasingly complex world, gathering, holding,
   and organizing vast amounts of information easily. However,
   this knowledge can also harden into rigidity, closing one's
   mind to change if a person fails to stay open to new ideas and
   the thoughts of others.

3. *Permeability* allows one to attune to the energy around them,
   registering the subtle cues, moods, needs, and connections
   among the people, plants, animals, and objects in the
   environment. However, this can become overwhelming
   if a person fails to close down enough to bring in proper
   boundaries.

4. *Ambiguity* depends on a fluid kind of intelligence that can
   stick with a situation that is unclear and persists in being quite
   vague for long periods of time. A more fixed mind will resist
   ambiguity and will miss out on any delightful encounters with
   the next tolerance, novelty.

5. *Novelty* is the most exciting state of all, but its intensity can
   seem overwhelming at times. If one has a high tolerance for
   novelty but a low tolerance for boredom, it is very easy to slip
   into addictive cycles instead of calming back down.

By now you may be wondering about your own relationship to each tolerance. If you suspect you might be *overdoing* one of these tolerances, here are
some suggestions to help you bring the flow back into your tolerance circle.

1. *To tame excessive boredom, work on the next tolerance: complexity.* When life has slowed down to almost total sameness, and you feel stuck and aren't even thinking about change anymore, it may be time to take a fresh look at your situation. Ask friends or advisors to help you see your life in richer and more complex terms. Seek fresh ways to look at old patterns, to question your current life, and to breathe new energy into it. Let it become more complex, more diverse, and more interesting, and then begin to get curious again about the rich possibilities for your future when you see yourself in this new way.

2. *To tame excessive complexity, work on the next tolerance: permeability.* When you find yourself too caught up in your own thought patterns, isolated from others, and preoccupied with complex ideas, perhaps it is time to open up to the world a bit. Reconnect with your body—begin exercising, improve your diet, get more sleep, get a massage. Expand your social life—make new friends, enjoy old ones, do volunteer work that helps people. Create new connections with nature—find trails to hike, relate with animals, get a pet. Look for ways you can engage with other cultures—perhaps folk dancing, ethnic cooking, even traveling.

3. *To tame excessive permeability, work with the next tolerance: ambiguity.* When you find yourself getting lost in the energy around you, so caught up with the personalities and demands of others that you aren't sure who you are, you may need to reduce your sensitivity to confusion. When you have a feeling of uncertainty and unpredictability, you can either call that feeling *confusion* or *ambiguity.* When you call it *confusion,* you can fall into feeling helpless and lose confidence. Then you are likely to lose your sense of self in a situation. However, if you learn to call the feeling *ambiguity,* you can relax more and realize that it is the *situation* that is unclear, not yourself. You

can simply notice that the world is a bit blurry and still hold a clear sense of self. Practice reframing this shift, moving from feeling confused to noticing ambiguity.

4. *To tame excessive ambiguity, work with next tolerance: novelty.* When your comfort with ambiguity expands to where it begins to interfere with your ability to bring ideas and passions to life, it can lead to a sense of apathy and indifference. Life can begin to seem pointless and depressing. It is time, then, to explore ways to put more fire back into life, to rekindle a delight in the unexpected, and to add a buoyancy or uplifted quality to each day. Consider creating opportunities for play, humor, and spontaneous acts. Begin to cultivate initiative, respond quickly to even fleeting ideas, and quit ignoring the urge to be creative. Spend time with friends who naturally seek novelty. With practice, you can learn to be more comfortable with the vitality and energy surges that arise when your life has been touched with novelty.

5. *To tame excessive novelty, work with the next tolerance: stillness/ boredom.* When your life gets so driven with high energy, excitement, unexpected events, and creative surges that you can no longer calm down or feel satisfied, you are very likely to turn to addictive patterns in an effort to keep the energy going or to finally unwind. Then it is time to find healthier ways to regulate your love of novelty. What is missing is the ability to self-calm. Begin to practice relaxation strategies, do stretching exercises or yoga, start gardening, take on a new skill that calls for repetition—learn a new language or take up a musical instrument. These practices can teach you to welcome an empty mind, a calm heart, and a relaxed body.

The next section will breathe life into these tolerances with stories of how my Naropa classes worked with each one. You might want to try some of those intriguing experiments yourself.

ENLIVENING THE FIVE TOLERANCES

Over the years, my Naropa students and I carried out many experiments, discovering ways to strengthen what we came to call the *five tolerances*. Here are a few of our favorite activities.

Boredom: Embracing Repetition

> [Music requires] years and years of practice in order to make what is conscious unconscious.
>
> **JAMSHED BHARUCHA**
> violinist and neuroscientist

Repetition can be challenging for us as adults. Staying engaged with each moment and resisting the temptation to become habitual isn't easy. In schools, the veteran teachers all know who are the master teachers and who are burned out. If a burned-out teacher declared that he or she had taught for twenty years, they would all say among themselves, "Not true. That teacher has only taught one year twenty times." The art of mastery involves repetition *without* sliding into habituation. It must remain lively with richer nuances each year.

It wasn't always that hard for us. As children we all loved repetition. It was our main strategy for getting to know the world, and play was our primary practice. It seemed to me that each kind of play had its own underlying gesture or motion path, so I created an activity with my Naropa class to explore this. Using blank paper and crude block crayons, they were asked to create a brush stroke that captured the movement of their favorite play activity from childhood. No words, no images, no name on the page, nothing but a sweeping gesture of some sort. Then we laid all thirty-plus pictures on the floor and silently proceeded to group them as if we were going to hang them in a gallery. The only rule was that every picture must be grouped with at least one other picture. If someone wanted to revise a grouping that was fine, and the shifting continued until there were no further urges to regroup anything. Then everyone went off to a different spot with the others in their gallery group to discuss their gestures. It was uncanny how often we would succeed in matching the felt sense of play gestures correctly. Almost always the swimmers, the tree climbers, the swing lovers, the speedy risk takers, and so on had been grouped with one another.

Over the years another pattern began to emerge. It seemed that those signature gestures had inwardly formed their minds as well. The tree climbers were consistently the visionaries who preferred to watch from afar, and the swimmers were usually very direct and goal-oriented. One day in class after tossing out an idea, I waited as usual for one particular student to challenge it by asking if the opposite could also be true. I thought a moment and asked if she had happened to spend a great deal of time in childhood hanging upside down on bars. "Of course," she said. Clearly this emerging pattern was worth exploring, but we just didn't have the time in those years to take the idea further. However, you might think about your favorite play gesture and whether in some way that is how your mind likes to play now.

Complexity: Collecting Your Pictures

[In high school] I had to use my pictures. What kind of pictures?
Well, you know. You might look over there and see a chicken
and some cattle and that isn't really important, but then in the
distance you see a horse running down a ravine just so. That was
a picture to remember . . . [pause] I have a lot of those pictures.

WALTER LITTLEMOON

We can learn to mine nature for pictures with the same kind of brilliance Walter Littlemoon did by paying more detailed attention to how nature behaves. You can approach this task in two ways: you can begin collecting elegant bits about nature that might come in handy some day or you can approach the task in the way my students did when they carried out an assignment called a *mind practice*. There was no way I could guide my students to collect the enormous portfolio of pictures Mr. Littlemoon possessed in just one semester, so I flipped the practice around. His pictures were potential answers awaiting the questions he encountered in life, but how about starting with the question and then searching nature for the answers!

They were to choose any question about themselves that seemed to have a psychological quality about it, the sort of theme they might explore with a close friend or in a therapy session. However, instead of asking their friends or a therapist for advice, they were to ask nature. Questions ranged widely: Is it true that I'm cold and prickly? How can I control my explosive temper? What does it mean to be clingy or to hoard or to be shunned? Why can't I create a warm space or a proper nest? Why don't I enjoy being in a group? They were instructed to stay completely away from any references to human behavior and just research how nature approached their theme. At the end of six weeks, we sat in a large circle listening to one discovery after another, being amazed at the interconnectedness of all the quests.

And their problems tended to dissolve as the natural wisdom beneath them was revealed. They no longer felt stuck. It had the effect of freeing them either to embrace their current behaviors or choose to make simple adjustments with ease.

Permeability: Matching with Others

This turning of thought into active listening—into interest—requires
effort. It is a willing-thinking process. Once accomplished, it
often activates our feeling toward the other, transforming our
natural sympathies and antipathies into an organ of perception,
into a feeling of understanding, an objective empathy.

CHRISTOPHER SCHAEFER
a leading Waldorf education scholar, former business mediator, and trainer

"Hit the ditch!" she warned repetitively. I was volunteering in an Alzheimer's unit at a local nursing home, and the speaker was a World War II veteran. One evening, I sat beside her trying to take in the emotion behind her rhythmic refrain. The urgency of the wartime setting became heightened, and I slipped a comment in between the refrains.

"That must have been *so* hard!"

She abruptly stopped her calls, looked me straight in the eyes, and slowly said, "You have no idea!" She soon returned to her chant state, but for a few moments we were connected.

I wanted to teach that matching skill to my students at Naropa, so I invented a practice called *listening by passing out*. It became one of their favorites. I would call for volunteers willing to come to the next class with a problem they would genuinely like fresh insights about. I needed one volunteer for each group of four or five students. That day, the class broke up into groups of four or five with one problem-giver per group. The problem-givers were to talk about their problem until I interrupted and then begin again until their listeners had faded away. The listeners were instructed not to speak at all, but to listen intently at first. Then I would interrupt the process with the sentence "Could you say some more about that?" and they were to begin *passing out*. First they were to drop their efforts to create answers for the problem-giver, then pull back to where the words lost meaning and were just a drone. The only thing remaining would be a felt sense of the problem-giver. Then they were to drop even that and rest in a light dream state until some fleeting story or image popped up. Once that happened they could sit upright again and wait for the others to "return" as well. Having no idea what those images could possibly have to do with the problem at hand, they shared their experiences with the problem-giver.

Year after year, we found that the images had remarkable similarities within each group, and no relation to the images of the other groups. One group might have images of the beach and shells, another about solitude and wind, and another about warmth and blankets. But each time the images served the problem-giver well. They seemed to be allegories that cut way below the conscious level of their question, to the seed question beneath it, and were seen as gentle, harmless, and very valuable offerings.

Ambiguity: Facing the Fear of Uncertainty

> Negative capability is when a man is capable of
> being in uncertainties, Mysteries, doubts, without any
> irritable reaching out after fact and reason.
>
> **JOHN KEATS**
> nineteenth-century poet, from a letter to his brother, George, in 1817

Each semester, I would set out to scramble my students' ability to take clear notes by jumping back and forth between related bits on a topic. If I hadn't already earned a reputation as a good teacher, they might have mutinied in those first few weeks. Instead, they relaxed, gave up any hope of nailing the information down, and allowed their minds to play with the seeming chaos. Since my overarching goal was to guide them toward being systems thinkers, I had to find a way to stretch their tolerance for ambiguity. They would need it in order to give their minds enough time to assemble the puzzle pieces of big ideas. Once they began to enjoy the art of pattern-seeking, I could offer more coherent lectures without having them lose their newfound *negative capability* that John Keats describes above.

Every time we commit to learning something new, we must gather the same courage we needed as children with new class lessons. Each new skill or idea would start out confusing, and there was no guarantee we would come through it successfully. As adults we may find ourselves avoiding that sense of confusion, failing to muster the courage to take on genuinely *new* learning. Instead we play it safe, learning new aspects of fields we already do well, and solidifying our sense of expertise.

As a way to stretch your own tolerance for ambiguity, consider trying to learn something you clearly won't excel at. If you've never danced, try ballroom or swing dance classes. If you aren't very flexible, try tai chi or yoga. If you have a terrible memory, try learning a foreign language. If you can't draw at all, take an art class. In each case, you will have the opportunity to discover what I did some years back when I took aikido for a couple of years. There was no chance I would advance to become one of the better students, so I explored my role as one of the less able ones. I actually shared that niche with one other student. There were things he was least able to do that I did rather well and vice versa. When he wasn't there one day, I found that we served a great function. His absence meant someone else would have to assume the role of the least able student for his weakest moves, and the anxiety in the class was palpable. We were the stress reducers for the class! So from then on, I decided to hold my role with dignity rather than embarrassment.

Novelty: Enjoying the Zone for Creativity

*Friend, please never lose your capacity for wonder and
astonishment in the world which you regard and in which you live.*

PAOLO FRIERE
from an interview published in *The UNESCO Courier*

Novelty can be intoxicating, driving people into cycles of overstimula-tion, lack of sleep, and attraction to addictive substances to cope with their surges of energy. However, most highly creative people have dis-covered a secret to staying in the creative zone for long periods without falling apart. Extensive research on the traits of highly creative people consistently leads to the same basic discovery—they have *paradoxical* traits that are allowing them to maintain an inner balance. While some people are introverts and others are extroverts, creatives tend to be both. While some people are high-energy types and others seem to prefer relax-ing, creatives do both. They are striking a balance between grounding and will-strengthening traits and their complementary opposites, traits that are uplifting and softer. We might even call these softer traits virtues because they can't be forced, only invited.

For several years my class would choose a will-strengthening practice to work on for six weeks and then follow that with a virtue practice for the next six weeks. They found the will practices to be straightforward. They chose one, declared their intention, and worked on it daily. But the virtue practices, the ones looking at the softer traits, weren't as easy. They discovered they couldn't force themselves to do it or that it lost its softness and became a will practice. They could only notice gently when they were actually displaying that virtue and make note of it. For instance, when students chose to work on a will practice like modera-tion or completion, they could hate it and still do it, but when they wanted to practice appreciation or simplicity, they had to embrace that idea and just hope they could look back on each day and find examples of incidents where they were indeed appreciative or living simply. Will practices seemed to strengthen character and were on the gravity or fixed side of the scale. These virtue practices were more tender, more uplifting and heart-opening, and tended to be on the fluid side of the scale.

If you find yourself lacking in creative spark, the challenge is to choose a virtue practice and work gently with it, so it can grow over time. You can say to yourself, "I have a good heart, and I can let it show." If you find yourself full of creative ideas but lacking the grounding to bring any of them to form, you need to choose a will practice and stick with it even when you don't feel like it. Your motto can be "I'm not enjoying this!" as long as you continue to work on it.

If you are eager to explore more facets of these five tolerances, you might want to consider how they relate to the five qualities of the healthy infant described in chapter 2—tranquility, curiosity, radiance, wonder, and delight. Could it be that babies who are tranquil will go on to tolerate boredom and stillness better, and ones who are curious will tolerate complexity more readily? Do babies who smile radiantly go on to be more comfortable with permeability, and ones who regard their world with wonder stretch their tolerance for ambiguity as they mature? And could the delight of the young child be a precursor to the love of novelty later? It's just a thought. You'd need to check it out to see if it's true.

My students and I continued to explore these tolerances for many years, unaware that twenty-first-century science would soon be making dramatic neurological discoveries that underpin the five tolerances and give us remarkable tools for furthering our own development.

NEW WINDOWS ONTO THE MIND

In recent years, brain research has made several extraordinary discoveries that are shedding light on how we carry out many of our finest cognitive skills. In this section, we will explore two of the three most profound ones. We will save the final one, the default network, for later.

The Presence of Mirror Neurons

In the 1980s at a laboratory in Parma, Italy, a research team led by Giacomo Rizzolatti was measuring the neurons monkeys used to control hand and mouth actions and made neurological history when they accidentally discovered that those exact same neurons would fire when the monkeys *watched* a person carry out the same movement. Their report was published in 1992 and has led to an avalanche of further research around the world on what came to be called *mirror neurons.* What began as a discovery about watching and carrying out motor actions keeps expanding as researchers find mirror neurons in more and more parts of the brain.

What makes these findings so exciting? They shed light on all kinds of imitative learning and are at the heart of all social engagement. They allow us to register and identify facial expressions and physical gestures, giving us vital cues for reading the feelings of others and for relating skillfully in social situations. They are deeply involved in formulating our overall sense of the other person, helping us to develop empathy and compassion for them. Even babies seem to have active mirror neurons. When one baby cries in a newborn nursery, it often sets up a contagion of others crying. Most babies will also mirror back when someone sticks out their tongue, sometimes as soon as forty-two minutes after birth! Clearly they are too young yet to have a sense of self that can copy the behaviors out of empathy or intellect, so this had left researchers at a loss for an explanation until now. Since these mirror neurons fire automatically and require very little conscious intention, many researchers now regard them as the most likely explanation.

These neurons allow us to learn important motor skills by copying the movements we watch. They serve us as we learn everything from golf swings and dance steps to refined listening and speaking skills. We feel inspired as we listen to powerful oratory or sensitive storytelling because our mirror neurons inwardly mimic the energy of the speaker. No wonder dynamic teachers are so much more effective at engaging children in learning. They offer more than mere words; they offer the inner choreography of their enthusiasm and curiosity, and that becomes as contagious to schoolchildren as the crying was to babies in the nursery. Consider the incredibly important role these mirror neurons must have played with nonliterate cultures in helping them transmit all of their practices and knowledge to each new generation.

Studies have tracked the activity of mirror neurons with individuals on the autistic spectrum, from Asperger's syndrome to more involved autistic conditions. These studies reveal that they either have fewer mirror neurons or their mirror neurons are not responding properly, especially when they encounter people or unfamiliar objects. Without the ability to read people's facial expressions, voice tone, or body language, social engagement becomes a very confusing and unrewarding activity. This gets compounded by another research finding showing that in autistic children, the amygdala grows far more rapidly in early childhood and may be adding to the hypervigilance, fearfulness, and avoidant behavior they exhibit. Those with Asperger's syndrome often manage to function rather well academically even though their lack of a strong connection to mirror neurons gives them more challenges in social situations. As a result, their observation skills often become incredibly refined, as they work to memorize as many social cues as they can. In the end, however, they must focus on the words a speaker says to fill in the missing elements and often end up taking those comments too literally. So far, we still do not know how to give them the experience that mirroring a warm smile provides—that dose of oxytocin that enhances our sense of well-being and makes social engagement so rewarding.

Theta-Gamma Coupling

The second finding took form gradually. It began in 2001 and has grown more fascinating with each new piece of research since then. It involves the discovery that the brain draws on two very different firing patterns in order to do complex thinking. We usually operate in a state called *beta* as we think about ordinary matters, and our brain is usually firing between thirteen and twenty-eight cycles per second to do so. If we relax into an empty mind or just close our eyes, we will drop down to an *alpha* state and slow down to nine to twelve cycles per second. But if we want to do complex thinking, neither of these states is very helpful. Instead, our brains must couple a very slow state called *theta* with an extremely rapid one called *gamma*. Theta hums along at a mere four to eight cycles per second while gamma ranges from forty to eighty cycles per second and can reach speeds of two hundred cycles per second or more. Our curious minds collect fragments of possibly related bits while operating in theta.

This dreamy browsing activity moves far too slowly to pull the collection of unorganized bits together. However, as the mind puzzles over those pieces, the pieces can begin to fire in unison, a process called *phase locking*. When that happens, it attracts a much higher speed to join in. This high-speed gamma has the power to scan those unorganized bits, act on them, and create the order or *coherence* that will reveal the big picture. Those moments when the puzzle suddenly takes form can almost take our breath away.

We have been experiencing these ahas since infancy. This coupling of theta with gamma helped our infant mind generate the coherence needed to turn sensations into perceptions. It aided us in the pairing of objects with their names and later with extracting meaning from spoken sentences. Eventually we began using this process to handle complex reasoning. It was this coupling that allowed us to learn *scaffolded* subjects like math, science, and languages. With those subjects we didn't dare forget any old information as we learned new bits because it all had to hang together if we wanted to succeed.

When these two speeds fall out of balance, we can have some problems. Some researchers are suspecting that attention deficit problems are rooted in sluggish and disorganized theta activity, leaving high-speed gamma to operate without a focus, creating distractibility and overstimulation. When we are sleep-deprived, we face a similar condition. The subtlety and nuance of those slow theta musings are lost. We have to speed up our brain activity just to stay awake. We are temporarily hyperactive and distractible until we catch up on our sleep.

There also seems to be a minimum speed below which we can't pull complex information together because gamma's ordering activity just won't happen. Here is a great example. Tai chi classes typically introduce each new move in extreme slow motion and continue to practice it that way. I was part of a class that was progressing in this dreamy fashion, and after about eight weeks very few of us could retain any more of the moves we were learning. Our minds kept dropping them, and we couldn't practice well between classes. Finally someone asked the instructor to lead us in doing all the moves we had learned so far *very fast* a couple of times. That was all it took for us to create the coherence that had been eluding us.

We don't always want to couple these speeds together, though. If we tease them apart, we can address two other tolerances. The first one is the tolerance for ambiguity, and for that we need to operate in theta for as long as possible before inviting gamma to come in and organize all the pieces. In research terms, we are trying to maintain a state of *self-organized criticality,* a state that borders on chaos but is still capable of pulling the pieces together at the last minute. The longer we can stretch that state of uncertainty and keep those pieces from coming together, the higher our intelligence turns out to be.

Now let's look at what goes on when we focus on gamma instead. Gamma is the spark behind novelty. Once we invite it to work with the unorganized fragments we have collected in theta, it acts like a neurological centrifuge, spinning the pieces into a coherent whole. It takes enormous amounts of glucose to fuel this activity, and the healthy, well-rested mind will have more fuel on hand. Think back to a time when you had an incredibly creative day. Quite possibly you were so engrossed you didn't even take time to eat much that day, so where did your brain get all that extra glucose? It turns out that your brain has a backup supply. It has special cells, called *astrocytes,* or *star cells,* located throughout the thinking and memory regions, and their main purpose is to provide a condensed form of glucose, called *glycogen,* on demand. Animal research demonstrates that regular exercise can increase the storage capacity of these star cells by as much as 60 percent, which can fuel a lot more gamma time. If you are longing to enhance your creativity, one obvious experiment would be to see what increasing your exercise level does for you.

A number of researchers are also intrigued with the physics involved in bringing large amounts of information together at one time. Their disciplines suggest that when we generate powerful bursts of high gamma to reach our new insights, we could be metabolizing enough glycogen to create actual sparks of light in our brain. This may be why we describe those aha moments as sparks, a light bulb going on, seeing the light of day, an idea dawning on us, and refer to people who have more ideas than most as being brighter or more brilliant.

A SURPRISING NEW BRAIN NETWORK

The third and most startling brain finding burst onto the research scene suddenly with a paper that was delivered in 2001 describing an entirely new brain network. Researchers had always assumed that glucose use was dropping any time the brain entered a resting state between tasks. However, Marcus Raichle and his colleague Gordon Shulman, neuroscientists at Washington University in St. Louis, began to notice that certain areas of the brain would *dim* whenever a task was being addressed. This led them to track what those dimmed areas were doing when no task was going on. They were surprised to find that large areas of the brain became extremely active during this *downtime.* As soon as the brain began addressing a task, these areas shut back down, so the team named them the *default mode network.* It's one thing for new research to uncover a small brain location that has a unique function. But this discovery was a vast new network, and it took the world's researchers completely by surprise.

How could they have missed it? Actually, it was largely hidden in the brain. The most prominent feature of the brain is the deep groove running from front to back, dividing it into two halves, or hemispheres. Much of this new network was tucked down in that groove. Picture that groove as a long canyon, and then imagine the canyon walls along its sides. This network occupied four huge portions of those canyon walls—one toward the front, one along the midsection, and the last two toward the back of that great canyon.

Let's take a quick tour of the canyon walls before discussing the astounding research findings that are emerging about this network. We can start by looking briefly at those back regions. We now know that those two rear areas contribute to creating a sense of self and an understanding of the other person and are very involved during meditation as well.

Moving forward along the canyon walls, we come to the midsection. The left wall of this wonderful region plays a huge role in regulating our mind's inner life. It allows us to take our own counsel, to pull away from the outer world to read and reflect on ideas, to make plans for the future, to retrieve what we know and combine it with new information, and to support our imagination. It helps with reasoning and brings clarity to our thinking. It needs to borrow as much downtime as possible to keep all the new information, ideas, and plans organized for us. One thing it does *not* do is engage in processing emotional information, leaving that to the frontal region.

The front end of the canyon contains our final default area. When it is working properly, this frontal region is quite elegant. It allows us to understand and appreciate ourselves, to attend to our own feelings, to make sense of the needs and feeling of others, to generate creative ideas, and to daydream. It organizes our intuition, our creative insights, and our emotional life. Whenever we aren't actively engaged in thinking, it will try to borrow some of that downtime to keep these domains organized.

Researchers soon began looking at the brain as housing two separate networks or operating systems: an executive network for attending to the outer world and regulating our outer life, and this default network for reflecting on that information and regulating our inner life. Almost immediately these researchers began asking a new question: If we have two networks, what allows us to switch between them? It wasn't long before studies around the world stumbled on the answer—the brain had a *third* network that contained a complex switching mechanism. It too had been hidden. If you have spent some time looking at brain images, you might have noticed a second deep groove along the side of the brain, starting above the ear and slanting upward toward the back of the brain.

This third network, sometimes called the *attentional network,* spills into that groove's canyon walls. When it works properly, this network's switching mechanism allows us to shift from the inner world of our default network to the outer world of our executive-brain network easily. Depending on the tasks we are addressing, we might choose one network over the other or alternate back and forth if we need to combine the best of both networks to do the job. It doesn't occur to us that anything could interfere with that natural flow.

With all of these moving parts, however, a lot could go wrong, and that has spurred groups of researchers in various parts of the world to specialize on different key questions. In this first decade, their work has already led to some remarkable discoveries linking these three networks with creativity, the meditative state, depression, schizophrenia, attention deficits, and social phobias.

For instance, in people with social phobias, the rear areas of the default network shut down, making it hard for them to read people quickly. It forces them to use the frontal region in trying to cope with the stress of social situations. But this region isn't well designed for the task and can trigger circular thinking. People with social phobias get stuck ruminating or repeating their thoughts over and over, making them even more stressed. This same pattern occurs with depression. People suffering from chronic depression find themselves locked in cycles of emotional thought patterns, rehashing memories and emotional issues with no resolution. This frontal region wasn't designed to trap us in these cycles at all. The breakdown occurs because the switching mechanism has gotten stuck. When it is stuck closed, it leads to the ruminating cycles of depression and social phobias.

Researchers are also discovering that it can be stuck half open, allowing a bleed-through between outer and inner realities that appears to be a major factor in schizophrenic episodes. Clearly we don't want our switching mechanism to be stuck shut or half open. However, there is a third possibility: creativity researchers are finding that it is also possible for some people to hold that switch completely open for both networks at the same time.

In this high-energy state, your brain is able to make incredibly rapid connections between outer information and inner reflections, resulting in intense creativity. The midsection of your default network is especially active during these episodes, tossing reflections back and forth with the executive brain very rapidly. If our brains really can generate sparks, it is clearly doing so at these times.

This vital midsection of your default network is ideal for new learning as long as it fires properly. When it fails to fire well, thinking is much more difficult. This seems to be the main problem with attention deficit disorder. These individuals then turn to the easily distracted frontal region with its emotional and intuitive tools instead. Teachers and researchers alike are searching for new ways to help these struggling learners. Strengthening this default midsection may hold the key to school success. If so, it will continue to be needed for new learning throughout life. Unfortunately, encouraging greater use of this incredibly important region is not easy in this high-tech world. The students' brains are drawn to the intoxicating cycle of emotionality available with texting, emailing, and social networking. These activities all engage the frontal region's emotional- and social-processing skills, further reducing the amount of time spent developing the midsection's gift of rational thought. When students fail to engage in learning, it impacts their neurological destiny as well as their academic destiny.

While all of the research on the default network was progressing, parallel research into the impacts of Alzheimer's disease on the brain was also occurring. The two paths intersected unexpectedly in 2004 when Randy Buckner, a member of the original default network discovery team, happened to attend a medical lecture on Alzheimer's. Typically such lectures would present case studies on the particular regions involved with each patient, but at one point this presenter showed a composite image of all the regions affected by Alzheimer's disease. Recalling that moment, Buckner said, "It was quite surprising. It looked just like the default network!"

What can we do with that information? We clearly don't want to lose the precious functions of our default network—our memories, our ability to relate to others, our creativity and imagination, the clarity of our thinking processes, and our sense of self. Yet Alzheimer's still has no known cure and little promise of slowing its progression once symptoms begin to appear. There is some room for hope, though, as some research-ers suspect it may be possible to delay the onset of those symptoms if we could give the default network more time to rest.

There is a catch-22 about trying to give it a rest, of course, since resting causes the default network to fire even more. Researchers have identified four activities so far that get around this problem, lowering the firing patterns of these default network regions dramatically. The first is engaging in new learning or focusing on outer-world tasks. The second is deep, dreamless sleep that typically occurs early in the night. Acu-puncture treatments are the third activity and have the effect of quieting all the default regions while activating our outer attention and body awareness. The final activity is a daily practice of meditation. During meditation, the rear sections of the default network are highly active and typically are operating in high gamma, but it dramatically quiets the default network's midsection and frontal region.

While you might be susceptible to Alzheimer's disease, it is more likely that you will have the opportunity to enjoy a healthy aging process, filled with new possibilities, new capacities, and new demands. With a reasonable amount of care and attention, you can look forward to enjoying the wonderful gifts of your mature mind discussed in the next section, the last one in our journey.

THE GIFTS OF A MATURE MIND

Aging doesn't mean diminishment or exile from the ranks of the living. As the period in which we harvest the fruits of a lifetime's labor, it gives us the panoramic vision from which spiritual wisdom flows.

RABBI ZALMAN SCHACHTER-SHALOMI
From Age-ing to Sage-ing: A Profound New Vision of Growing Older

This section explores the mind's last great frontier, and it will hold a different significance for you depending on your age. If you are below about age forty, you may have a somewhat detached interest, reading it with your parents, older friends, or neighbors in mind. However, if you are entering your fifties or beyond, it becomes much more personal, and it is from your vantage point that we will be discussing the major brain changes that pave the way for the mature mind.

With the specter of Alzheimer's at our backs, it is impossible to step into these later decades without a measure of anxiety. We worry a bit every time we forget a name or lose our train of thought in conversation, every time we try to keep pace with the faster processing skills of younger colleagues or our own children, or feel our brains collapsing into fatigue at the end of the day.

These events all remind us that we can no longer take our brains for granted. Changes are happening, and we need to understand them and find a way to work with them. If we succeed, we will experience more wisdom and better decision-making skills than ever before. Here is what we need to know.

The File Drawers Are Getting Fuller

Our minds are filled with more content, and that means we are more likely to have confusingly similar files than when we were younger. This can muddle our memories, making it harder to keep all the information straight. However, it also means we have a much wider perspective than before. If we take our time and reflect on situations, we can use our panoramic view to make wiser decisions than those with fewer files. We can also strengthen our minds by guarding against mental clutter just as we would avoid a cluttered desk. Sometimes, just listing the confusions, unresolved thoughts, and unfinished tasks that are weighing us down can clarify our minds. Then we can begin to address these unnecessary drains on our attention. As we bring more order and simplicity to our lives, it helps our minds operate with less stress and more grace.

Our Attention Can Short-Circuit

The scientific term for short-circuiting is *perceptual decoupling,* but we know it as the "Why did I come in here?" phenomenon. We start to go somewhere with a clear intention but end up reflecting on other thoughts along the way, only to discover that our brains have completely dropped our original intention. When we were younger, we could get away with this daydreaming, but no longer. We are especially at risk of this short-circuiting when we are tired. We need to face the reality that we can no longer handle sleep-deprivation and expect our brain to deliver for us. When we are well rested, there will be times when this distractibility can work to our advantage. While others are focusing tightly on a project, we might take in unusual side information that turns out to be extremely valuable for the team. While on vacation, we might be the one to spot a wonderful sidelight that others overlooked, enriching everyone's travel experience.

Processing Speed Slows Down

This trait of the mature mind has fewer workarounds. No matter how we look at it, our processing speed is slowing down. We need to drive more carefully, stop booking our day so tightly, and create more downtime so we can process important information fully. It doesn't have to make us less valuable than younger workers on a job as long as we resist trying to run adrenaline to catch up with them. If we stay calm, we can take advantage of our superior knowledge base and our ability to incorporate small details they might be missing. We can offer valuable big-picture perspectives and make wise recommendations that may have fewer errors than the quick decisions that are being considered.

The Wiring Is Changing

This is completely fascinating! The key changes involve two parts of the brain we haven't talked about too much, the amygdala and the hippocampus. The amygdala tracks danger and records very vivid images of what frightened us in the past. These images serve as wanted posters that help alert us whenever a situation like that occurs again. The amygdala pairs up with the hippocampus, our brain's memory center, to store these memories and also connects to the frontal lobes, allowing us to regulate our emotional responses to overly zealous fear warnings. This collection of wanted posters can become overpowering for those with post-traumatic stress disorder (PTSD). Their frontal lobes aren't functioning very well, which allows the amygdala to become so hypervigilant they can hardly function in the world. Researchers are beginning to discover therapy techniques to help those with PTSD learn to recharge their frontal lobes so they can calm their amygdala's overactive behaviors.

With normal aging, on the other hand, there are wiring changes that work to our advantage. The link between our amygdala and our hippocampus grows weaker, making it harder to store negative memories, so we tend to have a more positive outlook on life than before. At the same time, the link between our amygdala and our frontal lobes grows stronger, making it much easier for us to regulate our emotions. This gives us better judgment in emotional situations, so we can be a steady and grounding presence when others get overwhelmed.

Our hippocampus is also undergoing wiring changes of its own, and we need to address those changes more actively. For those of us who live a sedentary life, this vital memory center has been losing over 1 percent of its cells each year, from the time we were in our thirties. This adds up and begins to takes its toll in our later decades, but the very good news is that not only can we stop this decline, we can throw it into reverse! The hippocampus is one of two brain regions capable of *neurogenesis,* the ability to regenerate its own cells. (The other region is the olfactory bulb, and you may recall reading about that in chapter 2.) Two practices have been found to stimulate this regrowth of memory cells: meditation and aerobic exercise. We can actually take our pick here, but each practice has enough added benefits to consider trying them both. Done regularly, thirty to forty minutes of brisk walking or other aerobic exercise three times a week or daily meditation for the same length of time has been proven to increase the cell count in the hippocampus by 2 percent a year. This is a powerful impact and goes a long way toward preserving our memory system. Meditation doesn't suit everyone, but there is over-whelming evidence that exercise works just as well in this case. So those of us who have avoided carving out the time to start exercising have just run out of excuses!

Resilience Fades, Reserves Take Over

This last change sneaks up on us gradually. In earlier years, we could socialize long into the night or stay up all night writing papers or pre-paring for tests and make up all that lost sleep over the weekend. We bounced back. Now we seem to slither back when we overtax our minds. Somewhere along the way we developed an allergy to adrenaline. It began creating more stress than it was worth and took an increasing toll on our brains. If we kept insisting on working this way, pushing ourselves to exhaustion and recovering ever more slowly, we probably concluded that our brains had worn out. And we began to resent the aging process. However, there is another way.

We can simply shift to another paradigm, another model for work-ing with our brains. It's true that we no longer have the *resilience* we had in the past, but we can simply shift over to building up and using *reserves* instead. We can look at our brains as being like a well that refills overnight, so we can begin with a replenished amount of water or energy each day. Let's look at some of the activities that fill the well to build our reserves and then consider what drains or uses up those reserves.

Filling the Well (or Building Reserves)

We have three sources for gathering reserve energy—our bodies, our hearts, and our minds. Ideally we will choose a couple of activities from each source, just to balance our life out.

To nourish or replenish the energy of our *bodies,* we know we can exercise regularly. We can also pay more attention to self-care, eating foods that leave us feeling refreshed and energized, drinking enough water to keep our brain fully hydrated, and seeking out comforting touch. Hugs, massages, and time spent petting furry animals are all great ideas.

We nourish our *hearts* and receive renewed energy when we take up arts practices like painting, weaving, carving, playing an instrument, or singing. Creating beauty in our surroundings, arranging a few flowers, lighting a candle for dinner are all simple but powerful renewal activities. Another option is to seek out humor, both the gentle humor of quiet exchanges and the more whimsical and unexpected antics of slapstick comedy. Humor presents our brain with surprises, situations that are outside its predictable expectations. Researchers call this *cognitive dissonance* and find that after our brain is confronted with an absurd situation, it refreshes its pattern-seeking skills so it can make better sense of any other problem we are trying to solve.

There really is truth to the power of positive thinking as well. An uplifted heart can brighten our day, and research has found it can reduce our risk of mild cognitive impairment by an impressive 40 percent. One study found that when their subjects kept simple gratitude journals, they shifted into this positive state much more easily. They were just asked to list five things they felt grateful for each week, and within two months they reported feeling more positive and less aggressive. Even their friends and family had begun noticing a real change.

Finally, we can nourish our mind directly. We know it needs deep sleep so if we are at all sleep-deprived, we should take care of this first.

We can start by simply going to bed half an hour earlier or getting up half an hour later than usual each day. Within a week we'll know if we needed that. There are other practices as well. Whenever our mind becomes anxious and less effective, we can take a slow rhythmic break, like taking a walk, sweeping the floor, singing a simple children's song like "Row, Row, Row Your Boat" or "Twinkle, Twinkle Little Star," or sitting quietly for five minutes paying attention to the rhythm of our breath. Each of these activities can help our mind rest for a few moments and settle back down.

Our mind's self-talk deserves special attention too. If we are being self-critical and looking at tasks as being overwhelming, never ending, or too hard, we can shift our internal language. We can reframe the situation so we are calling the situation workable and temporary and are appreciating our mind for taking on the challenge.

If our daily life is fairly routine, our mind might really be nourished by new learning, from taking on a construction task to learning a language to taking a short course on something as low pressure as the care and feeding of llamas. That last suggestion was one I actually tried when I wanted to wind down after finishing my doctoral work. My brain was stuck in overdrive, and that was the perfect remedy!

Emptying the Well (or Spending Reserves)

We may be filling the reserves successfully and still feel depleted. In that case the problem is likely to be how we are spending those reserves. Some practices are just too costly to continue doing. If we are subjecting ourselves to unnecessary stressors each day, we can cut back. We can limit our exposure to the news and other adrenaline-producing concerns that we see no way to solve and agree not to let them take over our daydreams. Another alternative is to find ways to take effective action to support initiatives that are working on solutions to those problems that touch us deeply. We must find ways to drop the habit of worrying unproductively about situations. That is easier said than done, and you might want to consider sending a blessing toward the situation or people involved and then shift your focus onto other matters.

We can avoid *decision fatigue*. Sometimes we enjoy novelty so much that we do away with all routines. This forces our brain to make extra decisions. Reinventing breakfast each day can take its toll, and by the time we get down to the real tasks of the day we have already used up a good chunk of our decision-making energy. We can simplify those parts of the day by building in a few routines. There are also times when we have a dreaded task hanging over our heads. If we don't jump right in and tackle it, we can spend large amounts of time rehearsing that task, again wearing down our decision-making quota for the day.

Some people get so frustrated with their imperfect memories that they insist on wrestling with them constantly when reasoning might save wear and tear on their brains. When we can see that a situation will be calling on us to recall names or critical facts, we can jot this information down beforehand.

Sights and sounds can also wear down the mind. We can reduce our brain drain by filtering out as much environmental noise as possible and finding ways to reduce eyestrain. Last but not least, we need to recognize when we just need to take a break!

Cutting back on spending energy wastefully gives us more reserves to spend on living a full life! Aging can be an enriching experience if we are willing to give our minds the care and attention they need so they can serve us in these elegant new ways.

It has been a joy to bring you these wonderful adventures. While our journey is nearing its end, just as a great feast is never complete without dessert, you will find a sweet epilogue to savor before we close.

THE MERITS OF
AN EMPTY MIND

When we learn to stop, we begin to see, and when
we see, we understand. Peace and happiness are the
fruit of that. In order to be with our friend, a flower, or
our coworkers, we need to learn the art of stopping.

THICH NHAT HANH
The Art of Living

We cannot let another person into our hearts or
minds unless we empty ourselves. We can truly listen
to him or truly hear her only out of emptiness.

M. SCOTT PECK
The Road Less Traveled

THROUGHOUT THIS AMAZING journey, we have uncovered
many unexpected capacities of the mind, and always there have been
practices, showing how to acquire the skills that seemed most interesting.
This last offering proposes setting aside all these newfound skills, at least
for part of each day, to practice cultivating an empty mind. This strange
proposal raises a few reasonable questions: What is an empty mind? How

can it be experienced? What can it possibly offer that none of the other great skills could provide?

One of the United Nations' most revered past leaders, Dag Hammarskjöld, spoke eloquently of this gift at the ceremony opening the UN's meditation room, saying, "We all have within us a center of stillness surrounded by silence." Musicians often seek out their empty minds, too. I recently asked a passionate local guitarist, Adam Auriemmo, why he practiced, and he explained, "You're building a faith that when you quiet your mind, it will come." When Sonny Rollins, a renowned jazz saxophonist, was asked why he had been practicing yoga as well as his music every day for the past forty-five years, he had a similar response: "It has made me a more serious person, which I hope transfers into my music. When I perform, I try to have a blank mind so things come from my unconscious, surprising me."

This emptiness can be a great gift to our friends as well. The two opening quotes speak of using our empty mind when our friends need to be deeply heard. If we can step out of the way, there is more room for them to enter. So what is this empty mind anyhow? Picture all of your study and the practices you have been doing as working like the potter's hand inside the forming bowl, scraping away the rough clay to smooth the bowl's walls. Only when the hand is withdrawn at last, taking with it all the unnecessary clay remnants, will a refined, empty bowl remain. It is then that you discover you have crafted a perfect vessel to receive the wisdom of each new day.

As with all the other skills on our travels, this one calls for some simple practices. Eckhart Tolle proposes this one: "Look at a tree, a flower, a plant. Let your awareness rest upon it. How still they are, how deeply rooted in Being. Allow nature to teach you stillness. When you look at a tree and perceive its stillness, you become still yourself."

Sometimes animals can teach us as well. I once had a dog that loved playing stick, but he never quite got the game right. I would reach down to pick up a stick, and he would be delighted. I would then throw the stick, and he would eagerly fetch it and bring it back to me. But that's where the game broke down. I would ask him to "drop it," and he would dutifully obey, giving up all hope of our playing the game again. He was never able to realize that once he dropped it, the game would continue. Finally, I decided to learn from him since he wasn't learning from me. I learned how to "drop it," to ask my mind to surrender all hope of figuring things out, at least for a few moments at a time. Practicing these small interludes of no thought will help immensely as you strive to awaken your own empty mind.

That emptiness also brings with it a very important gift for our times, the ability to bless. I had always assumed that the ability to bless belonged only to young children, wise elders, and spiritual teachers, but I found myself questioning that in 1999. I was asked to be the faculty speaker for Naropa University's graduation then, and that was the year of the Columbine High School shootings. We were all filled with sorrow and the longing to be of service, to somehow heal the wounds of the culture. At the same time we also felt it wouldn't really be enough. I had this nagging impulse to encourage everyone to learn to bless, but it felt like an outrageous idea. I couldn't commit to doing it until I asked Rabbi Zalman Schachter-Shalomi, who was a member of our faculty at the time and whom we affectionately called Reb Zalman. He was not only a wise elder in the Jewish tradition, he was also deeply connected to the Sufi teachings and to Buddhism. Reb Zalman spoke for all these traditions when he explained that throughout the spiritual world this need to begin blessing was arising. The picture he gave me was of clouds of goodness hovering just out of reach above us longing to rain down. All we needed to do was acknowledge the presence of this higher wisdom, reach up, and allow our empty presence to call these blessings down to Earth.

Angelus Silesius, a seventeenth-century German Christian mystic, expressed the same wisdom when he said:

> God, whose extreme delight it is
> To dwell with thee, doth come
> Most willingly into thy house
> When thou art not at home.

I hadn't envisioned broaching this theme again, but as I write these closing words, the Newtown elementary school massacre has once again shaken our country to the core. It is likely to spur us to take many healing actions, and yet we know it will never be enough. Once again, learning to bless needs to accompany our efforts. I encourage you to add this last practice to the many treasures you have been gathering. While blessing may be quite different for different people, I can at least describe how I have experienced and practiced it. Perhaps that can give you a starting point for finding your own way to bless.

When someone I see or hear about or even think about awakens sympathy or antipathy in me, I will often respond by sending a blessing. First, I empty my mind in the manner we have discussed here, and then allow my heart to match with them. If I am feeling sympathy, I know to let that go. The quality of blessing that I invite down for them is like light, carrying strength and courage in its beams. But if I am feeling the aversion of antipathy, I need to drop that as well and return to a neutral state. Then I can invite down a quality of blessing that is more like warmth and carries love and a validation of their basic goodness in it. It's not quite as deliberate and conscious as this seems, and certainly isn't coming *from* me, but *through* me. It just feels like a wisp of an energy exchange with no outward activity.

This idea may have no appeal to you at all. If so, please let it go. If it has awakened a mild curiosity in you, you might just begin making a study of blessing. Ask others what they think of the idea and whether they have ever blessed or been blessed. In time, the idea might grow in you.

I would like to close our journey the same way I ended my classes at Naropa. For many years, a framed calligraphy of the Six Precepts of Tilopa hung in my office at Naropa, and we became good friends. It was the resting spot for my eyes and my mind. I always gave a copy to my students on the last day of our semester together. Had I given it to them at the outset, they could have taken it to mean don't bother cultivating your mind in the first place. By the end of our semester together, they realized it was showing the way to a deeper relationship with their mind, a recipe for experiencing an empty mind.

I offer it to you now. When you find your mind racing with unproductive thoughts, carve out a short interlude of time to let each of these strivings quiet down. Not only will it give your mind a rest, it will empty your wisdom bowl so you can be more open, meet the world afresh, and be of service once again.

THE SIX PRECEPTS

No thought

No reflection

No analysis

No cultivation

No anticipation

Let it settle itself.

TILOPA

an eleventh-century spiritual teacher in India

INDEX

ABOUT THE AUTHOR

DEE JOY COULTER lives on a small ranch just outside Boulder, Colorado. She has tended that land for nearly thirty years and has reached a sense of deep familiarity with it. She shares the ranch with her four Icelandic horses whose antics often remind her of a junior high lunchroom.

For nearly half a century, Dee has followed her passion for guiding learners into deep enjoyment of their minds. Equipped with a master's degree in special education from the University of Michigan, she began to impact the field of education. This path often involved creating programs and schools, beginning in the 1960s with a pioneering school for youth in a state mental hospital in Madison, Wisconsin. A decade later, during the idealistic times of Lyndon Johnson's Great Society, she directed an exciting school for dropouts in Colorado. She guided a group of parents into establishing a highly successful Waldorf school in Boulder during that decade as well.

Her ongoing curiosity about the influence of neuroscience in learning and cognition drew her back to school in the late 1970s to complete her doctorate in neurological studies at the University of Northern Colorado. She has continued to follow neuroscience research since then, weaving it into all of her teaching and speaking work. During the following two decades, much of her professional time was divided between national speaking engagements, student assessments, teacher workshops, and college-level teaching. Her son, Scott, was born in 1978 as well.

Helping him live into his destiny brought great joy to her life, and in the process he became one of her greatest teachers.

In 1983, Dee began her twenty-year tenure as a faculty member at Naropa University, a role she deeply enjoyed. She reluctantly stepped down from teaching in 2003, so she could prepare to write this book. Following a five-year period of preparation, she ended her public speaking and assessment work to begin writing. The actual writing involved an intense three-year retreat from public life, as she researched, incubated, and then drew forth the writing in this book.

For more about the book and Dee, visit originalmindbrilliance.com.

ABOUT SOUNDS TRUE

SOUNDS TRUE IS a multimedia publisher whose mission is to inspire and support personal transformation and spiritual awakening. Founded in 1985 and located in Boulder, Colorado, we work with many of the leading spiritual teachers, thinkers, healers, and visionary artists of our time. We strive with every title to preserve the essential "living wisdom" of the author or artist. It is our goal to create products that not only provide information to a reader or listener, but that also embody the quality of a wisdom transmission.

For those seeking genuine transformation, Sounds True is your trusted partner. At SoundsTrue.com you will find a wealth of free resources to support your journey, including exclusive weekly audio interviews, free downloads, interactive learning tools, and other special savings on all our titles.

To learn more, please visit SoundsTrue.com/bonus/free_gifts or call us toll free at 800-333-9185.